From your loving son

CIVIL WAR CORRESPONDENCE
AND DIARIES OF
PRIVATE GEORGE F. MOORE
AND HIS FAMILY

E. Dianne James

Elin Neiterman

Mary Ellen Hoover

Mary Ellen Hoover
Elin Williams Neiterman
E. Dianne James

iUniverse, Inc.
Bloomington

From your loving son
Civil War Correspondence And Diaries Of Private George F. Moore
And His Family

iUniverse books may be ordered through booksellers or by contacting:

iUniverse
1663 Liberty Drive
Bloomington, IN 47403
www.iuniverse.com
1-800-Authors (1-800-288-4677)

Because of the dynamic nature of the Internet, any web addresses or links contained in this book may have changed since publication and may no longer be valid. The views expressed in this work are solely those of the author and do not necessarily reflect the views of the publisher, and the publisher hereby disclaims any responsibility for them.

ISBN: 978-1-4620-3694-3 (sc)
ISBN: 978-1-4620-3695-0 (hc)
ISBN: 978-1-4620-3696-7 (ebk)

Library of Congress Control Number: 2011912553

Printed in the United States of America

iUniverse rev. date: 09/13/2011

From your loving son

George

To the men and women of Sudbury, Massachusetts,
who have come forward in the defense of their country.

Acknowledgements

The Sudbury Historical Society was instrumental in purchasing the Civil War letters of George Moore and his family, as well as the diaries of George and his soon to be wife, Sarah Elizabeth Jones. George Moore along with three of his brothers and four of his cousins joined the Union Army during the Civil War. George felt he was part of something momentous and asked his mother to save his letters. We thank the Sudbury Historical Society for permission to publish these letters and diaries and for their support in the writing of this book.

We wish to acknowledge the following people who gave us assistance in the course of our work. First and foremost we want to acknowledge the tremendous support of the Sudbury Foundation and especially Marilyn Martino for her thoughtful guidance as we began the process of creating this book. We appreciate the generous support of the Sudbury Cultural Council and the Massachusetts Cultural Council who believed in our project. Lee Swanson, Curator of the Sudbury Historical Society shared his considerable knowledge of the history of Sudbury in the mid 1800's. Chuck Zimmer, a talented photographer, helped us prepare many of the photographs and documents used in this book. Constance Smith of the Department of Veterans Affairs in Baltimore, Maryland, was able to locate the service records of the Moore brothers, which gave us valuable information in our search for George's descendents. Natalie Eaton, a Sudbury resident and great granddaughter of Rufus Hurlbut, George's cousin, generously shared her family genealogy and photos for use in this book. Toni Frederick from the Wayside Inn Archives graciously spent many hours with us as we searched for records of George Moore. We appreciate the help and information Richard J. Moore provided us concerning the family genealogy. Len Kondratick, Director of the Commonwealth of Massachusetts Military Division-Museum and Archives, shared with us records from the Adjutant General's office of the four Moore brothers. Rosalind Magnuson and Cheryl Price of the Brick Store Museum in

Kennebunk, Maine assisted us with information about George Moore during the years after the war when he lived in Maine. Kevin Frye, Andersonville Historian and National Park Service Volunteer located information on Curtis Smith, another cousin of George Moore, during the time he was a prisoner of war at Andersonville Prison. Susan Greendyke Lacheve, Art Collections Manager of the Art Commission at the Massachusetts State House, graciously spent time locating photos of the Thirteenth, the Thirty-fifth, and the Fifty-ninth Regimental flags. Mark Parisi of the Everett Public Library in Everett, Massachusetts located information on John Moore who spent several years as a resident of that town. Rich Baker of the United States Army Heritage and Information Center at the United States Army Military History Institute in Carlisle, Pennsylvania, assisted us in locating photos of Alfred Moore, and provided us with other relevant historic Civil War photos. Sharon McGilvery, reference assistant at the Auburn Maine Library, helped us in our search for family members of George Moore. Jill Cook, Nancy Jahnig, and Catherine Illi Seles provided us with many family photos. Jim Batchelder of the Andover Preservation Commission helped locate the family of Albert Jones Moore and his wife, George and Sarah's son and daughter-in-law. We also want to thank Frank Horgan who loaned us his 19th century Civil War books where we found remarkable etchings which have been used in this book. When we reached a dead end in our genealogical search, Judy Lucey of the New England Historical Society came to our rescue. The Town Clerk's office staff, including Rosemary Harvell, Judie Newton, Dorothy Oldroyd, Lauren Goddard, and Elaine Fortney, willingly helped to search out historic records for us. Elaine Taranto, in the Sudbury Town Assessor's Office, helped us in our search for the Moore family farm. We thank Quentin Masolotte, the North Dansville historian, who sent us an image of the building called "Our Home on the Hillside" in Dansville, New York. We thank Ursula Lyons, Mary Collins Vivaldi, and Debbie Keeney, for their proof reading talents. We are grateful to Paige Gilbert Goldfarb for her photographic skills. Curt Garfield, Town Historian, generously shared his extensive knowledge of the history of the town of Sudbury. We must particularly acknowledge the work of Virginia Maenpaa who transcribed many of these letters but passed away before this work was completed.

And last, but by no means least, we thank our many friends and family, especially our husbands, Stewart, Larry, and Dan, for their constant encouragement which has inspired us to continue this project.

Contents

Introduction

Mill Village, Sudbury, Massachusetts: photograph of an etching taken from a
painting by Alfred S. Hudson, Annals of Sudbury, Wayland, and Maynard –
Middlesex County, Massachusetts, 1891 by Alfred S. Hudson

In the years between 1861 and 1864, Mary and Uriah Moore, a farming
family from Sudbury, Massachusetts, sent four sons to the Civil War. All
four sons returned home at war's end in 1865. Correspondence, including
letters, diaries, and other original documents became available in the year
2000. The collection is now being published, not only for the residents of
this small Massachusetts town, but for all those who are interested in Civil
War history throughout the country.

War was no stranger to the town of Sudbury, Massachusetts. From
the bloodiest of all American wars, King Philip's war, to Bunker Hill,
and to Concord in the War for Independence, Sudbury had stood ready to
contribute its treasure and men. The year 1861 was no different. Between
1861 and 1865, with a population of only 1,691, this small town rallied
for the preservation of the Union. One hundred and sixty-eight men left
Sudbury to enlist in eleven different regiments, cavalries, or commissions

of the Union Army. Eleven men would not return home. More than one out of every ten citizens of Sudbury stepped forward for the cause of the Union.

Sudbury was first settled as a farming community in 1638 by the English. John Moore was one of the first settlers. In 1861 at the beginning of the Civil War, Uriah Moore, a direct descendant of John Moore, was a farmer in Sudbury. He and his wife, Mary Dakin Moore, had a family of ten children ranging in age from to 9 to 29 years old. Between 1861 and 1864 four of their sons left to fight in the Civil War.

There were many causes and events that led to the Civil War, but in 1861, with the inauguration of Abraham Lincoln, the division between the northern and southern states came to a head. For some time their differences had been building. The North was moving towards an economy based on industrialization while the South remained primarily an agrarian economy. The rights of the states versus the laws of the federal government had been an issue since the founding of the country. In the North there was strong anti-slavery sentiment while the South's economy depended upon slavery. In December of 1860, South Carolina declared its intent to secede from the Union and by February of 1861, seven Southern states formed the Confederate States of America. In April of 1861, South Carolina attacked Fort Sumter, and the war between the North and South began. Two months later, four more Southern states joined the Confederacy.

On April 15, 1861, President Lincoln called for 75,000 soldiers to serve for three months. The town of Sudbury voted to equip the "Wadsworth Rifle Guards," a Sudbury State Militia, in preparation for an immediate defense of Washington, D.C. When this engagement became unnecessary, twenty-five of the Rifle Guards volunteered for the Union Army and were mustered into the Thirteenth Regiment Massachusetts Volunteers, the largest number of Sudbury men to enlist at any one time during the war. The town voted to provide bonuses to the men, just as they had during the Revolutionary War, but the question of "will the town pay when the soldiers return?" became a great concern to the Moore family as the war drew to a close.

The Thirteenth Regiment arrived at Long Wharf in Boston aboard the steamer *Nelly Baker*. They then left by rail for New York on Tuesday, July 30, 1861, in two trains headed for Philadelphia.[1] Among these troops was George Moore's twenty-one year old brother, John Hayward Moore.

In 1862, on the 4th of July, the *Boston Journal* ran the following ad:[2]

Attention Recruits! A few more good men are wanted

to fill up Captain Andrews' Company, Fort Warren Battalion. Under the last urgent call of the President, this battalion will probably be increased and make up the Thirty-Fifth Regiment, so that there will be a chance for actual service. The following inducements are offered to all wishing to enlist:

$25 bounty in advance; also
$13, one month's pay in advance
$12 per month State aid; and
$75 bounty at the close of the war

Men of Massachusetts, citizens, privates, rally under the glorious flag of our country. Let the Old Bay State lead the van. Let our people rush forth in their might. Let us swell the Union ranks, maintain our proud position, that Massachusetts is ever foremost when duty calls.

Apply at once to the Recruiting Offices, No 71 Union Street, Boston or corner of Park and School Streets, Chelsea.

The following day a second notice appeared:

Fall in Recruits! Captain Nolan and Lieutenants Baldwin and Hudson are rapidly filling their company with first-class recruits for duty at Fort Warren

In response to this call, George Moore, 20, his brother, Albert, 26, his cousin Rufus Hurlbut, 20, and five others from Sudbury, William Bowen, William Bailey, Francis Garfield, George Hall, and Eli Willis, were mustered into the Thirty-fifth Regiment Massachusetts Volunteers in Company D on August 16, 1862, for a term of three years. The town of Sudbury promised each a bonus of $125 for signing up. Uriah Moore needed to sign a consent form for young George to enlist.

CONSENT TO THE ENLISTMENT OF A MINOR.

[This Certificate to be signed by the father, only surviving parent, legal master or guardian, as the case may be.]

I, *Uriah Moore*, do certify, that I am the *Father* of *George F. Moore*; that he is *twenty* years of age; and I do hereby freely give my consent to his enlisting as a soldier in the *Massachusetts* Volunteers, for the period of three years in the service of the United States.

Uriah Moore

Witness, *J. H. Moore*

Dated at *Sudbury*, this *30* day of *July* A. D. 1862

Consent form for George F. Moore, Sudbury Historical Society

Two years later, on March 31, 1864, Alfred Moore, who was now twenty years old, enlisted and was mustered into the Fifty-ninth Regiment. Uriah and Mary Moore now had four sons actively fighting in the war.

Between April 1862 and June 1865 there was a steady stream of letters exchanged between the family and their soldier sons. One son, George Frederick Moore, asked that his letters be saved and, in turn, he saved the letters his family sent him. Through the generosity of the Sudbury Foundation and individual contributors, the Sudbury Historical Society obtained 84 letters written to and from George, his 1863 and 1864 diaries, the 1867 diary of the girl he married, pictures, and patents awarded to George Moore after the Civil War.

The letters from George describe the daily orders to "pick up and move", the marching, often beginning at 4:00 AM, and the lack of food. "We got the last bread there is in camp today (nine crackers a piece) and I don't know when we shall get any more for our provision train has not got along yet." George describes in great detail his battle experiences and the hardships he and his fellow soldiers are forced to endure. In addition to the letters, George Moore's two diaries tell of the routine of a soldier's daily life when not in battle, of constant travel from town to town, the weather, and the lack of rations.. George never complained, no matter how much hardship he endured and many of his letters are sprinkled with humorous anecdotes. In most of his letters to his mother and father he signs off with the words, *From your loving son.*

The war is seen not only from the soldier's point of view, but also from the concerns of the five family members who wrote to George while anxiously awaiting news of the latest battles, and of the safety of their loved ones.

There are many spelling and grammatical errors in these letters, as well as missing capitalizations and punctuation, but they have been left as they were written out of respect to their authors.

In addition to the letters and diaries of George Moore and his family, the following documents are included: a list of Civil War soldiers who enlisted from the town of Sudbury, Massachusetts, a genealogy of the Moore family, a list of Sudbury citizens who donated money used for buying soldiers to supply Sudbury's quota, a list of payments to the soldiers of the Thirteenth Regiment by the town of Sudbury, a list of Civil War movements and locations of the Thirty-fifth Regiment Massachusetts Volunteers from 1862 to 1865, and a brief biography of Civil War Generals who were mentioned in the letters.

The story of George Moore, his three brothers, and the Moore family does not end with the conclusion of the Civil War. They were talented and ambitious. The final chapter describes their accomplishments after the war including George's U.S. patents for boot-making, his musical ability as the organizer of Moore's Military Band, and his work as a contractor and builder; Albert's occupation as an upholsterer; John's work as a builder and architect; Alfred's skill as an inventor who held patents for gear cases for bicycles and also owned a business under the name of the Moore

Shank Company; Mary, Harriet, and Ellen, all married and left Sudbury. Information is also included about George Moore's cousins, Rufus Hurlbut, Henry Smith, and Spencer Smith, who were all injured in the war, and Curtis Smith, who died in Andersonville Prison in Georgia.

A number of additional resources have been used to augment, provide context, and assist in the understanding of the war experiences of George Moore and his family. They include: *The History of Sudbury Massachusetts* by Alfred S. Hudson; *The History of the Thirty-Fifth Regiment Massachusetts Volunteers, 1862-1865*, written by one member from each company in the regiment following the war; *Three Years in the Army: The Story of the Thirteenth Massachusetts Volunteers From July 16, 1861 to August 1, 1864;* Sudbury town records; records of various military archives; ancestry records; and information from individuals in Sudbury.

---

[1] Charles E. Davis Jr., *Three Years in the Army: The Story of the Thirteenth Massachusetts Volunteers From, July 16, 1861 to August 1, 1864,* (Boston: Estes and Lauriat, 1894), xxix.

[2] Committee of the Regimental Association, *History of the Thirty-fifth Massachusetts Volunteers, 1862-1865,* (Boston: Mills, Knight & Co., 1884), 2.

The Moore Family in 1862

Mary and Uriah Moore and their ten children lived in Sudbury in the 1800's. In September of 1862 the Moore family was preparing to say goodbye to George and Albert as they left to fight in the Civil War. Their son John had been one of the first men in Sudbury to sign up almost a year before. By 1864 when twenty year old Alfred enlisted, four sons of Uriah and Mary Moore, George, Albert, John, and Alfred, were fighting in the Civil War.

Uriah Moore, age 56, was the oldest of Curtis Moore and Polly Nixon's ten children. At the beginning of the Civil War, Uriah had a large family and was a prosperous farmer. He and his wife owned a large farm in Sudbury, which was referred to as "the old place," even in legal documents and tax records. Somehow, though it is never made clear, at some point in 1862 Uriah was declared an "insolvent debtor." His home, land, equipment, and livestock, were scheduled to be sold at auction in the fall of 1862 to satisfy his debts. Uriah's loss of wealth noted in town records of 1861 and 1870 is startling.

> *Sudbury Town Records for 1861*: Moore, Uriah: House-400, barn-200, shed-75, 57 acres-2000, old place house-300, 2 barns-400, shed-15, corn house-25, shop-20, 99ac.-1800, Knights lot-20 acres-300, 3 horses-240, 4 oxen-170, 10 cow-220, 2 swine-20, chaise-25, 10 M lumber-110, Tax 38.15

> *Sudbury Town Records for 1870:* Moore, Uriah: House-500, barn-150, shop-50, land 3 ½ acre-450, horse-30, carriage-30, tax 13.13

The new land and house purchased from the proceeds of the auction were put in the name of his wife, Mary. Money became an issue for the family. Throughout the war the boys sent money home. Uriah was in poor health and without his grown sons he was left with much of the woodcutting and farm work to do himself. There are twenty-two letters in the collection from Uriah to his son, George, and undoubtedly he wrote just as many to his other three sons. Uriah sometimes asked, "When will you all be near each other? I want to see you." In early May of 1864, he visited all of his sons but Alfred. In his next letter to George he wrote, "It seemed like a dream." Uriah's letters contain many phonetically spelled words which may have come from his early 1800's education. Uriah was a very bright and hard working man who loved and missed his sons.

Mary Hayward Dakin Moore was just a year younger than her husband. She was a small, rather fragile looking woman with lovely handwriting whose letters showed she had a good education. Mary worried and prayed for the safety of her sons. She would often write to George saying, "take care of Albert" even though Albert was seven years older than George. When Albert was sick and left behind, she wrote, "I hope that Albert catches up with you." She sewed clothes for all her family in Sudbury and made shirts for George. Often it took so long for them to arrive that she imagined that someone else would be wearing them by the time George received them. During the war, fabric was scarce and expensive, so Mary frugally made over the older boys' clothes for the younger ones. She also sent her boys chicken pies that were often inedible when they arrived. When George became sick at the end of August, 1864, Mary traveled to be with him. Both Uriah and Mary wrote to George separately and he, in turn, wrote each of them individual letters. Mary always signed her letters, *Mary H. Moore.* Her obituary states that she was always proud of giving the service of four of her sons to the Civil War.

Francis Uriah at age 29 was the oldest child in the family. He suffered from an illness that was never explained beyond the fact that he had "terrible pains in his head." Because of this condition, he was considered unfit to be a soldier and did not enlist, nor was he drafted. He was a faithful correspondent to George, keeping him informed of family matters and the latest news from Sudbury. He read the Boston newspapers to gather information on the progress of the war, and relayed news that he learned from the trips he and his father made to Boston, talking with returning soldiers. George and Francis also exchanged newspapers to keep one another abreast of the news of the Civil War. Francis worked as a carpenter for the family, putting on an addition to the new house and helping his father cut wood. Town records show the town paid him for painting jobs and fence mending. Francis's letters are filled with commentary about the town of Sudbury and family activities and are often infused with subtle humor. Whatever his illness was, it became worse in early 1865, and he did not survive to see George and his other three brothers return home.

Albert Henry was 26 when he was mustered into Company D of the Thirty-fifth Regiment Massachusetts Volunteers along with his brother, George. Albert lived in Boston for a year before moving to Marlboro in 1860, but his enlistment was credited to the town of Sudbury. Albert was the tallest of the Moore brothers at 5' 11 ½". He and George were very close, serving all three years of their enlistment together. George named his two sons after Albert: Samuel Albert born in 1871 and Albert Jones born in 1873. There are no letters from Albert, but there is one letter to him that he was to pass on to George after reading it.

Mary Elizabeth at age 24 had started to take live-in housekeeping positions in Marlboro and Cambridge Port. In a letter to George, his mother wrote that the "girls had to earn their clothes," which was one more indication of the family finances. Mary wrote several letters to George filled mostly with stories about herself. Her letters have no punctuation or capitalization; however, the love shown for her brother in these letters is evident. The question of Mary's suitors is discussed in several of the letters between George and his mother with George showing great concern that his sister finds the right man, not necessarily her current suitor.

John Hayward at age 22 had been serving as a member of the Thirteenth Regiment Massachusetts Volunteers, Company F, for a little over a year by the fall of 1862. He had been a member of the Wadsworth Rifle Guards, a company of state militia belonging to Sudbury. Twenty-five members of this group were the first men from Sudbury to sign up for the war, and they became members of the Thirteenth Regiment Massachusetts Volunteers. The town had promised these enlistees from the Wadsworth Rifle Guards a sum of money which, when added to their government pay, would equal $20 a month. By the time George enlisted, the Thirteenth Regiment had been engaged in battles for a year near Harpers Ferry, the Shenandoah Valley, and the Battle of Cedar Mountain. From August 28 to 30, they fought in the Second Battle of Bull Run (Manassas). In September 1862, the Thirteenth Regiment, along with the newly formed Thirty-fifth Regiment, fought in the battles at South Mountain and Antietam. Often, in the next few years, the three boys would find themselves near enough to see one another. John drove a team of six mules carrying supplies and ammunition to the front, and later in the war became a saddler. George wrote home that he was glad that John would no longer be at the front, but, after completing his three years in the Thirteenth, John returned to the war as a member of the Christian Commission, transporting wounded soldiers off the battlefields until the war's end. There are no letters from John in the collection.

George Frederick was 20 years old and so young that he needed his father to sign a consent form for his enlistment. Along with his older brother, Albert, he was mustered into the Thirty-fifth Regiment, Company D, on August 16, 1862, listing himself as a laborer. His military records show that he was 5' 9" tall with a fair complexion and brown hair with blue eyes, the same as his brothers John and Alfred. George was an educated young man who, while in the army, wrote letters for other soldiers who could not read or write. He had musical talent and played the fiddle and the organ. Both George and Albert were promised a bounty of $25 paid in advance and $100 when they returned. This money became a very important topic in the letters as they neared the end of the war. This very personal description of a Civil War soldier and his family exists because George asked that his letters be saved, and he saved his family's letters through the war years.

Alfred Marshall was 18 and still in school, helping his father with the farm and tree cutting. When school was out, he also worked for a shoemaker in Ashland. According to Francis, his father had concerns about Alfred being away from home. In 1864 Alfred enlisted in the Fifty-ninth Regiment, Company I. Only a month after arriving at the front, Alfred was severely injured and spent sixteen months in Satterlee Hospital in Philadelphia. He was the last brother to return home. There are no letters from Alfred.

Harriett Amanda at age 16 was attending school in 1862. She was a great help to her mother, doing cleaning and laundry and, like many other women and girls in town, she braided straw at home which she sold or traded for goods at Hunt's Store, located on the corner of Concord Road and the State Road (Boston Post Road). Braided straw was used for making hats. There are no letters from Hattie, as her family called her, but many references to her in the letters.

Charles Herman was only 14 years old in 1862. There are no letters from him, but it is clear he had a definite opinion concerning the war. In the belfry tower of the First Parish Church in Sudbury there still remains a pencil drawing signed by Charles Moore. It depicts the Confederate President Jefferson Davis hanging by the neck.

Ellen Maria was 11 years old. There are no letters from her in the collection although George, in one of his letters, sent Ellen a ring that he had carved for her.

James Edgar was only 9 and the youngest of the Moore children. He wrote two letters to George asking his brother to "please write me some questions so I will know what to write about."

Beyond the Moore family, there were four cousins of the Moore boys who also enlisted. Rufus Hurlbut, age 20, was the son of Uriah's sister, Mary, and her husband Thomas Hurlbut. George and Rufus were close friends before, during, and after the war. Rufus fought in the same company and regiment as George and Albert. Uriah's sister, Olive, married to Joseph Smith, had three sons in the Civil War: Spencer Smith, age 20, served in the Thirteenth Regiment. His brother, Curtis Smith, age 21, a member of the Fifty-ninth Regiment, was taken prisoner and did not survive the war. Henry Smith, age 22, enlisted in 1861 in the Third Regiment, Company C, then in the Sixth Regiment, Company F, where he was a full sergeant. In 1864 he reenlisted in the Fifty-ninth Regiment along with his brother, Curtis, and cousin, Alfred.

When George, at the age of 20, left to fight in the Civil War, he knew that men in his family had often left Sudbury to fight for their country. His father, Uriah, had been a captain in the state militia. His great-grandfather, Lieutenant Uriah Moore, had marched alongside another direct descendent, Colonel Ezekiel Howe, at the alarm on April 19, 1775, and fought in the American Revolution. Another relative, General John Nixon, wounded at Bunker Hill, fought under General George Washington in New York. Many of these family names can still be found in Sudbury, Massachusetts today.

1862

"Ense petit placidam sub libertate quietem"

We drew the sword to gain enduring peace in a free land
Motto on regimental flag
Thirty-fifth Massachusetts Volunteers

Arriving at Camp Stanton in Lynnfield, Massachusetts on August 22, 1862, the young men who will form the Thirty-fifth Regiment Massachusetts Volunteers were issued uniforms after a surgeon's inspection to insure that they were fit for duty. The quartermaster then issued each man "a grey woolen blanket marked U.S., a light blue overcoat, rubber blanket, cap, dress coat, blouse, trousers, shoes, socks, drawers, shirt, knapsack, haversack, canteen, tin dipper, plate, knife, and fork."[1] Each man had to fit himself into one of only four sizes of uniforms that were available. Enfield rifles were then distributed and after the roll was called the men took the oath of allegiance.

> You do solemnly swear that you will bear true allegiance to the United States of America, and that you will serve them faithfully and honestly against all their enemies or opposers whomsoever, and observe and obey the orders of the President of the United States, and the orders of the officers appointed over you, according to the rules and articles for the government of armies of the United States. So help you God.[2]

George Frederick Moore was only 20 years old when he and an older brother, Albert Henry Moore, became part of Co. D of the Thirty-fifth Regiment Massachusetts Volunteers for the next three years. Co. D consisted of one hundred and two men, including officers, at the start of the war. The men believed the duration of their enlistment was for three years, while the government believed it was for the duration of the war. The war ended in the third year of the Thirty-fifth's service.[3]

Repeated calls for troops became familiar. The town attempted to fill their quotas and offered bounties. George and Albert Moore and the men who left in August 1862 were offered $125.00. Individuals in town gave money to fill the quotas and, when necessary, to buy men. A draft was instituted after the Moore brothers enlisted and it became possible to pay someone else to serve in your place.[4]

The regiment, under Colonel Edward Wild of Brookline and Major Sumner Carruth of Chelsea, left Lynnfield for the State House in Boston to pick up their Regimental flags, and then traveled by cars of the Old Colony Railroad to Fall River. There they traveled by the steamer *Bay State* to Jersey City, N.Y., and then boarded cars again to Washington. Only two days after leaving Massachusetts, with little experience as soldiers, these former farmers, carpenters, shoemakers, and laborers, found themselves marching in columns down Pennsylvania Avenue,

Albert H. and George F. Moore, Thirty-fifth Regiment Massachusetts Volunteers, Company D. Sudbury Historical Society, photograph reproduced by Chuck Zimmer

crossing the Potomac into Virginia, and spending the night sleeping in a field. The following day they moved near the fort where pickets[5] were posted, and for the first time cartridges were distributed. The men heard the booming of cannons nearby and were quickly set to digging entrenchments. They saw the ambulance trains rumbling slowly into the station with the wounded and thin ranks of men of the army of the Potomac. The returning soldiers, tired and tattered, told the new recruits of their fierce encounters with death in the Battle of Second Bull Run.

> Surely the crisis had now come, all the armies were about
> us and we were in good position to participate. But our

short time for preparation was spent; ready or not it was time for the Thirty-fifth to take the field, to keep it until the end[6]

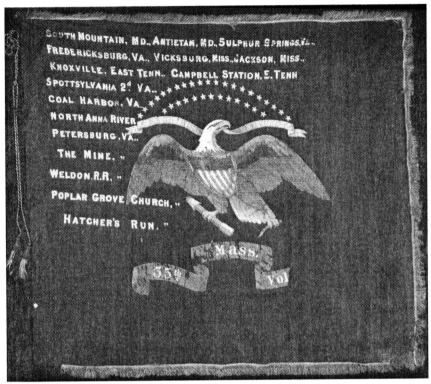

Regimental colors of the Thirty-fifth Regiment Massachusetts Volunteers, presented at the State House 22 Aug 1862 in lieu of national color, 1987-222, Commonwealth of Massachusetts Art Commission

General George McClellan, at President Lincoln's order, was now serving as Commander of the army of the Potomac. The new Thirty-fifth Regiment now became part of a much larger military unit, the Second Brigade of the IX Corps.,[7] under the command of General Ambrose Burnside. These fresh recruits were informed by the Second's older members that it was called "The Bloody Brigade," and it was certain death to belong to it.[8]

Explanation of military units:

Company = 100 men and is designated by a letter,

Regiment = 10 companies or about 1,000 men and is designated by a number,

Brigade = 3-4 regiments and is designated by a number,
Division = 2-3 brigades and is designated by a number,
Corps = 2 or more divisions and is designated by a Roman numeral[9]

In early September the Confederate General Robert E. Lee crossed the Potomac River and was camped near Frederick, Maryland. McClellan's plan was to protect Washington and Baltimore by heading to Frederick, forcing Lee back. On September 13, after days of marching, the IX Corps, led by General Burnside, passed through Frederick hearing choppy cannon fire and explosions of musket balls. In Frederick, General McClellan reviewed the troops while the citizens of Maryland came out to cheer on the men as they marched. The Union Army was in need of access routes through the passes on South Mountain in order to pursue General Lee. On September 14 the soldiers found themselves in the midst of the Battle of South Mountain where their commander, Colonel Wild, was injured and lost his arm, making him unfit for further field duty. The Battle of South Mountain was a

General George McClellan, Union Army, engraving, Pictorial History of the Great Civil War, 1878.

gain for the North but the loss of life was great. The Union lost 2,325 men, and the Confederates' loss was 4,343.[10] On the morning of September 15 the Thirty-fifth looked after their dead and wounded, retreating to the banks of Antietam Creek. The Army of Northern Virginia's first campaign in the North was stopped in the rugged mountain gaps of South Mountain.

On September 16, under heavy fire, the Thirteenth Massachusetts Regiment moved towards Antietam (also known as Sharpsburg in the South). John Hayward Moore was a member of Company F, the oldest chartered company in the regiment which included twenty-four other men of the Wadsworth Rifle Guards from the town of Sudbury, Massachusetts. The Thirteenth Regiment, who had been in the war since early 1861, was considered a highly trained group of soldiers. The regiment had a reputation of being capable of outmaneuvering the enemy.

At the Battle of Antietam, on September 17, the Thirteenth Regiment assembled in an open corn field in front of the Dunker Church when the enemy suddenly appeared. Under continuous fire the Thirteenth marched forward into heavy action in the corn field but was forced to retreat in order to refill their cartridge boxes. The Thirteenth Regiment took into this fight three hundred and one men and brought out one hundred and sixty-five,[11] a loss of nearly half their men. John Moore suffered a hand wound in this battle.

The same day the Thirty-fifth Regiment was also moving toward Antietam. The order was given to move both the older regiments, along with the new Thirty-fifth, across the stone bridge at Antietam Creek and up the hill to the line of battle. The Thirty-fifth laid down a supporting fire for the main assault on the bridge. Between four and five hours later, without additional reinforcements and running out of ammunition, the soldiers were in danger of being overtaken by the enemy at the stone bridge.[12] In a steady roar of musketry, and relying only on their bayonets, the men began to fall, but the position had to be held. General Burnside called upon General McClellan for reinforcements, but no relief came.

Antietam Bridge, Maryland. Soldiers and Wagons Crossing the Bridge. September 1862. Photograph by Alexander Gardner. #165-SB-19 National Archives, Washington, D. C.

We seem to be facing the enemy alone. It could be endured no longer. The regiment, among a storm of bullets, retreats to the hill. The enemy did not follow. The bridge was held. It had been an afternoon in the valley of death. We number eight or nine officers and three hundred and forty-eight men with the regiment, it was but one month since we had left Lynnfield, and two-thirds of our number were gone: at this rate how many would be left at the end of three years?[13]

The bloodiest single day battle in American history was fought on September 17, 1862. In the Battle of Antietam/Sharpsburg more than 23,000 men lost their lives. This battle came only three days after both armies had suffered total casualties of over 6,600 men in the Battle of South Mountain.

(Today a small monument to the memory of the men of the Thirty-fifth Regiment stands at the east end of the "Burnside Bridge.")

Although the battles of South Mountain and Antietam were two of the earliest and bloodiest in the Civil War, letters written by the Moore family and military records indicate that George and Albert missed both battles. It is known that Albert was delayed because of illness and never rejoined the regiment until October 3. To add to the confusion, army records show George as "missing in action," a report that reached Sudbury, but not before the family had heard otherwise. John Moore, however, was very much in the thick of both battles.

Mary H. Moore was concerned for her sons' safety after hearing news of the recent battles, and on September seventeenth, wrote to her son, George, unaware that John had been injured at Antietam. Reports that John had deserted reached Sudbury but proved to be false. In the following letter, George's mother wrote that John was sick and discouraged after the battles he had fought in during the past year.

President Lincoln and General McClellan in the tent after Antietam. #RG985 CWP4.1 U.S. Army Military History Institute, Carlisle Pennsylvania

Sudbury Sept 17 1862

From Mother.

Dear George

I sent a letter to you and
Albert, expecting you were both
at the same place, but found
out a few days after, that you
had moved with the regiment
and left him behind. I hope
he is able to join you by this time,
according to the reports in the
newspaper, you know what it is
to be in a battle. We are very
anxious to learn the particulars
about it. I hope we shall not hear
anything but good news. We have
had one letter from John, since
you left home, he spoke about
seeing you. He said it seemed
good to see you and the other

Letter to George from Mother on September 17, 1862, Sudbury Historical Society

Part two of September 17, 1862 letter, Sudbury Historical Society

Sudbury
Sept.17 1862

Dear George
   I sent a letter to you and Albert, expecting you were both at the same place, but found out a few days after, that you had moved with the regiment and left him behind. I hope he is able to join you by this time. According to the reports in the newspaper, you know what it is to be in a Battle. We are very anxious to learn the particulars about it. I hope we shall not hear anything but good news. We have had one letter from John since you left home, he spoke about seeing you. He said it seemed good to see you and the other boys from Sudbury. I think it must have been a happy meeting for you and him too. He writes that he is unwell and discouraged. I hope he will feel better soon. He has met with a great deal to make him feel bad of late, but seeing the rebels driven back, will put new life into him, I think.
   The 9 months men started for Camp today the Sudbury and Framingham boys have joined and gone together the girls went over to see them start. They will tell you about it when they write to you. You did not have much respect shown you when you started for Camp, but

you have the Credit of being among the first to answer the call of your Country. I hope it will not be long before the Rebellion will be put down, and the war come to an end. What glorious news that would be Tell Rufus[14] his folks are well and wishing to hear from him

Mr. Gerry[15] has written to his family that he is in Minisota and thinks of buying a farm there. Edwin has gone out to see him. If he should take all his children and grandchildren out there he would have enough for a whole town. It does not seem as though his family would want to go so far from here It is getting late and I must bid you good night. Write often.

From your loving Mother
M.H. Moore

The following is a letter from George's sister Mary Elizabeth.

Sudbury
Sept 25th 1862

Dear Brother
I now sit down to write you a few lines i have been expecting i should have had letters from you before this time we have not any of us had a letter from you for some time we have had two letters from John this week and one from Albert they have all writen to you since we have received a letter from you all the way we have known whither you was well or not war by Mr Balie[16] he wrote home that the boys were all well and it is about the same with Uncle Thommas[17] folks they have not heard from Rufus i guess since you wrote last i suppose you have heard about Johns getting hurt but Hattie had a letter last night and Father he has gone back into the company he has not seen Albert i suppose by his letter he does not know about you as well as do he wanted we should write and tell him all about you they have tried hard to have something happen to you they got the story round that you was taken prisoner and the rest that you was wounded i do not know what they will say about you next and they got the story that John had deserted he musnt do that the 35th Regt gets a good deal of praise theyes is something in the paper most every night about it. it is a stormy Sunday and i did not go to meeting and so i thought i must write to you i suppose Albert has got with you by this time i do not know of much news to write just now the last company that went into camp are most all at home now on a furlow Framingham Cattle show was this last week Wednesday Father carried a load over Mother and Charlie went with him and Hattie went with Frank he came home that afternoon on furlow and he come after Hattie you

*ought to have seen how she looked she had not combed her hair and we
had been baking and churning but poor me had to stay at home George
went and left Everett alone so he had to stay i did not care much for i did
not want to go their had got to someone stay i made a lot of turn overs
yesterday you and Albert may have one plateful if you will go into the
butery and get them i warunder if you remember how you used to tease
me if you found any cake or pie if you was whare i could send it to you
i would send you some every week i might send you a ginger snap in a
letter what if it should get miscarried and opened would i not laugh well
no i guess i shall wait till i have some other way to send i suppose you
have heard from Clara Gerry before now and know that they are agoing
out west they are agoing to start in about three or four weeks they are
agoing to join their Folks out there and what we shall do or where we
shall go i do not know this place is agoing to be sold and i am darned
glad of it if Mother can get up in town she will be contented and she
never will be here nor any of the rest of them but me i can make myself
contented i have enjoyed myself or will here or i did up to the other place
but i must close now write to me as soon as you can and i will answer for
you have not written to me at all*
    From Mary

On September 26 the Thirty-fifth Regiment moved into a regular camp
east of Antietam three or four miles from Harpers Ferry. On October 3
the first Grand Review of the IX Corps was held with President Lincoln,
General McClellan, and General Burnside, riding past. After the losses at
Antietam President Lincoln lacked faith in General McClellan and relieved
him of duty, replacing him with General Burnside as Commander of the
IX Corps.

Sudbury
October 3rd 1862

Dear George
    *I received yours of the 5th of Sept and was glad to hear from you and
that you were well and stood your journey so well I have wrote to you
cince but I have not received any thing from you cince though I have
heard from you cince that you have not been in a battle nor has Albert
but your Regt was in that big battle of Wednesday and done themselves
great honor it seemed to bad to have to go into battle so soon after
getting out there and to be so many killed and wounded so soon perhaps
you have not received my letter so I will write a few lines I have received*

*letters from Albert and John two or three times Albert is with you now
and John has seen you all and it must have been a happy meeting for you
all when John met you and you met John we stop at the old place yet and
we are ill at home but Alfred...he is at Ashland yet shoemaking I have
been a turning some potatoes don't yeald much and they don't sell in
Boston for only one dollar to one dollar and twenty five cents per barrel
and apples wount any more than pay for carting the property remaines
as it was when you left but I expect Curtis and Nancy-Jane[18] will sell soon
though they have not advertised yet Rufus Brighams[19] place is advertised
to be sold next wensday George Moore[20] is dead...he died thursday the
second day of October he was a seting up and reading a news paper a
few hours before he died he was over to the Cattle show last week I went
to the Cattle show and caried over a load of folks I was at Readville last
week where the nine months Regt is that the Sudbury boys are in there is
four Regts and a Batery encamped there they say when they move south
they expect to go to New Orleans Charles Gerrys folks are again to move
to Minasota in a few weeks Edwin Gerry has just returned from there his
Father sayes that it is the best State in the west for farming wee were all
well hope this will find you well write soon and tell me the news*
  your Father

The following letter is from Francis to George.

Friday
Oct 3 1862

Dear Brother
  *I received your letter Monday night and was glad to hear from
you and that you was all right. You was very lucky to escape being in
either of the Battles. The 14th or the 17th. The Battle of Wednesday the
17th is conceded to be the biggest and the hardest fought Battle that ever
took place on this Continent. They the Rebels were in a position where
they had to fight or be captured and Gen McClellan was determined to
capture them or drive them into Virginia and he succeeded in driving
them out of Maryland with a Rebel loss of three to our one. The 35th
Regiment is praised by everybody for its steadiness under fire and
gallantry during the fight. Being a new Regiment and not drilled at all it
is a wonder that they done so well. I was sorry to hear Col Wilde had to
have his arm amputated.*
  *I noticed when the regiment was on the march to the Fall River
Railroad Depot in Boston that the Col Major and Adjutant all had one*

arm in a sling but I little thought then to see either come back minus one arm. I hope the regiment will have a chance to drill. That is the remainder of it. The latest that we get about the Rebel Army in Virginia is that they are concentrated about Wincheston and are fortifying the hills in the vicinity. But now they can manage to stay where they are a great while in their ragged and hungry condition even if not attacked. I am not able to see but before this letter reaches you the aspect of affairs may be entirely changed. Letters received by the folks last night state that Albert has reached the regiment at last and that John has met him. I don't wonder Albert was glad to join the regiment after being left behind sick and then the long march without any news from the boys. I believe we do not realize anything about the War here at home we cant.

The nine months volunteers from Sudbury were sworn into the service one week ago and they go back to Camp at Readville[21] tomorrow their last furlough having expired. They are in the 45th Regiment (Cadet Regiment raised in Boston) which is not quit full yet.

The quota of Sudbury is 23 men and I understand that there are but 17 sworn in out of 22 that enlisted so there is six to be drafted as matters are now.

I gave Albert the names of a few of those who had enlisted in Sudbury and I believe that those I gave the names of have been sworn in. I saw the 43rd Regiment in Boston the other day on the common and accompanied by Gilmores Band[22] and a drum corps. The regiment is stated to be full and they were a serviceable looking set of men. They had not received their guns or equipments. They camp at Readville where there are four Regiments and a Battery. Gilmores Band has just returned from North Carolina.

The President has issued an Emancipation Proclamation[23] to take effect on the first of January next. So the Rebels can take warning in regard to slave property. All Loyalists will be compensated and Rebels will have their property confiscated. The next Congress will show what States are Loyal and what are not. I am going to send out home newspapers as I hear that they are not to be had in the army so you can read the news a week back better than I can write it. There was quite a rush of persons anxious to get exempted from being drafted on account of disability during the sittings of the Surgeons appointed to make examinations in this State in Marlboro the first day the surgeon examined 60 persons and everyone got exempted by paying the fee of One Dollar each. Certain persons in Sudbury also got exempted who are as able bodied as anybody I know of. I think the whole thing was a regular humbug. I do not think of any more news just now and I will close. The folks are all well and I hope this will find you the same.

I almost forgot to say that George W. Moore died last night quite suddenly of dropsy in the chest so the Doctor thinks.

I will close again
Remain yours,
Francis U. Moore

In early November the Thirty-fifth Regiment received daily orders to pack up and march. Through stormy weather they were on the move towards Virginia, tramping through frozen fields with little to eat. George often was on picket duty, a dangerous job at the front that required the soldier to be alert to any enemy movement.

On November 9, with two divisions of Stonewall Jackson's Corps on one side and Lee and Longstreet on the other, the IX Corps "found itself practically between them and far in advance of their base."[24]

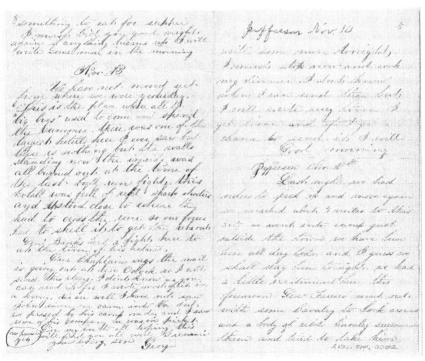

Partial Letter from George to Father from November 10 – 13, 1862, Sudbury Historical Society

All the towns in the following letter are in Virginia.

Orleans
Nov 7ᵗʰ 1862

Dear Father (and all the rest)
    It is a stormy day a regular snowstorm it has snowed all day it fell to
the depth of two inches and it is awful cold we have to build large fires
and then build our tents around them to keep warm we make out to keep
quite warm when we march we have our great coats on to keep warm.
I don't know as we shall see any winter quarters this winter I don't care
much if we don't if they will only keep going ahead. I hope they will keep
on until we get to Richmond then take possession of the housing and
winter there We could get along well enough if we had enough to eat they
have to keep sending the baggage trains back for provisions and then we
have to go on short allowance until they catch us again the Gen'l rode
through our Regiment today and told us to be saving our bread for the
train had not got up with us yet and he didn't know how soon it would
that is consoling this stormy day. We have got orders to pack up and be
ready to march so I must close now. I will write some more when we stop

Amesville Nov 8ᵗʰ 1862
    We started last night about four oclock and marched in a snow
storm about four miles without our supper we came to a streem that we
could not cross then we had to turn around and march back again and
go another road we went into a woods to camp about 10 oclock at night
we made large fires and tied our tents to trees around them to keep the
wind off then we cooked our coffee and ate about two hard crackers
then spread our rubber blankets and laid down and went to sleep we
got up around 7 oclock this morning cooked some more coffee ate one
hard cracker about 8 Oclock we got 6 hard crackers for a days ration 2
to a meal about 9 clo we started to march we got orders to pack up and
march about 8 ½ oclock we marched about 5 miles and came to a streem
halted and built a bridge then crossed into a village called Ten Mills,
passed through that Village and marched about 8 miles to this place and
camped cooked some more coffee ate the last cracker we have got going
to bed good night I will write you again tomorrow

Amesville Nov 9ᵗʰ
    This is a pleasant day but cold some of the boys in this company
went last night and got 3 hogs and brought into camp so we had quite
a breakfast the hogs here run all over the fields so we have a good
chance to get some pork only we have to look out for the guard for they

guard all the property here as fast as they go along the people here take confederate notes and they don't know a counterfeit one from a good one so some of the boys get a great deal of good money for counterfeit notes it is about noon now and we have not got orders to march yet perhaps we shall not march today if we don't I will write some more tonight I must stop now and cook my dinner. I don't know when I can send this but I will write every time I get time and if I get a chance to send it will Good morning

Jefferson Nov 10th
Last night we had orders to pack up and move again we marched about 5 miles to the city we went into camp just outside town we have been here all day today and I guess we shall stay here tonight. We had a little excitement here this forenoon Gen Ferrero went out with some Cavalry to look around a body of rebel Cavalry surrounded them and tried to take him but he drew his sword and told his men to pitch in and give it to them and they did and got out all right, and took one prisoner then the Gen rode into camp and sent out one Reg't and two pieces of Cannon they sent a few shells after the rebs and they "skeedadled"

We got the last bread there is in camp today (9 crackers apiece) and I don't know when we shall get any more for our provision train has not got along yet

Nov 11th
No provision yet we killed a cow yesterday so we have got some fresh meat we have not moved yet from where we were yesterday nothing of importance has happened today so I will not write much I will wait until tomorrow.
Good night

Sulphur Springs
Nov 12th *1862*
This morning about two Oclock we were ordered to pack up and move again about 4 Oclock we started back towards Warrinton we marched about 3 miles to this place stoped laid out our camp and here we are I don't know what we marched back for unless it was to get provisions but I have not seen any yet, only fresh meat only some "hoe cake"[25] *Albert got of a "Black man" this morning I don't know where our baggage train and provision train is or when they will get here but I hope they will today for I cannot live on meat always. We (Al and I) got some flour today so we can make something to eat for supper I must bid*

you good night again *if anything turns up I will write some more in the morning*

Nov 13

We have not moved yet from where we were yesterday. This is the place where all the "big bugs" used to come and spend the summer there was one of the largest hotels here I ever saw but there is nothing but the walls standing now the inside was all burned out at the time of the last bull run fight this hotel was full of rebel sharp shooters and it stood close to where they had to cross the river so our forces had to shell it to get the rebs out Gen Banks had a fight here to at the time of his retreat.

Our Chaplain says the mail is going out at ten Oclock so I will send this along. I don't know as you can read it for I wrote most of it in a hurry. We are well I have not seen John since we came into Va. but we passed by his camp one day and I saw some of his company he was on picket

Give my love to all hoping this will find you all well I remain your loving son

George

(no provisions yet)

Letter from sister Mary to George on November 9, 1862, Sudbury Historical Society

Marlboro
Nov 9th 1862

Dear Brother
 I now sit down to write my third letter tonight if i get this done soon
enough i shall write one or two more certain but it is between eight
and nine and i shall have to go to bed early for i shall have to get up
by five in the morning i am well and hope this will find you the same i
am out to work yet and in Marlboro you see by my letter and am in a
good place also i am at work for Mr Charles Witt Albert knows him i
have not heard from home since Monday and i do not know whether
they are well or not but i guess that they are or i should have heard of
it what are you up to bothering Albert i know how you used to like to
bother and i guess you have not forgot how i have got through to Elisha
now and thankfull am i for I was a fool to go in the first place for what
i did i did not have but a dollar and and quarter and had all the wood
and water to get in and four pigs to feed at that besides (———) the other
worker did not think much of it but i could not help myself without going
home and i did not want to do that she wanted me to stay another week
after i had engaged to come up here but i did not see fit to stay i do not
know certain whether i shall work out any more after i get through here
or not but i hope not Elisha has bought one of George Moores Horses
the one that was sick last Summer he will lie and cheat like a bucher
and mean as dirt i never want to work where he is again what sickened
me was to see so much whispering when he was in the house it used
to make me (———) the best of it was they did not get me to eat pudding
and milk i did not like it nor know how to make it end so they did not
have any while i stayed Elisha is talked about everywhere i go they say
that down in Brighton they call him the Hag it was someone that had
been down there and herd them call him so that told of it i Saw Miss
Betsy Brigham the other day and she inquired about you and Albert
and John i might have told her that we talked of sending out a box for
you although (———) and perhaps she would have sent you a pie and it
is not to late now i guess i will send her a word when we send the box
i suppose you would want her to mark it so you could be shure and get
hers first i expect we Shall not get so many of your letters this way as
we used to now a certain family are going away i suppose that they are
agoing to start in a day or two i do not know what will turn up next
Emily Brigham has gone to Brighton to work and Katie Tower is agoing
to Weston i believe the girls will all be gone as well as the boys pretty
soon but i do not care lately where i am or what i do i had as soon be

*in one place or another as long as i have got to work out and i hope
that will not be a great while longer i believe i have written all the news
that i know of now how is Albert he wrote he had been sick again i am
afraid he cannot stand it but i hope he will if he has got to stay the yrs
one of the Marlboro boyes come home that got wounded he went out in
the regiment that John did i believe he has got his discharge and so has
Morris Mary Stones Husband Well i must begin to think about stoping
my writing for i must finish my other one and then go to bed it is getting
to be towards ten and the fire is out and it is could*

*Write back as soon as you can and forgive me for not answering
your letters before good night be a good boy and mind your Marm take
good care of Albert and yourself also answer soon from your loving
sister*

Mary

On November 15, the Thirty-fifth Regiment under General Burnside began
to advance toward Richmond by way of Fredericksburg,[26] one of the most
difficult marches of the campaign. As the Thirty-fifth traveled over the
hills, missiles came whizzing by, while guns were set up, and artillery
fired from both sides. Eventually the cross fire was too much for the
Confederates and they decamped. Rations were still scarce and the men
were told they would each receive one hard bread (an almost indestructible
cracker).[27] For the next six days the regiment camped in the rain on the
frozen ground.

> On Sunday the twenty-third, after Governor Andrews's
> Thanksgiving Proclamation was read, the entire regiment
> was required to repeat in unison the final words, "God
> save the Commonwealth of Massachusetts!" We did so,
> but felt all the time the Old Commonwealth was safe
> enough at home, and what most needed saving, or a little
> Thanksgiving comfort, was the Thirty-fifth Regiment.[28]

Meanwhile in Sudbury, Uriah Moore, George's father, had been
declared an insolvent debtor. John H. Dakin of Sudbury, and Horace Heard
of Wayland, assignees of the goods of the estate of Uriah Moore, sold his
land, home, and goods, at auction. They allowed Mary Moore $500.00 first
and then his property was purchased in parts by Martin Goodnow, Prescott
Willis, John Goodnow 2nd, and Charles Haynes.

Sudbury
Nov 27 1862

Dear Brother

I received a letter from you Nov 8th and wrote to you but I don't know whether you received it or not. I wrote in regard to the state of affairs at home at that time. Thinking that you and Albert would be anxious to know how things are. I take the earliest opportunity to write you. The Real Estate was sold Yesterday by the Assignees at auction. In consideration of the sum of 500 dollars given by the Assignees, Mother quits all right and title to the estate and the whole was sold giving a clean title subject to no encumbrances. Heard refused at first to allow more than 300 dollars but we decided to take 500 or claim a homestead besides Mothers right and he finally made terms. I don't think Father could of got a homestead anyway and he would have had to contend in law for it. We have bought the Stone House and a lot of land in front. The house Father bid off for 550 dollars and the lot of land containing about 3 ¼ acres which extends to a line from Sewells south wall strait across the mowing to near a pair of bars at the hill for 131 dollars per acre. John Goodnow obid off the rest of the mowing about 5 acres next to the Spring Pasture for 78 dollars per acre. Prescott bid off the Spring Pasture for the sum of 282.50. What we bought is what Father proposed to have and therefore he is satisfied and Mother also. The conditions of the Sale was 5 per cent down the rest next month. Stone occupys the house till the 1st of April next. Nothing has been said in regard to the family occupying the house where they are. Probably will stay till then. I don't think of anything else in regard to the sale to write now, if there is, you and Albert will please write at once and what you think about it, etc

The folks received letters from John a day or two ago. He is well. He has not heard from you for some time he says and was about writing. There is no news here at present. The papers say that a draft will be had here on the 8th of December and the number required from Sudbury is 21 more.

I will close hoping this will find you well. The folks are all well I believe.

Yours
Francis

I wrote to Albert on the 22nd but do not know whither he has received the letter or not.

F. U. M.

Sudbury
Dec 18th 1862

Dear George
I received your letters that you wrote from the 7th to the 13th the 21st of the month and they were very interesting getting the particulars from day to day so but not very pleasing on the part of your living it must be pretty tough marching and living on so short alowence I wish we could get a box of victuals out to you we will send a box out as soon as we know that there is a prospect of geting it to you the Family were all together at the Old place Thanksgiving day but George Albert and John and partook of a Thanksgiving supper but then to see those vacant seats at the table it would bring to mind those dear ones that used to fill those seats in former times that they are far away in the war perhaps nothing but hard bread and coffee for their supper but I hope that wee shall all set down to a Thanksgiving supper together next Thanksgiving at our new home up in the middle of the Town and then it is consating to think that you were engaged in a good cause I wrote to Albert cince the sale of the property and about our purchase of the house and part of the land up there and I wrote to Albert that when I wrote you I would give a further account of the sale I think I wrote Albert who the purcherers were but I have not had time to figure up so as to know the whole amount but the Asenees say that if Nancy Jane and Curtis could not come in for a dividend and if I was liable to the banks for that sum that I don't orter pay the proceeds of the sale would pay out one hund per cent at the low price the land sold for I expect we shall stay where we are this winter we are all at home now except Mary she is at work at Cap Brighams now Alfred is a goin to School this winter the Meathodiest Society held a fair last Thursday evening but it was a slim affair George Moores personal property is to be sold tomorrow everything is very high now here as to clothing and groseres don't think of much news this time we are all well and I hope this will find you well write soon as you can and write all the news
From Your Father

In preparation for the battle of Fredericksburg, shoes that were worn out from the march were replaced by new boots received by mail. By December 9 and 10 the First and Sixth Corps infantry of General William Franklin's Grand Division arrived. Among them was the Thirteenth Massachusetts. The entire army was gathering at the Rappahannock River and the Thirty-

are plaques showing the history of Meigs Field, www.wikipedia.org/wiki/Readville-Massachusetts/CampMeigs.(accessed 11-29-2010).

22. Patrick Gilmore (1829-1892) born in Ireland. Established the band that served as the Twenty-fourth Mass. Regt. band in the Civil War and also served as stretcher bearers during battles. He wrote "When Johnny Comes Marching Home." www.psgilmore-society.org. (accessed 11-29-2010).

23. Emancipation Proclamation freed the slaves in the Confederate states but not those loyal to the Union. All slaves were freed with the Thirteenth Amendment in 1865.

24. Committee of the Regimental Association, *History of the Thirty-Fifth*, 65.

25. cornmeal flatbread

26. Committee of the Regimental Association, *History of the Thirty-Fifth*, 67.

27. Hard bread was a 3"x3" square of bread made with flour, water and salt, so hard the men soaked it in coffee. It was used when perishable food was not available.

28. Ibid., 73.

29. Ibid., 89.

30. Ibid., 93.

31. Ibid., 98.

1863

I understand you have been promoted on account of your bravery in the field of battle. It sounds rather better than it would if you had run, but I am glad I did not see you stand in that dangerous place, and I feel very thankful that you was preserved from harm.

Letter to George from Mother – October 5, 1863

Sudbury
Jan 3rd 1863

Dear Brother
    I received a letter from you some time ago. I have just come out of the woods from chopping and as I am too tired to do anything else so I take the opportunity to write to you.
    I received a letter from Albert the 29th Dec and another New Years day and one from John last night. Mother has received that money all safe and I believe she wrote the same evening. That bundle that Albert sent by Mr. Draper¹ I have received all safe. Mother and I sent a Package to you and Albert this morning by mail. It contained some dried apples, Sugar, Tea, Pepper, Two Diary's and some Paper and Envelopes and we want you to let us know whether it all arrives safe. John writes that he has seen you and Albert lately and says you both are in want of under clothing and Shoes now if you want some under shirts drawers and boots we will send some by mail if you will let us know. We can send them for a cent an ounce by leaving the ends of the package open. We have a box and fixings all ready to go whenever there is a chance for a thure conveyance.

There is nothing different in regard to affairs at home since I wrote to Albert last. Father continues to have his old spells yet. He told Mother the other day that he should take all that he gets from the Estate and go off somewhere but did not <u>say</u> out <u>west</u>. Edwin Gerry sold his farm at Auction the other day. George Heard bought it for 1690 dollars. Hunt & Gerry have sold some of their old stock at Auction. Hunt continues the business and Gerry goes west in the Spring.

I will mention that those deeds have all been passed and the house and all the land is secured to Mother by deed. She proposes to sign or give each of us her note without interest for the amounts that we severally put into the land. There is but little War news here at present. Banks Expedition has arrived at New Orleans it seems and Butler[2] is coming north. There has been some Victories gained in North Carolina by the Federals lately. The 45th Regiment took part in them but no sudbury boys have been killed or wounded that I have heard. Harriet & Alfred are at home most of this week on account of no school.

It is the old story of poor teachers. Geo Thompson commenced the school and taught about a week and left. Chas Thompson then came in for a few days till another could be got but left _before_. I believe a fellow by the name Brackett comes to try it next Monday.

The girls are all very anxious to find out how he looks and as he has been seen in the neighborhood somewhere lately inquires are being instituted daily in regard to him

I see in the papers that there is some talk of having a railroad or an extension of the Western Railroad from Worcester to Boston independent of the Boston & Worcester road and that two routes are being surveyed. One through Framingham and the other through Sudbury. If it should go through Sudbury Real Estate would have a rise. Some don't think it could go through the Village because that Library Building would be in the way unless they took it for a switch house. The Village folks are rather ashamed of the building I hear and perhaps would give something to have it moved up in town if it could be but the Centre folks would not consent probably. John Goodnow must have been a little out of his head or he would have devised a larger sum for the building for such a Library. If it had been located in the Centre the Town I think would have granted an addition and had a creditable building. We are having very pleasant weather here now for winter. There is a light snow on the ground but no sleighing. We have had one or two days only of sleighing which was in the fore part of December. Every day since Christmas has been pleasant. I guess this will do for this time and when I hear any

*news I will write again. The folks are all well I believe. I will close with
the hope that this will find you well.*

 Francis

In the 1860's the schools in the town of Sudbury had a winter term and a
summer term. The winter term began in early December and ran to March
1 and was taught by a man, while the summer term ran for two months and
was usually taught by a woman. The summer term was for the younger
children only, because the older children were working in the fields. On the
first day of school the students were asked what grade they had completed,
what studies they had taken, and what they expected to take in the current
year.[3] There were many different age and grade levels in the classroom
which was a challenge for the teacher.

 John Goodnow of Boston, formerly of Sudbury, bequeathed in his
will money to build a library for the town. Mr. Goodnow gave $20,000 for
the library's operation and $2500 for the building, as well as three acres
on which to build. It was the second public library in the state and at its
opening contained 2300 books.[4]

 The Forty-fifth Regiment had a number of Sudbury men: Sergeant
Marshall L. Eaton, age 30; Sergeant Homer Rogers, age 22; Corporal
Arthur Dakin, age 22; Corporal Bradley Hemenway, age 26; Frank H.
Hunt, musician, age 18; and Albert B. Richardson, musician, age 19; Asa
B. Bacon, age 41; James B. Butterfield, age 22; John H. Eaton, age 24;
Theodoric A. Jones, age 18; Alpheus Puffer, age 22; William Scott, age 19;
and Charles C. Spaulding, age 24.[5]

 The railroad that Francis mentioned in the above letter never came to
Sudbury until 1870 when the Framingham and Lowell Railroad stopped
at three depots in town.[6]

*Sudbury
Jan 22ed 1863*

Dear George
 *I received yours of the 31st and was glad to hear from you I have
had a letter from all of you cince the Battle at Fredericksburg have had
two from John after seeing the report of that Battle I felt very anxious
to hear from you all I am glad you was not in that Battle...it would have
been better if they had not been any of the Soldiers in it for they was
a telegraph despach came on Monday last that Burnsides Army had
crossed the Rapahanac again cince we have had it contradicted but his
Army is in motion and had been ordered three days rations looks like*

a great Battle looked for soon I hope you have got some shoes if you have to march it is to bad that the Soldiers cant get their full supply of clothing and rations that the government provides for them I think they will be better provided for for the President is a looking into this matter a little closer it is reported that the President has orderd all the officers around Washington into the field all that is found absent from duty to be discharged from office and the officers not to draw their pay any oftoner than the privets I wish you could have been at home at Thanksgiving to have took diner with us it was sutch a Thanksgiving as I never expearance before to have so many absent although we had a good supply of the luxuries of the land but those vacant seats at the table I hope I shall see you all at home before next Thanksgiving sound and well and this rebellion put down I am glad you had so good a meal at Cristmus I wish we could have got a box out to you Thanksgiving so you could of had a good dinner as we had I am very much obliged to you and Albert for the twenty dolls you sent me but don't send any money if you need it to make you comfortable for we get along pretty comfortably so long as I am well and able to labor I think that we shall have money enough to pay for that place I wrote to Albert about the dividend and my discharge and how the affairs stand I think I expect we shall receive our dividend in a few days then the little farm will be paid for if you have not received that box when you get this write me we are all well hope this will find you well write soon

From Your Father

By most accounts the Thirty-fifth Regiment was in the Battle of Fredericksburg, although there is a note in the *History of Wayland* that at some point before the battle the regiment was ordered to guard the wagon trains and support the Second New York Battery.

After the costly defeat at Fredericksburg in December, morale in General Burnside's army was dangerously low. Everyone in the army from generals down to privates blamed Burnside for the debilitating defeat. But because he accepted responsibility for mistakes, he was left in command. He planned to push the army ahead rather than settle in to winter quarters. His plan was to re-cross the Rappahannock, attacking Lee, and on January 16, 1863, the regiment received orders to be ready to move with three days' rations. The mild temperature combined with severe rainstorms and sleet left the unpaved roads deep in mud. The men struggled for two days, advancing their wagons and artillery, often pulling and pushing the cannons themselves when the horses could no longer move. After three days Burnside abandoned the idea and the men returned to camp. The order for winter quarters was issued and the men banked up the sides of their tents for warmth, created little chimneys, and waited the entire month of January for weather conditions to improve. This fiasco became known as Burnside's "Mud March."[7]

On a hill opposite Fredericksburg, on the banks of the Rappahannock River in the town of Chatham, was the deserted home of Confederate Major James Horace Lacy. In his diary, George notes that he slept in the Major's house on January 27.

On January 26, General Burnside was relieved of command of the army of the Potomac, and was replaced by General Joseph Hooker who assigned General John Sedgwick to command the IX Corps. The Thirty-fifth Massachusetts Regiment was part of the IX Corps. Although General Burnside had been relieved of his command of the army of the Potomac, he remained in command of the IX Corps. The Corps, now under General Burnside, left for Aquia Creek, the military depot for the army stores. On February 9 the men boarded the steamer *Louisiana,* towing two schooners containing the Fifty-first New York and the Eleventh New Hampshire. They headed down the Potomac through Chesapeake Bay to Fortress Monroe where there were ships of war all around. It was here at Fortress Munroe, not quite a year earlier on March 8, 1862, that the battle between the ironclad *Merrimack* and the Union wooden frigates, the *Cumberland* and *Congress,* took place. The soldiers were able to see the topmasts and charred timbers of these ships.[8] George wrote home describing the *Monitor* as a cheese box on a breadboard, an observation similar to many who saw it. From Fortress Monroe the regiment landed in Newport News and remained there for the next six weeks.

February 17, 1863
Camp Mead
Camp at Newport News

Dear Mother
I received your letter Sunday and was very glad to hear from you I received the box Friday with a letter from Hattie and answered it Sunday. The box was in good condition excepting the pears and two of the pies they were a little moldy on the crust but the rest was good. I am very much obliged to you all for it and will remember it when we are paid off

Rufus received a box from home the same day we got ours He had a chicken pie in it but it was all spoiled and most everything else his box was on the road a week or more longer than ours the reason we did not get them before was because we were going to move

I am writing on our box it makes a first rate table. Albert is making rings we have nothing to do today for it is raining and we don't have anything to do when it is stormy unless it happens to be our guard or picket day

We are some way from where we were when I wrote you last we are about six miles from Fortress Munroe this is a splendid place wood and water is close to us and we are close to the beach there is one of the Monitors close to here it is a queer looking craft it looks like a flat board with a cheese tub turned bottom up on it only a great deal larger

I don't see how we happened to get in this place unless the war is going to close for we are in a fighting Brigade and I should not think they would like us out of the field and put others in but strange things will happen sometimes. I don't know whether we are going to stop here the rest of our lives or not but I think we shall stop here a few months at least for they are bringing us winter tents

I wish John was here to but he is driving teams and I shall not have to think of his going into battle. I must write to him today to let him know where we are.

I would not swap this place with the 45th boys for I guess we have as good living as they do one look at our bill of fare flour bread, fresh & salt meat, pork, beans, potatos, rice, molasses, onions, tea, coffee, sugar, salt and dried apples it seems like dining a fine class hotel to what we have had This is what will make a fellow weigh a plenty to eat and not much to do. then them Barkers[9] are running wild again well they ought to have something for excitement in Sudbury but if it is dangerous to have such animals as them around Barnum ought to have them he would make money for a little while I guess. I wonder what Sudbury will do when this war is over and a lot of wild boys come home sensitive people will have to keep their eyes and ears closed. I think them Barkers would be good persons to have out here they would supply the place of a balloon and bullet could not hit them either. I should like to have been to the court I'll bet there was some sputtering

I believe I will close now for I don't think of much else to write

Love to all

Goodbye for a while

From your loving son

Fred

P.S. I have a ring that I made sometime ago for Ellen I will put it in this letter. Could not make the letters very good it was so small

G.F.M.

The close feelings of family and the ties to life back in Sudbury were always interwoven with the news of the war in George's letters. He let his mother know that her son, John, will be spared going to the front for now. He displays his sense of fun with the imagery of the Barker boys with balloons as a target in a circus sideshow, and he jokingly signs his name "Fred" (his middle name) in one letter.

Rufus H. Hurlbut Company D Thirty-fifty Regiment Massachusetts Volunteers, Courtesy of the Marian Hurlbut Eaton Collection

Sudbury
March 3ed 1863

Dear Brother
I received yours dated the 12th of Feb on the 17th and I will try and give you now the state of affairs that were in Sudbury. It is snowing hard now as I write. We have had quite a number of little nasty snows here lately not enough for sleighing , but just enough to keep a fellows feet wet when out at work in the woods or in fact anywhere out of doors. I went up chopping this forenoon but had to bring my dinner home to eat it.
I am writing in the old kitchen. Mother is mending some old pants. Ellen and Edgar are also in the room. Edgar is writing to somebody. Ellen is braiding. Their school finished the other day. Harriet has just gone to school. She has been helping wash this forenoon. Father has been having a jaw at Cyrus Hunt. I suppose that you know that Cyrus bought the Place of Nancy Jane well he came here about a half an hour ago and wanted to see Father in private. He offered to sell this Place to Father for 3 or 4 hundred more that he gave Nancy Jane[10] for it. After Father got Cyrus's price and everything else he could out of him he commenced blowing him up, told him what he thought of him, told him he never would buy the Place of him, accused him of meaness in other transactions and

in fact blowed him <u>*sky high*</u> *and when he landed that peculiar* <u>*smile*</u> *was gone and that nose took a bee line toward town, he following it.*

 Father feels pretty bad about leaving this Place as the time approaches and you must write him an encouraging word or two. Alfred is at Ashland. He went to work a week or ten days ago the man sent for him to come and he would give him a permanent job and as school was almost done he concluded to go. Father had two or three minds about his going <u>*as usual*</u> *but finally let him go. He came home a few days ago for some shirts to be made and Father carried him back this forenoon. Mary went a week ago to Sawyers, the Warden at the Poor Farms, to work for a week or two. Some of the Folks received a letter from John on the 24th. He said he was driving a six mule ammunition team and sleeps in his wagon with powder shells etc under his bed. His cough sticks to him yet but otherwise is well. He had not received his box but expected it every day. I also received a letter from Albert last night. We went to March Meeting Yesterday. All the Republican candidates were elected with one exception, Town Clerk – Jonas J. Hunt. Selectman Abel B. Jones, George Goodnow, Hiram H Goodnow. Treasurer – Edwin Harrington. Assessors – Samuel A. Jones. John H Dakin. James Moore. Overseers of Poor - Samuel Puffer. Dexter C. Jones. Alfred N. Thompson, Constables - Samuel A. Jones. Charles E. James. John H. Harriman. School Committee - Jonas J. Hunt. Charles Thompson. Librarian of Goodnow Library was let out to the lowest bidder, bid off at 84 Dollars for the year by Samuel Puffer. The Library is to be open only two half days in each week.*

 Josiah Gleason[11] is in Town. He arrived here day before yesterday. He looks rather slim, has been sick a long time and just got well enough to come home. He says that he expects to have his discharge. Says that the <u>*papers*</u> *are not filled out yet. The Surgeon advised him not to have them filled out until he got paid off. Says he has not been paid at all since he has been out.*

 Edwin Gerry has not gone out West yet. He has been sick and is rather feeble yet. His wife says she shant start until he is well. I guess that the undertaking has affected him not a little. Have you read the Boston Weekly Journal of Feb 26th. The accounts look as though something was to be accomplished soon in giving the Rebellion fits, especially at Charleston, Vicksburg and other Places also. It seems that a Conscription Act has passed the Senate and will become law probably, so that the men will be forthcoming to reinforce the present Army. <u>*Coloreds*</u> *as well as White men to be enrolled. My sheet is about full and I will close. We are all well and I hope this will find you the same.*

 Francis

The men of the Thirty-fifth continued to live in camps located near malarial swamps. Men who had escaped measles as a child now suffered from black measles, while some died of typhoid fever, leaving fewer men fit for travel and battle.

On March 20 the IX Corps was sent to the Department of the Ohio under General Burnside's command. Burnside's Department now included parts of Kentucky and Tennessee. The Thirty-fifth was assigned to Eastern Kentucky. The regiment's duty was to provide protection of the railroads and communication for General Rosecrans's advance on Chattanooga. On March 26 the regiment traveled by steamer to Baltimore. There they rode on top of boxcars heading to Pittsburg and then to Cincinnati, Ohio where they received a collation[12] from the local citizens at each stop. The soldiers waved their caps from the tops of the boxcars to the townspeople who waved back. They crossed the Ohio River into Covington, Kentucky, and lay down and slept on the sidewalk for the night. The people in Kentucky were equally divided, Union and Confederate, even within families. Kentucky was a loyal state and thus not affected by the Emancipation Proclamation, even though it was still a slave state. The men discovered during their first march on macadam[13] turnpikes.[14] how much more painful it was to walk on roads made of stone and tar than on grassy fields and dirt paths.

The Conscription Act, signed by President Lincoln on March 3, 1863, led to draft riots in New York as many felt the act was unconstitutional. All males, ages twenty to forty-five, with few exceptions for specific employment or for health reasons, could be drafted into national service. The act allowed a drafted man to pay $300 to buy a substitute to serve for him, which favored the well-to-do, causing much resentment. As the government called for more men to serve, some towns were unable to fill their quotas from volunteers, so some local and state governments voted to pay the $300 to men to fill the quota. In Sudbury, local citizens gave money to be used for the buying of men when needed, (see Appendix H) but by 1864, the ability to pay for a substitute to avoid service was given only to conscientious objectors.[15]

Covington, Kentucky
March 31ˢᵗ 1863

Dear Father
    I received your letter last Wednesday and was very glad to hear from you. When I got your letter we had struck tents at Newport News and were all ready to leave when Mr. Campbell[16] came along and gave

me the bundle you sent and the mail came in at the same time and I got a
letter from Mary and Alfred

We are a number of hundred miles from Newport News now. We took
the boats wednesday night for Baltimore and Thursday night we took the
cars at Baltimore for Cincinnati we arrived there about 9Oclock last night
took supper then crossed the river into this place we arrived here about
3Oclock this morning then lay down on the side walk and had a good sleep

We received a collation at about every city on the route we had a
tiptop breakfast at Pittsburg Tenn. and supper at Cincinnati last night I
don't see but what the people of Penn are as patriotic as they were when
I went through there before but I don't think the people of Ohio are as
loyal as they are in Penn and here they are worse still

This is a pretty large place and plenty of business is done here

We are waiting for the cars now to take us to Lexington, which is
about 100 miles from here. I don't know what they are going to do with
us here but I suppose we are going to join Gen'l Rosecrans[17] Army at any
rate we are going with Gen. Burnside wherever he goes I suppose you
will know where that will be as soon as I shall I never saw fellows act so
as they did on this journey they didn't know what to do with themselves
when they arrived at any city- place you could have seen them all over
it in less than five minutes and then when the engine whistled you would
see them run, some of them would get left and would take the next
train and catch up again they told us at Baltimore that when the 2ond
Maryland Reg't (that is in the first division) arrived there they staked
about 290 guns and waited for the cars, when they got ready to start they
could not find but about 90 fellows the rest had deserted the people there
are just as much "sesish" as ever but don't dare to show it but if they
could help a fellow desert they would any time

I must close now I will write again as soon as I get a chance. Good
bye love to all from your loving son
     George

Sudbury
April 26th 1863

Dear George
     I have not received a letter from you cince March 31st that was wrote
from Covington K.Y. I have wrote to you and Albert cince but I don't
know as you have got them Alfred got a letter from you dated April 11th

*from Mt Sterling your Mother got one from Albert giving an account of
his long march I got a letter from John last Friday dated April 21ˢᵗ he was
at the same place driving teem and was well he wrote that he expected to
move the next day at the time of closing his letter he had got to take his
teem and go and get a load of tents the reports we get from all sources
look much more favorable to our cause I think the Federal leaders are
taking about the right course that is to surround those strongholds so
as to prevent running supplies in to them it was reported yesterday that
our forces had effected a pashed in to the rear of Vixburg and I think the
experiment that our Fleet made with their Moniters and iron clads upon
Fort Sumpter and Charlestown was very sucesfull wul I will rite a few
lines about home now I have got setled down at my new home up in town
now and a very pleasant location and I have composed my mind to make
myself contented and happy as I can as John said he should rather have
a location on Peakham than to have land joining on them Willises but the
Rebels still follow me the farm of George W. Moore¹⁸ was sold yesterday
a Auction and it was sold in three separate lots the buildings and 60 od
acres were sold in one lot subject to the old ladies right of dower and
Edwin Hearington was the purchaser and then the ¾ of acre lot that the
little Barn stood on next to my house was put up next and then the lot
that the old shanty of a house Barkers used to live in and that hill pasture
first pasture joining the house lot was sold we had raised money enough
to buy them two lots if they were sold and did not bring any more than
they were worth to any living man but that P. Willis reported to certain
persons previous to the sale that revealed it to me that if he knew that I
wanted those house lots he would out bid me let the sum be what it would
so I got your Uncle John to come over the sales and procure some one
to bid for me but he mistrusted they were bidding for me and Prescut
risen them up to the enormous sum of seven hund and fifty dollars and I
let them go I did not go out to the sale myself at all wal I made him pay
over three hund dolls more than they were worth to any man the ¾ acre
lot no one bid on me but Prescut and the other lot no other one bid on
that but Webster M (illegible) he did not over two hund and fifty dolls on
it the ¾ acre lot he had to pay two hund and fifty dolls and the other lot
he paid five hund dolls for but I dond care they cant get the place away
from us that we now live on so he has thrown away over three hund dolls
and gained nothing by it I have made up my mind to pay no regard to his
doings he who cannot be happy without taking great pains will always
find his paines greater than his happiness I must close hoping that I can
write you a more pleasant letter next time hoping this will find you well*
    Your Father

Uriah's neighbors at "the Old Place," the Prescott Willis family who had outbid him on land that he wanted, were now going to be his neighbors at his new house up on Peakham Road as well.

The Brigade was now under Colonel Hartranft. Colonel Wild, recuperating at home from his wounds, sent a national flag from Boston to the regiment to replace the flag lost at Antietam. On May 23 the regiment left for Crab Orchard, Kentucky, passing many other troops camped along the way, preparing for an advance into East Tennessee.

The following letter from George to Francis describes in humorous detail some of his time spent marching in Kentucky. This march along the Kentucky River is clearly detailed from early May in George Moore's 1863 diary.

May 24-1863
Camp at 35th Regt

Dear Brother
I now sit down to answer your letter which I received some time ago I was very glad to hear that you had received that money. I guess the folks were in need of it I don't see how you got along through the winter. I understand that we are going to be paid again soon for my part I don't care if they don't pay us for 6 months then I shall not spend it.

Yesterday we started on another tramp we went about 10 miles and went into camp then our marching order was countermanded and so we are stopping here for further orders they don't seem to know what to do with us here in old Kentuck they march us a little way then we lay still a few days then march us again first forward then back. I guess they want to show us around the state. I wouldn't care if they would only let us ride. We are about a mile and a half from a place called Craborchard.

We have just got some good news about the taking of Vicksburg. I hope it is true but I am afraid it will turn out to be the same as taking Richmond did.

How is old Sudbury and all the folks do they have any trouble there now days I understand they are all getting married. I wonder if it is to escape the draft poor fellows some of them may want to be drafted in a few years

I expect every mail to hear that you are married although you need not be afraid of the draft they won't take you or Alfred the first call, perhaps they won't call for anybody. I hope they wont need to for I don't want to see any more have to come out here, but if they do need any more I hope they will take every man there is north then we all could go home in a little while

I must close now for we have got to change our camp. Give my love to all write soon

From

George

A few days later, George received the following letter from his sister, Mary.

Marlborough
May 31st 1863

Dear Brother
I have been writing to Albert and thought I would write to you also I am well and hope this will find you the same there is not much going on here any more than in Sudbury I have got to my home for the summer I suppose and if I like or will or I have the three weeks that I have been here I shall be contented they seem to think a good deal of me Mr Leimom Weeks Father and Mother and Brother live in the other part of the house I call them Grandpar and Grandmarm and Billy Leimons[19] Brothers and myself are getting along nicely he wants to go down to Sudbury some night and have me go with him and get Hattie[20] and we will have a ride she came up and brought me home Election night and we got him in and we had a ride and he thinks he would like another he has been to war and he got wonded in the foot he came home last winter he has been on cruchers ever since till last week he has got so he can go with a cane I calculate to have some good times if I stay here this summer and guess I shall George you would have laughed if you had been here Monday morning I went into the Chamber to get the clothes and was agoing to get the sheet on the bed and I went in not knowing that any one was in there I was going to open the window and I heard some one a laughing and I looked round and there was Billy in the bed a laughing away I bet I was not long comming out I cannot help laughing every time I think of it he looked

so qurar their is a fellow that works for Mr Weeks he is the ordest thing that I ever saw yesterday he had been to work on the highway and he had drinked a lot of cider and he was about half crazy last night he came up stairs to go to bed and he jumped out of the chamber window and stayed out awhile and then came back and went to bed they Sent for the neighbors to come and stay in the house for Leimon was sick and they wanted some one else in the house it did not worry many I bet you What did you do Election day I hope you had a good time as well as myself I went home about noon got there soon enough to get my dinner and in the afternoon Emily Brigham Lucreta and Hattie and myself went to the Village and went into the Library and into Mr Jones new House and when we was comming home Father overtook us with the horse cart and we got in and rode and he got the horse to troting and I thought I should shake all to pieces but I made out to stand it til I got home I did not fire any guns this year but I should if I had been at home but I was not you see When you write you direct your letters to Marlborough in care of Mr Leimon Weeks and tell Albert to also I shall get them better I walked up in town after yours the other night it is a little ways up in town it is three miles but I heard that their was one for me and was bound to get it they do not go up more than once a week so you see I do not get my letters as I should if I was at home you said you thought I looked poor you knowed I am not as fleshy as I used to be and I do not have much chance to grow fat for I have to work hard most of the time I wonder what will be agoing on here the 4 of July I supose you will not be here then but I wish you was going to be it will seem lonesome enough. I do not much expect to go any whare that day Hattie talks of going out to work if she can find a place a little while but I do not think she will find any very easy now for it is so late unless she gets a place in a shop some whare I suppose you have heard from the father before this time so you know that they have got your money and it did not come before they needed it either when you write write me all the news that theyr is because you know I am not at home and shall not get it unless you write it to me I have not much of any news to write for I have not heard any the folks were all well when I went home they have been up to see me twice since I came up here I must close now for I want to write a number more letters if I get time answer soon and I will write as ofton as I can

  from your loving sister Mary E Moore

Mary was working as a housekeeper for a family in a neighboring town in order to earn money for her clothes and upkeep. Later in September her mother wrote to George that she hates to have the girls go out to work, but it is necessary, and it is better to have them do housework than to work in a store.

On June 3 the regiment was told to pack up and be ready to move out at a quick pace. It was not long before they discovered that the battle site was some nine hundred miles away. They were "on loan" to General Grant, who was in need of more troops in his campaign to capture Vicksburg. They marched thirty-four miles in twenty-two hours to reach the cars at Nicholasville, Kentucky, which took them to Cincinnati, and then to Illinois. On June 9, in the town of Cairo, where the Mississippi and the Ohio Rivers converge, the regiment boarded the steamboat, *Imperial*. Eleven steamboats traveled, in sight of one another for protection, five hundred miles down the Mississippi. They passed Missouri, Arkansas, Kentucky, and Tennessee, and landed on June 14 within view of Vicksburg. The Union Army was throwing large mortars and shells from rafts further downstream, towards the front of the city, while Generals Grant and Sherman planned to attack the rear. After a night spent in a Louisiana swamp, they moved up the Yazoo River and formed a camp where General Grant visited the next day. The Yazoo River runs parallel to the Mississippi and joins the Mississippi just north of Vicksburg. Breastworks were built and artillery set, establishing an impregnable line. Grant had encircled the city with his reinforcement troops, overpowering the Rebel Army and on July 4 cannonading ceased. The Confederates had surrendered. Losses to the Confederates had been over 40,000 men, 31,000 of whom were at the garrison of Vicksburg, along with enough arms and munitions for 60,000. The Confederates' supply line had been severed.[21] This Battle at Vicksburg took place at almost the same time as the Battle at Gettysburg.

Sudbury
June 14th *1863*

Dear George
 I received yours of May the 9th *and was very glad to hear from you and to know that you enjoy so good health you must be pretty well to stand such long Marches but the secenery in traveling through new Countries has a tendency to keep ones courage and strength up and the excitement of war I should have answered yours before but I have been so unwell and have had so much to do hope you will excuse me this time*

as I am apt to be more out of health about this time of year just before green sauce and fruit comes which I expect to pick a mess of green peas in the course of this week prospect of good crops of everything fruit in abundance they say I have got the best garden they is in town I wrote to Albert cince I received yours and directed it to Cincinati stating we had received that money that you sent home and was very gratefully oblige for it it came in a time that it done us a grate deel of good and those pictures that you sent I could see quite a contrast between them and those that you left when you went away John sent home his picture cince I received yours he was well he is not a driving teem now he has got a saddlers berth now received a letter from John just after the Battle of Fredericksburg gining a detailed account of the Battle from day to day for seven days which I would give to you but I don't feel able to write it and suppose you have got the particulars before this time your Mother received a letter from you and one from Albert a few days ago yours was wrote from Cairo waiting fa the Boat then you have seen the King of Rivers the Missisipa River the two years and nine months men seem to coming home now but I have not heard a man say but what they ment to reenlist and go back again I saw Henry Smith cince he came home he says he shall enlist again says most of that Regt will the 44 Regts came into Boston on Tuesday night last some 20 of the Framingham boys went out and they came up to Framingham on Thursday Morning and met with a grand reception their I went over was a large prosesion escorted them from the depot to the grove and there they partook of a bountaioses collection of eatables the prosesion consisted of a horse Comp Fire Engine Comp. Military Comp. Citizens and Richardson Band and a band of little drummers well it is pretty still times just now in old Sudbury they have got the tomb of John Goodnow done and makes quite an improvement to the Cemetary the cost I have not learnt I think some two thousand dolls. John Goodnow has built a shoe shop between the blacksmiths shop and the meeting house the Library is in great Circulation and is a good collection of Books speaking of the war it looks as though it was a coming in favor now more than it ever was they feel here to the north if they can subdue Vixburg it will be a discisive blow all at home but Mary and Alfred Francis is building an adition to the barn all well hope this will find you well

    From your Father

P.S. Excuse me this time hope I shall be able to write more next time

After General Grant's victory at the Battle of Jackson on May 14, Confederate General Johnson began to gather troops and moved towards the rear of Grant's troops. Grant ordered General Sherman to clear Johnson from the area and by late afternoon on July 4, the IX Corps was on the move towards Jackson, Mississippi. Drinking water along the way was said to be "poisonous and malarious"[22] and continued to be a problem throughout the march. The heat was unbearable and the skies were filled with lightning and thunder. By dawn on July 11, the troops were advancing towards the city:

General William Tecumseh Sherman, Union Army. engraving, Pictorial History of the Great Civil War, 1878.

> A soldier in a faded blue uniform rode quietly by. He is
> General Sherman – even then an object of curiosity; but
> where was the immense staff, the flash and glitter which
> we were accustomed to associate with the chief of a great
> army? Evidently our great commander had come out to
> see and not be seen.[23]

On the outskirts of Jackson, Mississippi, the Thirty-fifth continued to
support the skirmishes for two weeks, being relieved daily by other
regiments. The Confederates decided to evacuate the city rather than be
captured, and on the morning of July 17 the Thirty-fifth was the first
regiment to enter the city. The national flag Colonel Wild had recently sent
from home was raised to the top of the capitol. In his diary entry for July 17,
George writes "marched into Jackson at daybreak...our Regt first there...
took a lot of prisoners...raised our flag on court house"

> The members of the regiment think it rather a hard joke
> upon them when the Northern papers gave the honors to
> the Thirty-fifth Missouri, the editors thinking that it was
> not possible for a Massachusetts regiment to have been
> present here. The city of Jackson was then made useless
> to the Confederates by the tearing up of the rails leading
> out of the city.[24]

The regiment was now ordered to return to Kentucky. The men were
exhausted in the extreme heat and weakened by lack of food and water
and the long wait for the steamboats. The hot weather was so oppressive
that they started their marches at half past three in the morning, but still,
the men dropped beside the road. During this wait one man received a box
from home that had been sent the past winter and everyone was curious as
to its contents. In the box were pairs of mittens for every member of the
regiment, knit by the ladies back home. "Could fortune have timed a gift
more inopportunely?"[25]

When soldiers needed supplies or personal items, they often bought
them from the "sutlers," vendors who followed the troops showing up
especially on payday. George mentions sutlers in his diary.

Street Scene Showing Sutlers Row, Tennessee. #111-B-512
National Archives, Washington D.C.

In early August, the regiment boarded the steamboat *Planet* along with the Eleventh New Hampshire, Fifty-first and Seventy-ninth New York, and a company of the Forty-fifth Pennsylvania. The men were uncomfortably crowded onto every foot of deck space. The Thirty-fifth Regiment was assigned to accompany a train of two hundred wagons to Hickman's Bridge, Kentucky. After the heat of Mississippi, only six officers and two hundred men, including George Moore, were fit enough for this assignment, which took eighteen days. Malaria still plagued the soldiers. Men that had remained in Kentucky, and were now well enough, rejoined the regiment as they headed toward East Tennessee. On Thursday, September 3, after the Battle of Jackson in Mississippi, George Moore was promoted to Corporal. Orders arrived on September 9 for the regiment to proceed to Crab Orchard, Kentucky. When these orders and other directives to proceed to Knoxville were countermanded again and again, the men, now becoming discouraged, began to build winter quarters. When the order arrived on September 13 to proceed over the mountains towards Knoxville, only one hundred and fifty men of the Thirty-fifth Regiment were well enough to make the trip.[26]

Sudbury
Sept 13ᵗʰ 1863

Dear Albert and George,

I believe I have received a letter from both of you since I wrote to you, so I will try and answer them. I am very glad to learn that you are having some time to rest after the hard time you had in Miss. I read a letter in the Marlboro Journal, written by a member of the 36ᵗʰ Regt, which gave a dreadful account of their sufferings in the campaign to Jackson.

I am glad I did not know your situation at the time; I should have been discouraged about ever seeing you again. It seems as though I would not be thankful enough that your lives were spared. I hope it will not be your lot to go through another siege like that. Some people think the war is nearly over, and I hope it is, but I suppose the rebels will hold out as long as they can.

I received a letter from John a few days ago. he writes that they are having quite an easy time, and growing fat. He seems to think the army of the Potomac have not done as much good as the western troops, but I tell him he ought to feel as though they were all doing great service to their country. I don't think any of us realize yet, how much good the soldiers are doing, but the history of this war will tell us how much good they have done, and how much they have suffered.

You say they are giving furloughs to some of the soldiers, how glad we should be to see both of you to come home. I hope you will try to get a chance to come if you can.

I believe I told you in my last letter that Hattie had gone to Ashland to work. She likes her place very much as yet. It seemed rather hard to have her go away from home, but she must earn her clothes some way, and I think it is better for her to do housework than to work in a shop. I think it is quite remarkable, that you got the bundle I sent out so long ago. I should have thought some one would be wearing those shirts before that time. I am glad you found them for it will be growing cold before long, and you will need them

Mr. Edwin Gerry and his family have got back to Sudbury. The climate out west did not suit him. Mrs. Gerry tells some amusing stories about the customs out there. You know she has a good faculty for describing. She says the people there ride to meeting with oxen. I think she would enjoy such a ride quite well. I don't know whether they will settle down in Sudbury, or go some where else

Mr. David Lincoln is dead and they say Prescot has got about all his property, but I don't think any one will envy him, if he is rich. It requires something besides money to make people happy. We are having quite sudden changes of weather lately, which makes a great many people sick with colds. Your Father is troubled with neuralgia, now the weather is growing cooler, but he keeps about his work most of the time. He has been to Boston every week for some time. He has a large garden, on that piece of land front of the house, and has raised considerable stuff for the market. When he has not a full load of his own, the neighbors supply him with apples or something of that kind to make up a load. Old Charley makes a first rate farm horse, but I hate to see him work so hard.

Francis stays with us yet, he has been doing jobs for other people, so he has not quite finished our carpenter work yet. He does not eat any meat yet, but lives on graham bread and potatoes and fruit. He thinks his health is better than it was when he ate meat. He finds the flour for his bread so he is not much expense to us, and he does not charge any pay for his work on the barn-My sheet is about full, so I must bid you good bye for the present. Please write often.

M. H. Moore

Although Francis' poor health kept him from being drafted, he was well enough to work on carpentry and painting projects for both the family and the town.

Crab Orchard
Sept 19ᵗʰ 1863

Dear Brother
I received your letter a few days ago and it was good to hear from you and to hear that you are well. I am glad you didn't have to come out here for I think 3 out of our family is enough if it is not let us do double duty. I don't know whether you would stand it out here or not I know that our kind of living would suit you our food I mean but sleeping on the ground with a little shelter tent over you would soon use you up. Sometimes we don't have that over us sometimes we have to lay down with our equipment on and guns at our side without anything over us and when we get up in the morning our heads would feel as though it had been in a vice. Has Everett got well yet and is he coming out here. If he pays 300 dollars and stays at home he will catch it when I get home

that is if Mary isn't around with the broom if she is I won't dare to say anything I don't blame him if he don't want to come but then the people ought to come if they are drafted for that is the fairest way to get them if they draft you may know that you are needed there are some men that don't ought to come out here but I think an able man to come as he is had ought to come. Well this draft will make a great many show their patriotism. I am glad I came out when I did. I am not sorry I came yet although I have been discouraged about the war but I think there is some prospect of its closing now. We are doing garrison duty here now and I think we shall stop here sometime part of the Regt is on duty in the town the rest of us are just out of town the 51st PV is here with us one Regt of the Brigade is at Camp Nelson about 23 miles from here the other Regt (11th NH) has gone to London, the 9 corps is divided along between Cincinnati and East Tenn. We are about 30 miles from the Railroad at Nicholasville so we can get our mail pretty regular we are having a tiptop time.

There was 2300 prisoners went through this place yesterday that Burnside took at Cumberland Gap. they were the same dirty set of greybacks that we see everywhere or a part of them at one or two houses the ladies waved their handkerchiefs to them but all they got by it was a guard on their house

I must close now for I have got to go on duty. give my love to all the folks and friends write soon and all the news

From George

The following letter was sent to Albert and he passed it on to George.

Sunday
Sept 20 1863

Dear Brother
Your letter dated the 11th I received night before last. The box I received some time ago all safe. The contents were a little damp when it arrived but after a little airing they were all in as good condition as could be expected. Tell George I am much obliged for the music. One piece I have learned and it is tip top. You spoke in your last of enclosing a receipt but there was none in the letter.

Eli Willis called here today and gave me a bundle of letters from you. He arrived in town last night. He looks exactly as he used to with the honest frown and not much the worst for wear either. John wrote home a few days ago. Says that he got a letter from you the other day. The first for a month or two. Says that Spencer Smith[27] had just arrived back to the regiment and had a high old time with him talking over matters and things at home. Says he feels 90 per cent better after hearing Spencer tell his story. I wrote to George that Lieut Hudson[28] had called here. He gave a first rate account of you boys. So does Eli. So George is promoted to Corporal. I hope he will prove worthy of the <u>high</u> honors conferred. Eli says that the order to go to Tennesee is countermanded, so you will probably stay in Kentucky for the present. I hope you will not see another fight.

I have been thinking that you might like to have me write and let you know <u>precisely</u> how matters stand here at home now. Therefore I herewith submit my report. First I will state in regard to the money that you boys have sent home that it has mostly passed into Fathers hands. All that has been sent addressed to Mother she has paid over to him after using some for family nescessaries and all that has been sent addressed to me I have paid over to him after deducting some due me, as you wrote me to. I think that Father is using the money for the subsistence of the family. Mother has taken up some of her money and also used for the same purpose. There was also a dozen good pear trees bought and they were transplanted out in front.

Father has cultivated about ½ an acre of the piece out in front as a garden and it is one of the best gardens in the neighborhood. Part of the Blackberries and the vegetables, Beans, Corn, etc above what the family used he has marketed and got the cash for. He has also raised considerable produce on the Daniel Moore Place and marketed.

The Hay crop was good. It is all stored in the barn. Whether there will be more than enough to keep one horse and cow through I don't know. Father has hired the cow pastured the past summer. The excellent crop of hay and grain on the Daniel Moore Place is stored there. There is a good crop of fruit there also. I think that Father intends to hire that Place another year as he sowed some rye on it lately. In regard to the taxes on this Place Father agrees to pay the first installments, the whole amount is about 10 Dollars I believe.

The extension that I am putting on to the Barn, Kitchen, etc. Mother finds money to buy the stock for and I do the work without charge. The cost of the stock for the extension will probably be about 70 Dollars. In regard to the stock that Father has sold and taken the cash for. I will

*state the amount as near as I can. The Mowing Machine 50 Dollars,
Horse Cart 16 Dolls, Ox Cart (that I built partly new) 25 Dollars,
Winnowing Mill 4 Dolls, The Dickenson horse 30 Dollars, Pung sleigh
and extra top 2 Dollars. This money and also the allowance, 50 Dollars
etc. is quite a little sum to have laid up. He has now to use a Horse cart
which I built, the Charlie horse, the Chaise (he has had the wheels new
rimmed and tired) The Sleigh and Harnesses and all the farming tools
that he used to have and the one horse hay wagon he bought back for a
small sum.*

*John Eaton wants to settle with his creditors. He offered to settle by
paying 15 cents on the Dollar. I understand that most of them favor the
proposal. Mother has not decided yet whether to settle on those terms or
not. Some of his Creditors say that the Real Estate is fixed so that if he
goes into Chancery they can't get hold of it.*

*I still continue to live on the mode of diet that you recollect I adopted
when you was at home, only a little more so. I am living on two meals a
day on a diet composed of nice unleavened bread made of wheat meal
and water only, with fruit and occasionally vegetables. Therefore I have
to buy my own subsistence flower with the exception of a few vegetables
from the garden now and then. Mother is kept pretty busy with her
needle in order to keep Father and the children presentable. Mary,
Harriet and Alfred are still at the same places they have been. None of
them have been home for a fortnight. News both locally and War are
scarce here at present.*

*I almost forgot to state that I am keeping a Cash Account in one
of your Books of all items of Debt & Credit as exact as I can. You will
excuse this letter. My paper warns me, and I must close. The folks are all
as well as usual. Hope this will find you the same.*

Frank U. M.

George Moore played a number of instruments and asked his mother to
send his fiddle to him. He says the fiddle was played by many of his friends
and provided entertainment for all. During the war George played the
organ in a Baptist church in Kentucky. After George returned to Sudbury
he played the accordion when he visited Sarah Jones, and participated in
several singing groups in town. George organized his own band, "Moore's
Military Marching Band," and they played all over the Northeast and
in Canada. A great many songs came out of the Civil War, some easily
recognizable such as the "Battle Hymn of the Republic" by Julia Ward
Howe, and the "John Brown Song."

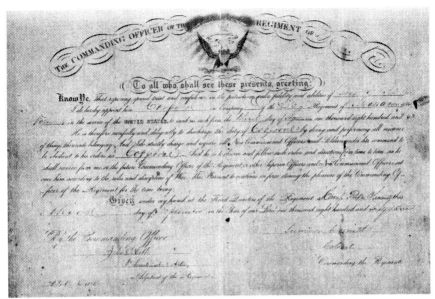

George Moore Promotion to Corporal, Sudbury Historical Society

Crab Orchard Ky
Sept 30th 1863F

Dear Mother
We received your letter day before yesterday and was very glad to hear from you. We have been having a pretty good time but I believe we are to start for Knoxville, Tenn tomorrow it is nearly 200 miles from here so we have quite a tramp of it most of the way is over mountains I don't know certain yet whether we shall go or not but that is the story. I thought when we came here we were going to have an easy time but they can't get along without the (———) so I suppose we shall have to go
We have just got a good camp with board tents as housesn an everything comfortable but it is our luck I don't suppose they would have sent for us unless they needed us so we hadn't ought to complain
Some of the officers have sent home for their folks to come out here and they are on the way now but they will have to go home again without seeing their friends
How are you all getting along nowadays I suppose Alfred and Hattie are at Ashland yet and like as well as ever

Albert received a letter from Francis yesterday stating that Eli Willis had been there to see you folks I suppose he surprised most of Sudbury folks I should like to get a furlough but I suppose I shall have to wait my turn which may not come for 2 years well if I get home then all right I shall be satisfied and I think there is some prospect of it now

What is going on in old Sudbury now do they have anything there to keep the place alive I want to have Eli get back so I can find out about the place

How does the Library get along do Middletown folks go down there for books or do they get along without them I want to see that building

I must close now give my love to all the folks write soon and write all the news

From your loving son
George

Sudbury
Oct 4ᵗʰ 1863

Dear George
I will take this opertuneity to write a few lines to you now and send by Mr Willis I was so glad to get hold of his hand it seemed almost as though I had got hold of your hands came to here him talk about you and one right from among you it is a long time cince I have written to you you will see in Alberts letter that I tried to excuse myself poor excuse has been a long time cince I have had a letter from you I think I have not had one cince you wrote from Camp near the big Black River Miss and I think not from Albert cince landing from the boat in site of Vicksburg

Captain John Hudson, Company D,
Thirty-fifth Massachusetts Regiment,
Photograph SC579-RG98S-54.87
courtesy of U.S, Army Military History
Institute, Carlisle, Pennsylvania

Lieut Hudson called on me when he was on here he spoke very highly of you and Albert and all the Sudbury Boys you had a chance to

exercise your courage and firmness at the Battle of Jackson Miss and
you did it with honor to yourself

I think I have wrote to you cince you and Albert sent your pictures
to me and that twenty dolls which I was very much obliged to you have
used all of the money you have sent in providing for the family except
paying up Francis what you oed him I was glad to hear that you had left
that unhealthy State Miss I hope you can stop in Kentuckey if you have
got a heathy location I should like to come out and see you Mr Willis
gave me an invitation to come out with him I had not got my harvesting
done so I could not very well leave have not much news Mr Willis will
give you all of the news of the present give my best respects to the
Sudbury Boys and the members of your Company D and members of the
35 Regt in general you have Won an Honorable and Noble spot in history
that cannot be blotted out in the present generation we are all well hope
this will find you well write as often as you can

From your Father
P.S. we will send out a few articles perhaps of not much interest to you

During the war, parents and wives traveled to visit their soldiers when
they knew they would be in a place that they could reach in a few days'
travel time. It was not uncommon for officers to have their wives with them
and there are photos of civilian spectators picnicking while watching the
battles from the hillsides. Uriah traveled to visit his sons when they were
all together, at least once, and his mother traveled to see her son, George,
when he was hospitalized in Philadelphia.

Sudbury
Oct. 5th *1863*

Dear George
I have been writing to Albert this evening and am going to write a
few lines to you. I understand you have been promoted on account of
your bravery in the field of battle. It sounds rather better than it would
if you had run, but I am glad I did not see you stand in that dangerous
place, and I feel very thankful, that you was preserved from harm. I
often think how many mothers have been called to give up their sons,
who were just as dear to them, as mine are to me, and I hope I shall
never forget to acknowledge the hand of God in spareing their lives. Eli
Willis says the 35th *Regt does not number two hundred now. It does not*

seem as though so many of those healthy looking men I saw at Camp, had died so soon, but I hope they will not have to see another battle. I think they have done their part of the fighting, and I hope there will not be much more fighting for any one to do.

You will not see many of the Sudbury conscripts out there. Part of them have been exempted, and about all the rest have paid their $300. I suppose all the brave men volunteered before the draft commenced. Poor Everet has been examined and accepted so he has paid his $300. but he feels very bad about it. He will be likely to put off being married a while longer now. I don't know but Mary will have to work out all her days if she waits for him

Aren't you and Albert going to have a furlough as well as the rest? Perhaps you intend to take us by surprise. You will find us very glad to see you any way, if you do come home, but the worst of it would be to have you go back again

The children have grown considerable since you went away. Charley wears a pair of your pants that were large enough for you when you left home and they fit him quite well. Alfred is as large as any one of the boys now. He tried on one of Johns coats the other day, and said it was to tight across the shoulders for him.

I believe you gave leave, when you went away, for the boys to wear your clothes, so you will not expect to find them all when you come home. The old clothes I had in the house, have saved laying out money for new ones while cloth is so dear. I hope things will be cheaper when this war is over.

Mary is at Marlboro yet but I don't know whether she will stay much longer or not. Mr. Jonas Hunts store was broken open last night, and some things stolen, but I have not learned all the particulars about it yet. I do not think of any more news this evening so I will bid you good night. From your ever loving Mother

Mary H. Moore

Albert H Moore and George F. Moore, Sudbury Historical Society

Camp near London, Ky
October 6th

Dear Father
I have not received any letters from you for sometime so I will take this opportunity to write and let you know where we are. I wrote to Mother a few days ago that we were going to Knoxville since then we have traveled about 35 miles over the roughest road I ever saw. the first day we traveled 12 mile it took us about 7 hours the 2ed day we went but 5 miles that took us 3 hours the 3rd day we traveled about 10 miles over the roughest part of the road it took us most 8 hours yesterday we traveled 8 miles in 2 hours and 40 minutes that is the fastest traveling we ever done. we had to carry our knapsack with woolen and rubber blankets, overcoat, shirt, stockings, and a few little trinkets, had 8 days rations 40 rounds of ammunition canteen full water and Gun and equipments. the whole weighing about 50 or 60 lbs we didn't have to march today we are waiting for the battery's to come up, so as to all go along together there will be only one Brigade of us and 2 batteries. our Brigade contains 4 Regts the whole making about 500 men for duty I think we haven't 100 men for duty in this Regts the Miss campaign wore us down we had most 500 men for duty when we went down there. the Sudbury boys are all well except Mr Garfield[29] and Harry Hall[30] they are back to the hospital I don't know anything about Wm Bailey[31] he has not been with us since we left Arlington Heights there is Rufus, Wm Bowen, Albert and myself left in the company out of 8 that came from home Wayland had 14 men in this company and there is but 2 here now Waltham had 33 and there is but 5 left we are the largest company in the Regt we have got 21 men Officers and all
I must close when you hear from me again I expect it will be from Knoxville write soon and all the news from your loving son
George

In October the regiment left Crab Orchard, Kentucky, heading over the mountains through the Cumberland Gap. The winding ascent was one of the roughest the regiment had traveled. The wagons became mired in the thick mud caused by early snow storms and ice, making it slow and difficult for both the men and the animals. On one steep ascent ten mules were required to pull a single wagon. The Cumberland Gap, through the southern Appalachians, provided wild mountain views and colorful foliage reminding the soldiers of New England.

The Cumberland Gap is located just north of where the states of Kentucky, Tennessee, and Virginia, meet. For the Thirty-fifth Regiment, the first experience fording a wide river came at a point in the Cumberland, the Clinch River. Each man had to make the decision whether to face the discomfort of going barefoot and bruise his feet, or to keep his boots on, and face the discomfort of marching in wet boots for some time to come. Travel for the next few days was difficult in the rain and snow. Marching in cold, slippery mud the regiment was finally within sight of the Gap by October 14.

Camp near Tazewell East Tenn
Oct 15th 1863

Dear Brother
We are in camp today and I have nothing to do so I am going to improve my time by writing to let you know where we are and that we are all right
We have been on the march for Knoxville about a week or ten days. We are within about 40 miles of there now we have marched about 115 miles over the worst road I ever saw we went over a number of mountains yesterday we went through the Cumberland Gap Parson Brownlow[32] and family went through the Gap at the same time we did or rather he passed us as we were going through. when he passed us the Band played a patriotic tune the Parson bowed to us. he said he thought a great deal of Massachusetts boys. he stopped in the town last night
We don't get any mails now so we don't get much news there is a rumor here that Rosa has had another fight with Bragg and whipped him they say that there is 15000 prisoners coming through here today I don't know whether it is true or not but I suppose I shall before night
We want to hear from the Ohio Election most of anything now for we consider it of some importance
Who have they got for candidates for Gov in mass this year tell us all the news and how you are all getting along at home and excuse this short letter
from George

George notes in his diary that on October 16 the regiment arose at one o'clock AM to march through stormy weather over twelve miles, crossing the Clinch River towards Knoxville. By October 19 the regiment arrived outside Knoxville after marching more than one hundred and forty miles through Tazewell and Maynardville, Tennessee. Some houses displayed red flags on their doors, signifying small pox.[33] Soldiers on both sides feared small pox, and primitive forms of vaccination were used to attempt to keep the troops free of disease. One case of small pox could spread quickly through a company. Deaths from disease were greater than deaths on the battlefield.

Sudbury
Oct 25th 1863

Dear George
    I received yours of the 6th and was very glad to here from you and to know that you have stood the changes of Climates so well it must be very trying to change Clyment as ofton as you have to it seems a great while cince I have had a letter from you before I know I have not wrote to you for some time I wrote and sent by Ely and gave my reason for not writing I suppose Ely has got out there now not much news returns a coming in favorable from the Border States and the reports from the seat of War comes in favorable it is genealy pretty healthy now have had a number of deaths in Town of late of old people the Old Revolutionor is gone Mr John Goodnow was buried a week ago last Friday Mr Samuel Hill was buried today we are getting along very comfortably the labor of myself and the labor of the old horse has supported the family pretty comfortably so far with what you Boys have done for us although everything has been very high that wee have had to buy and I think we shall get through the winter very comfortably if we remain well have got pretty much through with my harvesting had good cropps plowed up about one and a quarter acre of the land last Spring planted about two thirds of it to corn and potatoes Sold besides the Corn and potatoes enough for the family to eat through the season untill the crops come again if they come as usual and the turnips beets beens cabbages cucumbers squash pumpkin tomatoes watermelons sweet corn and pees sold about thirty dolls worth besides from the acre and a quarter pretty much all the amusements we have is temperace Meetings and temperance Lectures the Library is a pretty successful thing so far the Copperheads[34] say but a little I will close after stating that it is reported that you have had a Promotion in the Company am glad to here that you have done yourselfs honor so far I hope you will

be spared to do more good write as often as you can we are all well and
hope this will find you well
from your Father

By October 28 the regiment was part of a four-regiment detail ordered
to take down a pontoon bridge. The bridge was a series of box boats that
were dragged out by mules and then loaded onto flat cars attached to a
locomotive that had been taken in pieces across the river and rebuilt. There
was not enough time to bring the train back to Knoxville and so, with a
full head of steam, the cars and locomotive headed down the track where
the bridge had been:

> A full head of steam was gathered – the driver jumping
> off and leaving the train to its fate – the engine roaring
> like a wild bull – leapt into the air and plunged headlong
> into the river.[35]

After watching the train and cars plunge into the Tennessee River, the
regiment moved on to Lenoir Station where they would spend the winter.
General Burnside stopped a few days in camp with the men. At three in the
morning, on November 14, the men were rousted out and told to pack up
and be ready to move as quietly as possible. It appeared that the regiments
were now headed toward Knoxville instead of Loudon. They waited in
the pouring rain for orders when a locomotive arrived from Knoxville,
and Generals Burnside and Ferrero jumped from the tender. Again, orders
were changed and the fighting troops were turned around and directed
toward Loudon. The news that General Longstreet was crossing the river
just below Loudon sent the regiment to the aid of the Twenty-third Corps to
help delay the enemy so the Union trains would be able to reach Knoxville
to help fortify the city.[36]

Travel was so difficult and slow that part of the ammunition at the
rear was destroyed along with officers' baggage and books to prevent
it from getting into enemy hands. Of more immediate concern to the
soldiers was the destruction of a hundred wagons filled with food and other
supplies, so they would not fall into rebel hands. Food was already in short
supply and the men were issued half or even quarter rations. On reaching
Campbell's Station, General Burnside had a mile-long line designed to
delay Longstreet until the Union trains could get through and fortify the city
of Knoxville. General Hartranft's Thirty-fifth Massachusetts and Eleventh
New Hampshire Regiments were deployed along a north-south line. After
three days of skirmishing around the clock, this was accomplished. "On the

outer slopes of our hill a line of entrenchments was drawn, and all hands
went busily to work, including local citizens who came and took places
alongside the Union soldiers for the defense of their homes. Volunteers
included men, recently under the yoke of slavery, who were now lending
their help for the Union cause. Burnside let it be known that Knoxville was
to be held to the last man."[37]

The Thirty-fifth Regiment was assigned to assist Lieutenant Samuel
Benjamin's Battery,[38] moving the gun-carriages through the mud at a
snail's pace. The horses were so overworked that the men "broke ranks and
caught hold of the muddy rims of the wheels or parts of the gun-carriages,
wherever a hand could seize them and pushed and shoved to assist the
animals."[39]

Sudbury, Nov. 29, 1863

Dear Albert & George,

*We received three letters from you last Tuesday evening, one for
Francis, and two for your Father, and we got one from John the same
night. It seemed quite reviving to hear from all of you at once, for it had
been some time since we had heard from John. I fear you do not get all
our letters. We have sent quite a number since you left Crab Orchard I
sent two by Eli and Hattie sent two and your Father sent one or two by
him. Your Father has sent letters since the Election, and Francis has
written to you two or three times since you left Kentucky. I don't see why
Eli does not return to the Regt. He appeared quite patriotic when he was
here, and pretended to be anxious to get back, before you moved. We sent
a few small articles by him besides the letters. Your Father saw him at the
store, the night before he left town, and he bought two handkerchiefs for
him to bring to you, and Francis sent some books and papers, and I sent
each of you a new towel. I hope you will get them, although they are not
of much value, they might be some benefit to you, out there.*

*Your Father received one of Parson Brownlow's papers last
wednesday night and was very much interested with it. He read it
through before he went to bed that night, and he has lent it to Mr.
Dickenson and others. He says it ought to be read in public, for every
one to hear.*

*We have received some papers from you before that, and some
flowers. That bunch of cotton was a great curiosity to us, I shall take
special care of all such things that you send home.*

*I wrote to you a week or two ago, and mentioned about Everett,
feeling very bad about having to pay $300 or go to war. I believe I hinted
that connection between him and Mary, was like to be given up, but I*

suppose I must call that a mistake, for he came home at Thanksgiving and called as usual. He left town without letting her know where he was going, and has not written to her since, and he had been gone so long, I think she had nearly made up her mind that it was all done with. She threatened to give him a piece of her mind if she ever saw him again, but I don't think she talked very hard to him. Hattie says she would not make up quite so easy, if any one should treat her so.

What kind of a Thanksgiving did you have out there? I thought of you a great many times that day, and comforted myself with the hope that the war will be over before next year at this time, and you will all be at home. If it should be so, we shall have such a Thanksgiving as we never had before. The meeting last Thursday, was at the Methodist Church, and the house was pretty well filled. All three ministers were there and expressed their feelings with regard to the war. They appear confident that our cause is prospering, and that this dreadful struggle will soon be over. They had a contribution, for the benefit of the prisoners at Richmond, who are suffering for food and clothing, many of them have already starved to death. The rebels will not allow government to do anything for them, but have consented to permit a few private individuals to go to their relief. Those who go, will run quite a risk, but I hope they will be prospered in their kindness to their suffering fellow men. It seems dreadful to think of those young men, who left their homes, to defend their country, now starving in prison. I hope their cruel oppressors will soon have their reward.

We expect a lecture in the town hall tomorrow evening from Mr. Coffin who has been an eyewitness to a great many battles out south and west. I expect it will be very interesting. He has been a correspondent of the Boston Journal, for some time, and has written some very interesting letters. His name is called Carleton, in the Journal. Very likely you have read some of the accounts of the battles he has seen. I have been thinking you would like to know how the Goodnow library looks so I got Francis to draw a little picture of it, so you could judge something about it. It is a mean looking building, for one that cost 2500 dollars, but it is fire proof, and that is why it cost so much. It is eight cornered, like the cupola on the barn, at the old place. The walls are built of brick, and the roof is tin, it is lighted by two large windows in front, and eight windows at the top of the building. That square, marked over the porch, represents a piece of marble with this inscription

Goodnows Library
Erected 1862

The interior of the building is much prettier than the outside, it has shelves enough to hold a great many thousand books, I believe they have bought over 3000 volumes this year, and expect to increase the number yearly. there are all kinds of books, some religious books some on agriculture, and a great many story books for young people and children. The Library is open wednesday and saturday afternoons and evenings, & gives the young people a good excuse to take a walk. Mr. Samuel Puffer is Librarian, but his health is rather poor, so Alpheus has taken his place of late.

I don't think of much news this time, but perhaps I can find more when I write again. we are all well, and I hope you are enjoying the same blessing. Ellen says, "tell George to write me a letter and ask ever so many questions, then I can think what to write when I answer it." Please write often and we will do the same.

From your loving mother
M H Moore

THE GOODNOW LIBRARY, SO. SUDBURY.
See page 28.

Goodnow Library in Sudbury, Massachusetts. Alfred Hudson. History of Sudbury Massachusetts (1638-1889), Photograph reproduced by Chuck Zimmer.

Knoxville East Tenn
Dec 6th 1863

Dear Mother

    I suppose you are all anxious to hear from us so I will improve the first opportunity I have by writing I suppose you got the news a long time ago that we were surrounded at Knoxville by the "Johnies" we have been here 17 days the rebs left us yesterday it seems as though we had just got out of presion I will try and give you an account of events as they happened commencing with:

Nov 14th
This morning about two oclock we turned out packed up everything we were at Lenoin about 6 miles from London & about 23 miles from Knoxville we heard that the "Johnies" were crossing the river at London we had a brigade of the 23rd Army Corps stationed there under Gen. White they retreated to this place about noon. they said the rebs were coming about 2 PM Gen Burnside arrived from Knoxville he ordered Gen White back and sent the first Division under(Ferrerr) with him they found the rebs had crossed the river with a large force it rained all day

Nov 15th
This morning we turned out at two oclock and started for London we arrived there at daylight we found the rebs had crossed the river with a large force so Burnside thought it was best to fall back to Knoxville and hold the place if he could so the 2ed Division was ordered to hold the rebs in check while the rest of the troops retreated which we did until most night then we started to retreat we caught the rest of the troops at Lenoire here we were relieved by the first Division we were ordered to help get the Artillery through the mud we worked most all night the horses have been living on short allowance so they could not draw at all we had to take them off of the Artillery and draw it up the hills by hand

Nov 16th
We arrived at Campbell's Station this morning this is about half way from London to Knoxville here we had to stop and fight the "Johnies" again we had 4 men wounded in our Regt. The 1st Division had a heavy loss towards night we started on a retreat again

*Nov 17*th

*This morning we arrived at Knoxville, we are fortifying the place. the 1*st
Division is on the left of the town we on the center or front and part of
*the 23*rd *Corps on the right We have to get forts at each end of the town*
and we are building some in front we expect the rebs here tomorrow

*Nov 18*th

I went on picket today there is some pretty heavy firing down on the
left but the Rebs have not got up here yet they will be along tomorrow I
guess this is a pleasant day

*Nov 19*th

I was relieved this morning before daylight firing commenced all along
the lines today so I suppose we are surrounded, we went into the rifle
pits today the rebs fired a few shots from their batteries today one shot
came near hitting Burnside

*Nov 20*th

Today I was detailed as sharpshooter and was put into a house with 9
other fellows out in front of the rifle pits so as to pick off the officers if
they attacked here. The rebs fired with their batteries this evening one of
their shells hit the house that I am in it lodged in the chimney but it didn't
burst so it didn't hurt anybody

*Nov 21*st

it is stormy today not much going on today had a little firing. the pickets
fire at one another most all the time

*Nov 22*ed

Pleasant today considerable heavy firing down on the left not much
going on in front of here we keep pickets on skirmishes out about ¼ of a
mile

*Nov 23*rd

Pleasant day. had pretty heavy skirmishing today the rebs charged on
*our skirmishes and drove them in this evening the 35*th *was ordered out*
to hold them in check which they did till most morning we burned quite
a lot of building so the sharpshooters couldn't occupy them and pick off
our men

*Nov 24*th

*This morning the 21*st *Mass Regt - 48*th *Penn & 35*th *Mass were ordered to charge on the rebs and drive them back they had dug rifle pits so our men were ordered to drive them from the pits which they did in good shape capturing quite a number of provisions we lost one man killed in Co. I, Albert and Rufus were the first to reach the rifle pits picket firing all day today*

*Nov 25*th

Not much doing today but picket firing burned a few houses this evening

*Nov 26*th

Thanksgiving day you may believe we feel pretty blue today we had pork soup for dinner we made some pudding so we had quite a dinner there was considerable firing today not much of anything else stirring

*Nov 27*th

not much going on today we expect reinforcements in a few days considerable firing this evening

*Nov 28*th

strong considerable firing today Gen Longstreet sent to Gen Burnside to have him surrender so we expect hard work tomorrow

*Nov 29*th

*Longstreet attacked our left this morning about 3 Oclock and was driven back with a heavy loss he tried to take the fort on the left it was garrisoned by Lt. Benjamin's regular Battery and part of an Ohio battery the 1*st *Division was in the rifle pits around the fort they had a lot of telegraph wire strung along on the stumps in the front of the pits so when the "Johnies" came up they tumbled over it then our boys let them have it... they piled the dead up in heaps Gen Ferrero fell back and let the rebs come up to the fort then Lt. Benjamin poured the grape and canister to them he let them come up so near that he lit the shell and threw them out among the rebels with his hands one rebel officer came in and put his hand on a gun and told Benjamin to surrender, the gun was loaded so Leut. Benjamin fired it and killed 11 men our whole loss in the fight was reported at 17 men the rebels loss was about 1000* we took 200 prisoners there is no fighting today the rebels are burying their dead

Nov 30th
not much firing today we had good news from Gen. Grant today

Dec 1st
not much firing today had a little this evening had some more news from Grant today. we expect reinforcements every day the ground froze last night

Dec 2ed
Not much firing today I guess the rebs got enough of it the other morning more news from Grant

Dec 3rd
Considerable firing today pretty cold last night water froze no reinforcements yet thawed a little today

Dec 4th
Considerable heavy firing today heard from our reinforcements today they will be here tomorrow

Dec 5th
the rebs left last night they went towards Va. we went out 5 miles but didn't see anything of them our Cavalry are after them Gen Sherman is after them we have taken a large number of their deserters I suppose you will get the news before you get this

Dec 6th
We have been living on half and quarter rations all this time the boys have had to go on picket every other day and night and it has been pretty cold so they have had a pretty hard time but they did their duty without grumbling for which we received a compliment from Gen. Burnside. I must close for now for I have got so tired that I cannot write anymore I don't know as you can read what I have written, and I don't know when I can send this but I shall as soon as I can. I forgot to state that Sudbury boys were all right. Give my love to all...from your loving son
   George

On November 26, the national Thanksgiving Day, dinner consisted only of "pork soup and pudding," a very different affair from the previous year when they had beefsteak and potatoes. The assault on Fort Saunders on November 28, resulted in Confederate losses of over "eight hundred killed and wounded, and four hundred taken prisoner. The Union lost not more than fifty. An armistice was held from 10 am to 8 pm to bury the dead, and care for the wounded."[40] General Burnside allowed the Rebel Army to use his ambulances for the transport of their wounded while his own men assisted the Rebel doctors. George writes in his diary that on this day "Longstreet gave Burnside until 5 pm to surrender." This, of course, did not happen.

Sudbury
Dec 6ᵗʰ 1863

Dear George
    I received yours of the 6ᵗʰ of Nov and one from Albert at the same time about ten days ago and was very glad to hear from you have wrote twice to you cince that one by Ely I received a letter from John dated Nov 20ᵗʰ at the time I received yours he was well I have just closed one for Albert and cut out some late news of the battles and enclosed in his and so I will write a short letter now and enclose some more Newspaper News in yours and will write again soon I wrote in Alberts in reference to the Recruiting business and the prospects of volunteering which I think is good and also spoke in his of the Election that I had wrote to you cince the election and gave you the returns of this State and also of Sudbury and this District which was a great gain on the Republican side I will close by saying old Sudbury remains about the same not much enterprise here we went through the ceremonies of Thanksgiving Supper and partook of the bountyes of the Earth but those vacant seets we were all to home that day but Alfred and you three boys but Alfred is at home now it is pretty cold now but no snow yet we are all well hope this will find you well write soon and give me the account of Burnside Battle
    From your Father

Sudbury
Dec 9 1863

Dear Brother
 Your letter dated the 5th of November I received some time ago. Father also received three one night from all of you boys and also a copy of "Brownlows Knoxville Whig". I had been anxious to read that paper when it came out and I was glad of the opportunity. Brownlow is determined to show up the rebels. I can see Mr. Dickenson borrowed the paper to read when he heard that father had a copy. John wrote about the middle of November the last time. He wrote that he is well and tough. He is in Virginia near the Rapidam River. He said that it was expected that a forward movement would take place soon and I see by the papers that they crossed the river and skirmished with the enemy but with what result I do not know.

 He said that he wrote to you and Albert just before he wrote home. The papers say that General Grant has gained a victory over Braggs Army and expected to capture Braggs whole force. The Banks Expedition has arrived in Texas and has captured a number of cities on the Rio Grande River and also had a big haul of cattle. Fort Sumter is being hammered upon yet and is about demolished by this time probably. Charleston has to have a taste of shells now and then but they don't agree with her, "The Charleston Mercury" says that it should like that Gen Gilmore might get blown to the "eternal shades" with one of his own shells. I have written to you and Albert since you state that you have received my letters, so there must be letters on the way. In my last letters I wrote all about the Elections throughout the North etc and also about the new call for 300,000 more men and if not Recruited by the 5th of January, 1864 a Draft will be (———) to make the numbers. So the President is determined to keep the army up to its present standard in numbers at least. The North will uphold the Government in <u>all</u> its measures for putting down the Rebellion you may depend. Recruiting is quite brisk in some places. In New York City 1000 men volunteered in one week. Some of the towns in Massachusetts have filled their quotas and a surplus over. Sudbury has not done much yet in filling her quota but War Meetings are to be had according to a vote of the Town at a Meeting day before yesterday. There are some who state that they will enlist before suffering their names to appear in a Draft.

 I also wrote in my last letters all about matters at home. We are all as well as usual Thanksgiving day came on the 26th of November throughout most of the Northern States Appointed by both President and Governor and was generally observed. It was a very pleasant day here. The three Societies in town all met at the Methodist Meeting House on that morning and listened to a sermon from Mr. Trinton (Methodist) and at the close of the service a collection was taken up for the benefit of the starving Union Prisoners at Richmond. The money goes into the hands of the "Christian Commission" who have recently obtained permission of the Rebels to distribute food and comforts to the poor fellows. I see by the latest papers that Burnside is pretty closely pressed at Knoxville by Longstreet but has been able to hold Longstreets forces in check. I hope that reinforcements will be forthcoming. I am anxious to hear from you. I have received papers from Albert and Mother has also. Eli Willis has papers for you the letters you wrote that he has sent forward to you

 I wrote in my last letter that Mary and Everett were not on very good terms, but they are as <u>thick</u> as ever again now. Harriet says all he came back for was to get treated to some <u>Thanksgiving pie and cake</u> (Everett I mean) but she did not say what she went directly from church down to the village for with a certain young fellow <u>before dinner</u>. We had a treat last week Monday evening at the Town Hall in shape of a Lecture on "War Scenes and (——)" by F. C. Coffin (Charleton) the Correspondent of the Boston Journal whose interesting letters from the army we have all read in the Journal. E. Stone and family have moved down to Somerville for the Winter. Whether they will come into town again I do not know. Wheeler Haynes bellowing calves and swearing Irishmen were a little too much for their peace especially <u>nights</u> and they left. The schools in Town all commenced the Monday after Thanksgiving. The Teachers give good satisfaction generally I believe. The Upper school in the Centre is taught by a Parmenter from Wayland. Alfred came home the other night. He is out of a job. You say you are <u>fat</u> on half rations. I should judge so for you weigh 14 lbs more than I do. 142 lbs I weighed last month. I shall be obliged to close. I hope this will find you well as ever.

 Francis

Sudbury Centre: Unitarian Meeting House, Town Hall, Methodist Meeting
House photograph of an Etching taken from a painting by Alfred S. Hudson
Annals of Sudbury, Wayland and Maynard. Middlesex County, Massachusetts
1891 by Alfred S. Hudson

General Sherman arrived in Knoxville on December 6, and General
Longstreet retreated toward Virginia. The IX Corps started after the enemy
on good roads, making good time on half rations, and by December 9
Longstreet was only twelve miles ahead. The men waited in an open field
in the cold and rain, and spent the days devising ways to augment the short
rations. The coffee was gone and the men had only the corn left on the
ground by the horses which they ground and cooked in their tin dippers. As
soon as the regiment arrived at Blaine's Cross Roads on December 16, they
formed a line of battle, the mounted infantry arrived, and an immediate
attack was expected. It was pouring rain and bitterly cold. The tents had
been left back in Knoxville, and the men's knapsacks and baggage would
not arrive until six days later on December 22. The men had been on the
march for some time in terrible weather, and, by now, with shabby clothing
and almost barefoot, they anxiously awaited the supply trains. The mail
did arrive, and the men discovered that the country had been following the
siege of Knoxville with great interest in their morning newspapers.[41]

Henry S. Battles, George T. Smith, John H. Moore, Members of the Thirteenth
Regiment, Massachusetts Volunteers, Sudbury Historical Society

Sudbury
Dec 29th 1863

Dear Albert and George
*   I received a letter from each of you last evening and was rejoiced
to hear from you. We have been to the office every night for a long
time, but could get no tidings from you. I tried to look on the bright*

side and think it was because the communication was cut off. Still I could not help feeling very anxious about you, for I knew there had been a dreadful battle out there and the paper said the 35 Regt were in the fight. I suppose I felt more low-spirited on account of some bad news we heard about Henry Dakin[42]. You recollect he was in Camp at the same time you was there, and left for the south, soon after you left. He was very healthy for a while after he went out there, but lately he has been suffering from what is called chronic diarea, and his Wife felt so anxious about him, she went out to find him and get him home if possible. She went as far as Washington, and they told her there, that it was not safe for her to go to him, but promised to bring him to her if he was able to be moved. She waited a week expecting him every day but he did not come, so she got a pass to go to him, but just as she was going to start, the news came that he was dead. It must have seemed hard to her to think she was so near him and could not see him before he died. He knew she was there, and was overjoyed at the prospect of seeing her. He said it would do him more good than medicine, but he was too far gone to have anything help him. His wife succeeded in getting his body, and it is on the way home now, and will probably be here in a day or two. I hope he was taken good care of but I suppose we shall never know certain about that. If you should happen to meet the 38th Regt any where, I wish you would inquire about him. You speak of cold weather out there. I expected you was so far south, you would not know much about cold weather this winter. We have had some very cold days here this winter. We had a hard storm, week before last, it commenced with snow but turned to rain and froze on to the trees so thick that the heft of this ice broke off quite large limbs from elms and other large trees, and the weather has been so cold that the ice has not all melted from the trees yet. The sleighing is first rate. There has been one or two marriages here since I wrote to you. Smith Jones and Juliette Johnson were married a few days ago, and Laura Moore is married to a gentleman by the name of Bowen. She got acquainted with him at the Arsenal. I believe he works there now. Alfred is at home now. Your Father has bought some wood of Elisha Goodnow, and Alfred is helping him cut it off. You did not write whether you had received any letters from home lately, but I hope you have, for we have written quite a number. Has Eli Willis got back to the Regt yet? We had a letter from John a few days ago. He is in Virginia yet, and says they are building houses for winter. He says he weighs 179 pounds, and grows handsomer every day. He says the soldiers are getting furloughs but he thinks he shall not come home till his time is out, and I hope you can all come home by that time. If half the reports are true it seems as though the rebs could not hold out much longer. When I read in my letter, about your triping up the Rebs with that telegraph wire, your Father said "the yankees will outwit them yet". I am thankful I did not know your situation at the time of the battle. How did you feel when you knew you were surrounded by the enemy? We see that He who has guided you through so many dangers was able to protect you even then. I hope we shall never cease to be grateful for past merries, and to pray for future blessings. May the time soon come when our Country will be at peace and our friends return to their homes in safety.

Please write every opportunity. From your ever loving Mother Mary H. Moore

Those men who still had covering for their feet and were able to volunteer for picket duty found that they had the advantage of being able to forage. The men began to stack logs along the sides of their tents, build chimneys, and cut firewood for camp, in an attempt to keep warm in the cold and snow.[43] The regiment was still short on rations and no food other than a piece of beef was issued for Christmas dinner.

1. Private Frank Winthrop Draper (1843), Wayland, MA, Massachusetts Thirty-fifth Regiment, Co. D, promoted to full Captain, March 25, 1864, mustered out March 28, 1864, commissioned officer in Co. E, US Colored Troops Thirty-ninth Regiment, March 28, 1864. Mustered out June 3, 1864.

2. Benjamin Franklin Butler (1818-1893), Brigadier General of Massachusetts Militia, with the Eighth Massachusetts Regiment, one of the first troops to reach Washington, 1861. Commanded Fortress Munroe. Controversial General.

3. Alfred S. Hudson, *History of Sudbury, Massachusetts 1838-1889* (Salem, MA: Higginson Book Co., reprint), 502-503.

4. Ibid., 528-529.

5. Ibid., 549.

6. Ibid., 532.

7. Committee of the Regimental Association, *History of the Thirty-fifth Massachusetts Volunteers, 1862-1865,* (Boston: Mills, Knight & Co. 1884), 100-101.

8. Ibid., 105-106.

9. Cyrus E. Barker, 23, resident Sudbury, credited to Acton, Private Thirteenth Regiment Massachusetts Volunteers, wounded, Antietam, Sept.17, 1862. Discharged for disability, April 15, 1863. Enlisted 59th Regiment Massachusetts Volunteers, Jan. 14, 1864, wounded July 30, 1864, Petersburg, VA. Taken prisoner Aug. 19,1864 at Weldon Railroad. Exchanged March 19, died April, 1865. http://www.actonmemoriallibrary.org.

10. Uriah Moore's sister.

11. Private Josiah Gleason enlisted July 1862 at the age of 35 in Co. G, Thirty-second Infantry Regiment, Massachusetts Volunteers, received a disability discharge on February 25, 1863.

12. Collation is a light meal served by local people as the troops stop when traveling, usually at rail stops.

13. Form of pavement invented by Scotsman, John Lowdon McAdam, 1820, layers of stone covered with a binder as tar, (tarmac).

14. Committee of the Regimental Association, *History of the Thirty-fifth*, 113, 123.

15. The Columbia Electronic Encyclopedia, Sixth edition, 2007, Columbia University Press.

16. Charles Campbell, 38, Private, Co. D, Thirty-fifth Regiment Massachusetts Volunteers.

[17.] William S. Rosecrans, (1819-1898), graduate West Point, 1842, Colonel Engineer on McClellan's staff, 1861, Colonel Ohio Infantry, Brigadier General Regular Army, Major General of Volunteers, 1862. Defeated at Chickamauga.

[18.] George W. Moore (b. Nov.3,1827 d. Oct.2,1862), Sudbury, MA, wealthy farmer, wife, Mary Jane Bent, daughter, Georgette Bent Moore b. 1863, distant relative of George F. Moore.

[19.] William (Billy) Leimon Weeks age 28, Marlboro, Thirteenth Regiment, Massachusetts Volunteers Co. I, discharged for wounds on Nov. 24, 1862 at Washington D. C.

[20.] Harriett Moore, (Hattie) sister of George F. Moore.

[21.] Committee of the Regimental Association, *History of the Thirty-fifth,* 127-138.

[22.] Ibid., 139.

[23.] Ibid., 142-143.

[24.] Ibid.,150.

[25.] Ibid.,151.

[26.] Ibid., 142-154.

[27.] Spencer Smith, Thirteenth Regiment, Massachusetts Volunteers, Co. F, cousin of George Moore, son of Olive Moore and Joseph Smith, member of the Wadsworth Rifle Guards.

[28.] Captain John Williams Hudson, 29, Lexington, MA, commissioned an officer in Thirty-fifth Regiment, Massachusetts Volunteers, Co. D, Aug 16, 1862, Captain, Apr 30, 1863, Major, Aug 16, 1864, Lieutenant Colonel, Nov 14, 1864.

[29.] Private Francis Garfi eld, 32, Thirty-fifth Regiment Massachusetts Volunteers, Co. D, Aug 16, 1862. Transferred Seventh Regiment, Veteran Reserve Corps, Co. D, Dec. 31, 1863. Disability discharge, April 1864. Ancestry.com.

[30.] George H. Hall, b. 1840,Thirty-fifth Regiment Massachusetts Volunteers, Co. D, Aug 16, 1862-June 9, 1865, machinist. *Massachusetts Soldiers and Sailors in the Civil War.* Vol. III, 668. Harry Hall picked up a Confederate soldier's Bible on the battlefield. It is now part of the Sudbury Historical Society collection.

[31.] William Bailey, shoemaker, Thirty-fifth Regiment Massachusetts Volunteers Aug. 16, 1862-June 9, 1865, *Massachusetts Soldiers and Sailors in the Civil War.* Vol.III, 666.

[32.] Parson William Brownlow of Tennessee, editor of *Brownlow's Knoxville Whig* (newspaper which rejected secession and the Confederacy). He supported Temperance Societies. Charged with treason for his editorials on secession was jailed in Knoxville. After the war, elected Governor and State Senator of Tennessee.

[33.] Committee of the Regimental Association, *History of the Thirty-fifth,* 171.

34. Copperheads: a group of Democrats in the North who opposed the Civil War and advocated a peace settlement with the South.

35. Committee of the Regimental Association, *History of the Thirty-fifth,* 174.

36. Ibid., 174-177.

37. Ibid., 185-193.

38. Lieutenant Samuel Benjamin led Battery E of the Second U. S. Artillery that fought at the Second Bull Run, Antietam, Fredericksburg, Knoxville, Campbell's Station and Fort Sanders.

39. Committee of the Regimental Association, *History of the Thirty-fifth,* 181.

40. Ibid.

41. Ibid., 197-199.

42. Able Henry Dakin, Co. I, Thirty-ninth Regiment Massachusetts Volunteers, musician, died near Kelly's Ford, December 20, 1863 at age 31, cousin of George Moore.

43. Committee of the Regimental Association, *History of the Thirty-fifth,* 199.

1864

I hope the time will soon come when I shall see you all at home safe and sound and the Rebellion put down and every Man free white and black.

Letter from Father, May 8, 1864

In January of 1864 the Thirty-fifth Regiment was located at Blain's Cross Roads, Tennessee. This location was so far from their base that supplies were nearly impossible to obtain. Although foraging provided small amounts of food, the regiment's suffering was the worst that they had yet experienced. Throughout January and February, George wrote, "no clothing yet."

The anticipation of drawing supplies such as pork and coffee for the New Year faded as each man was issued two ears of corn in place of his ration of bread. Every day two men from each company were issued a pass to go beyond the pickets and forage. Many men went nearly barefoot and each man was issued two squares of rawhide to fashion himself some sort of foot covering to protect his feet in the cold rain and snow of January. Small pox had become such a threat that each man was vaccinated.[1]

General Ambrose Burnside, Union Army: engraving from Pictorial History of the
Great Civil War-1878

Camp near Blanes Crossroads
East Tenn

Jan 4 1864

Dear Brother
I have got a chance to write at last and I am going to improve it too
so I will commence with you. I have got a lot of letters to answer but
I thought I must write home first. I wrote to mother after the siege of
Knoxville and gave her an account of that affair the next day we started
on a tramp after Longstreet and have been traveling most of the time
since we left our knapsacks and tents at Knoxville we took nothing but
our blankets and it has been rainy and cold so we have had a pretty
rough time of it we have been living on half rations also We are in camp
in a Valley about 20 miles from Knoxville Gen Longstreet is in the valley

above here they say he is surrounded I hope it is so. if we could only capture him we would be willing to live on half rations a long time to come. I think he will get away somewhere for he is a pretty smart fellow his army is deserting him and coming into our lines and taking the Oath of allegiance to the United States 300 came in a few days ago, and they come in small numbers I saw two fellows a few days ago that left him they say they have not had any rations given them since they came into the Valley they have lived on what they could get in the Valley so I guess we can live on half rations as long as they can live on nothing for they will soon forage all there is in the Valley

New Years day the ground was covered with snow and it was awful cold but it is warmer now so we get along first rate. Al and I built a tent and fireplace yesterday so we live quite comfortable

The old 3 years Regiments in this corps have all reinlisted the 21st Mass starts for home today there is 12 Regts enlisted that is all the old Regts there is here there is 6 of the last 3 years Regts here. Col Hartranft (commanding this division) said this morning that those 6 Regts were going to Newport News to stay while the others went home he said we should start in a few days. I hope it will turn out so. I think we shall go somewhere out of this Department if Burnside takes another Department we shall go with him. I had rather be under him than any other Gen in the Union Army and I had rather be in any army than the army of the Potomac

How are you all getting along at home now I have got some money that I am going to send to the folks just as soon as I get a chance and I hope I shall have a chance soon for I hear you are in need of it The young folks are all getting married there aren't they. I suppose my schoolmates will all be married by the time I get home. well I don't know as I care. I heard that Al Willis had got a child and I heard that he said he wished he had come out here when John did poor fellow why didn't he come he had as good chance as the rest. that will do to talk. he has got a chance to come now if he wants to I should be happy to see him in this Regt any day. "ahem"

Mother wrote that she was saving the "curiosities" we sent home. I have got some Reb money that I will send her in this tell her to put it with the rest I will look out for more things to send if she is saving them

I must think of closing now for my sheet is about full. you must not think that I am finding fault because we don't have more to eat for I am not I have got done finding fault for I know it can't be helped. give my love to all. write soon and write all the news for we don't get any. I hope we shall be out of this before I write again.

From George

Strawberry Plains, East Tenn
Jan 20th/64

Dear Mother

 We received your letter a day or two ago also one from Francis we were very glad to hear from home they are the first letters we have received for nearly 6 weeks. I received one from George Jones the same day I got yours so I thought I done very well to get 3. When I wrote last we were at Blanes Cross roads that is about 10 miles from here. we left there Saturday. we are in camp near the East Tenn. Va. Railroad and about 15 miles from Knoxville we are having first rate weather There is a little snow on the ground. we have had two or three snowstorms and some pretty cold wither

 We are having a pretty good time nothing to do we are getting half rations yet, but we make out to get enough to eat by foraging we have been paid off since we were at Knoxville and I have got some money to send you whenever I get a chance. I don't want to send it by mail for I am afraid I shall lose it if I do if reports are true that we get I shall have a chance to bring it myself it is reported that the whole 9th Corps are going to be sent off to recruit each Regt is going to its respective state. this is only a report and I don't place much confidence in it, although I think we are going out of this Department and that soon to if it is true you have probably heard of it before this time the sick have all been sent off and the teams are going over the mountains into Kentucky today or tomorrow so I think we shall soon follow.

 We have not got any clothing (only some shoes) yet. but we can get-along very well with them. How the time passes it don't seem only a few days ago since we were surrounded at Knoxville here it is almost 2 months you wanted to know how we felt while we were surrounded. I felt a little "blue" especially Thanksgiving Day but then I knew we had a good general and I know the rebs had got hard work to take the place. I never saw the boys in better spirits when there was a fight depending on them they were there they didn't grumble at all they got just enough to eat to keep them up and they had to do picket and skirmish duty 24 hours out of every 48. I don't know as I felt any worse when I left home than I did Thanksgiving Day but then I am alright now pretty well contented and growing fat on half rations a little ragged and independent as a "gentleman darkey"

 How are you all getting along there now days how I should like to step into the house there today and not have anybody know I was coming how does Mary get along now with Everett I wish she didn't like him any better than I do, but then he is a gentleman to some fellows I know I will say that for him. If she likes him I suppose it is nobodys business but this I know it is none of mine by the way how does Hattie get along with that little man from South Sudbury I hear he was around Thanksgiving day as well as Everett. I suppose he had to sit in the high chair didn't he now don't let Hattie see this letter if you do she will give me fits when she sees me. But then she must not get mad for I am only joking. What is going on in old Sudbury this winter do they have any Temperance meetings this winter I heard they were going to have a dancing school there. I must think of closing now for my sheet is about full. Give my love to all the folks and all my friends, write soon an write all the news I will close hoping to be with you all soon

From your son
George

P.S. I had to write this with a pencil for I didn't have ink enough to dip the pen into

Sudbury
Jan 24th 1864

Dear George
 I have not received a letter from you cince one dated Nov 9th don't know if you get my letters but I will keep a writing you may get them sometime Francis received one from you and one from Albert last night dated Jan 4th that you were still in camp in poos valy but sometime expect to move to Newport News I hope you will get out there to stop awhile there it would seem as though you were nearer home and then should think you could get a furlough to come home this Winter if not perhaps we could get you a box of eatables and could get full rations I received a letter from Albert Dec 14th and have wrote to him cince I wrote to you in Nov after the Nov Election and gave you the returns of the Election in this district and in the State we were filling up the Quota of the last call in most of the towns around us and some of the towns have raised a surplus as more men came forward than was required except Sudbury we have not done much as yet here had a letter from John about ten days ago he is in prety comfatable quarters he has a shop that he works in he is in a village his shop fronts on a publick Street and he hires his washing done he was well I saw Col Leonard²

of the 13*th* Regt in Boston two weeks cince and spoke with him he thinks that the Rebels cannot hold out much longer he crossed the River with the Regt at the last Battle that they had with Lee he sayes what he saw of Lees Army they were a portion of the privates barefoot and raged he sayes he thinks if those 300,000 men come out at once could close up the War soon Gen Burnside was in Boston this last week I was in Boston at the same time and did not know it at the time they have several Regt arrived home on a furlow that have reenlisted Boston is pretty full of Soldiers now it looks quite Warfied there was a Telagraph dispach to Boston last Friday the day I was in Boston that Longstreet had Serendred it is reported that the confederate Capital is a going to be removed to Collumbia South Carolina it is Reported that Charlestown South Carolina must come into our hands soon as for News here there is not much about now the wether is quite moderate today the wind South and snow thawing but very little snow on the ground had but very little this Winter had tip top sleighing for several weeks and pretty cold wether I have improved the snow for the most part I Bought a small lot of wood standing of Elisha Goodnow which I paid one hund & twenty two dolls for and have cut and hauled in to the mill saw logs enough for five thousd feet of lumber all with the little horse Sorrel and shall have from 60 to 80 cord of mostly hard and pitch pine wood card wood is seling in Marlboro for 8 dolls per cord must close will write the next of the news next time we are all well and all at home but Mary E she went to CambPort last Wk to work hoping this will find you well write often if you can

    from your Father

P.S. your couseon Emely Smith is dangerously sick with a fever and liver complant

Emely Smith is Curtis Smith's younger sister and George's cousin. Uriah was now almost 59 years old and in poor health, yet in the midst of a New England winter he had cut enough lumber to build two or more good size houses plus sixty to eighty cords of wood.

The following letter is to George from his young brother James Edgar Moore.

Jan 24ᵗʰ 1864
Dear Brother

how do you do we are all well and hope you are the same it is nice skating now I went skating last night. I wish you wood rite to me as soon as you can and tell me what is going on out there. and tell me whether you have had any fighting out ther since I rote to you be fore. Francis had a letter from you last night that had some rebel money in it. I never see any rebel money be fore. Mary is gone out to work at Cambridge Port for Mr Newman. There are 37 schoolers in the lower school and there are 41 in the opper school Miss Abby A. Long keeps the lower school and Mrs Parminter keeps the opper school I have rote all I can think of now so good by

from your loving
Brother
James Edgar Moore

Although George's brother James writes "that Mrs. Parminter keeps the opper school", usually the school master for the winter term, or for the older children was a man. The school day began with roll-call and a reading of the scriptures by the scholars (students). Classes began with reading, arithmetic, and writing, with a short break for recess mid-morning. Lunch, or "nooning" as it was called, was from noon to one. Afternoon classes began with reading, followed by geography, grammar, history, and spelling, with a break mid-afternoon. The boys often played "round ball," an early form of baseball in which teams pitched to themselves, ran the bases in the opposite direction from today's game, and could be out by being hit with the ball. "Three strikes and you're out" was still the rule. The last day of school was examination day and the school was scrubbed and decorated for the occasion. After the students presented their recitations, everyone sat down to enjoy special treats brought in by the students.[3]

Thomas Prentiss Hurlbut, Father of Rufus Hurlbut: Photograph Courtesy of the Marion Hurlbut Eaton Collection.

Through January and into February the regiment lived with few rations and continued waiting for clothing to arrive. They marched short distances each day in the cold and rain as they pursued Longstreet, skirmishing along the way towards Knoxville. Many of George's fellow soldiers in Company D were now ill.[4] By February, both Albert Moore and William Bowen were so lame that they could no longer walk, and were left at the old camp. George, however, continued on with the regiment, some nights sleeping on straw in a corn barn to keep warm. General Ferrero arrived in camp and announced that Longstreet was not going to attempt to take Knoxville again, so camp was set up on the outskirts of Knoxville. Colonel Carruth arrived back from Boston, and Captain Hudson had returned to the Thirty-fifth from the hospital at Knoxville. Longstreet was now headed to Virginia.

The letter below to Francis was one of the first times George wrote about wanting to return home and get on with his life. Thomas, referred to in the letter, was Rufus Hurlbut's father, Thomas P. Hurlbut, who was 44 years old at the time he attempted to enlist. At the dedication of the Civil War monument in Sudbury in 1897, Jonas Hunt, in his address, stated that Thomas P. Hurlbut had done more than anyone else to ensure that the town filled its quotas during the war.

Camp of 35th Regt
East Tenn
Feb 5-1864

Dear Brother
I will now try and answer your letter which I received sometime ago I should have answered it before this but I have been sick part of the time and we have been traveling most of the time so I didn't feel much like writing but I am all right now we are in camp now and we don't have much to do We are in camp about 5 miles west of Knoxville we have been here about 2 weeks we had to leave here one day and go after the "Johnies" but we came back again everything is quiet here now we don't hear much from the rebs in fact we don't hear much about the war anywhere guess it is over wish it was all the news we get is through Brownlowes paper and that is not much. He is a "brick" there are a plenty of his stamp in this state only you don't hear so much from them. The Union people here say the rebel citizens have got to leave or they will make them they say the state cannot hold both parties and they (the union) will not leave there was a reb citizen shot yesterday by some

unknown person and quite a number of others have been fired at they
think it is some of the 6th Tenn Cav'ly (union) that fired at them they (the
rebs) begin to think that it is getting to hot for them here.

There is considerable talk of our going home to recoup. I don't know
whether there is anything in it or not but think there is if it is so you
probably have heard of it before this. I hope it is so for I want to get out
of this place

How do they get along with recruiting there now has Sudbury filled
her quota yet. I hear that Uncle Thomas enlisted but the doctor wouldn't
accept him. I should think some of the young folks would feel cheap to have
him enlist and they stay at home he has shown his patriotism. I should think
Everett would feel a little cheap. What is going on there now days. anybody
else get married or have they all got married. I don't suppose there will be
anybody left by the time I get home well never mind I can come out here and
get someone it is sometime since I have had any letters I wish some of you
would write each week so we could get the news. I must close now

give my love to all
From George
P.S. I have some reb songs that
I will send in this letter tell...
mother she can put them with
the other things

Sudbury
Feb 14th 1864

Dear George

I have not received a letter from you cince one dated Nov 9th /63 I
received one from Albert dated Dec 14th but I will keep a writing perhaps
you may get them sometime you wrote that you received one from me
through the Mail and one that I sent by Ely Willis⁵ Albert has written
home that he had received a small bundle that we sent by Ely but he had
not come the Regt yet we sent two small bundles by him I wrote to you
after the returns had come in pretty fuly of the Nov Election and gave
you an account of which the Republicans carried with an overwhelming
Majority a great gain in this District as well as this State over last year
which I have repeated in letters that I have sent cince I received a letter
from John dated Jan 27/64 he wrote from Culpeper C H Va he was
well he wrote that they was no war news to write me so he gave me a
description of the Town and his quarters which were very comfortable he

has a shop in the Town that he works in he thinks he can pass this winter away very easy if they let him stay there he has had an invitation to reinlist again for three years more he said he would think of it during the next five months it seems by the accounts that you write home that they keep you moving most of the time it is rumered that you were a coming home to recruit up I hope it is so by the accounts this States propotion of the quota is about full for the 300,000 I was out to the Camp at Readville they have got up quite a villadge of Barraks there and quite an Army of Troops there went out there about two weeks ago with Curtis Smith[6] to get his furlow extended for the reason of his Sister being very sick his sister Emely she is but just alive now I was in Boston last week a Monday and saw the 16th Mass Vetteran Regt come in they numbered a little over a hund Privates I spoke with Col. Leonard the other day in Boston Col of the 13th Regt he spoke that the prospect for putting down the Rebs seemed to him very promising now he thought if they could get the 300,000 men rite out there now could close up the rebellion soon Mr Rogers wished when you wrote to me again if you knew where Hary Hall[7] was to write and inform me of his whereabouts it was reported last week in the papers that they had been a battle down at Newbern and the rebs hold Newport have had a very mild Winter here this is Spring like wether now not any snow on the ground except the north side of hills fewer woods now have had quite mudy traveling most of the time for two or three weeks we are all to home except Mary Elizabeth she is to work at Camb-Port doing housework I am in the wood business yet that is a chopping wood the schools have closed there Winter term so I spose I shall have more Chopers now we are all well and I hope this will find you well write often as you can I am going to write to Albert again as soon as I can get time

From your Father

John Moore was a saddler, making and repairing saddles and harnesses for the animals used by the cavalry and the wagon trains. It was a skilled trade and kept him away from the front lines except when he had to deliver ammunition to the front.

By and large, it was the Democrats who favored immediate peace, wanting to keep everything as it was. They were often called "Copperheads." However, most of the Republicans supported the Union cause in the Civil War. John Andrews was elected Governor of Massachusetts in the November 1861 elections with Joel Hayden, Lt. Governor, and Oliver Warner, Secretary of State. Erastus Dickinson, minister of the Evangelical Union Church, was elected Representative to the General Court Sixteenth

Massachusetts which represented the towns of Sudbury, Stow, and Wayland, in the legislature.[8] It was Reverend Erastus Dickinson who officiated at the marriage of George and Miss Sarah Jones.

On February 16, 1864, George Moore was detailed for guard duty on the ammunition train.[9] Three days later, his brother Francis wrote the following letter to him.

Sudbury
Feb 19 1864

Dear Brother
I received a letter from you last night and dated Feb 5. I was glad to hear we were looking for letters every day. Father received a letter from Albert a short time since but it was dated a long time ago when you were at Poor Valley. It is now a fortnight or so since we have received a letter from John. His last stated that he had received his box that we sent out to his order which came with money for expense. His letter dated Jan 20th says that he received a letter from Albert dated Dec 29th. Was well and having a good time. Stationed near the Rapidan Va. some ways from the regiment therefore did not get his letters regular. He says that if he has his health at the expiration of his term of service that he shall go out to you and work for the Government. Those War songs you sent are a curiosity to we Northerners. They prove that there are talents among Southerners as well as among us and are used to a purpose.

The family are all as well as usual and also all of our friends with the exception of Emily Smith who is but just alive. Dr. Goodnow[10] who has attended her gave her over and a Doctor from Boston was sent for who after two or three visits now says he has some hopes of her. Mother has watched about every other night with her for a fortnight back. Father and Alfred have been at work in the Lot of Wood that he bought of Elisha Goodnow. He has paid the cash for about half of it being 54 Dollars I think dont know for certain whether he has paid for the balance or not. He says that he is now hard up for money to use for <u>family necessaries</u>. Mary is at Cambridgeport. Harriet is sewing straw at home. Fathers old fits continue yet with <u>short</u> intervals between. However you know that they are not <u>very dangerous</u> if not noticed. War news is quiet just now. Grant is preparing for striking blows somewhere soon. Mobile is threatened by Banks. Charleston is being in (––––). Butler has sent a body of troops to release the Prisoners at Richmond but the *attempt was frustrated when within 10 miles of Richmond by a Yankee deserter who gave the Rebels information of the <u>good time coming</u>. Burnside is organizing in his Department (with headquarters at New York) troops for some quarters. He lately reviewed the regiments now at Readville. The latest report about Burnside is that he is to command in Kentucky. In regard to recruiting I will state that under the call for 300,000 some places have filled their quota and others have a surplus. Sudbury expects that theirs is filled by buying the men. The money being raised for the purpose by private subscription. However I judge by what I hear said as the Town has nothing to do about it but to find a hall and a Speaker as the business was taken out of the hands of the Town by private parties. A few facts in regard to Uncle Thomas. You probably have heard but one side of the story. Everybody here thinks that he knew before he enlisted that he probably would not pass examination by the surgeon, but after enlisting he was so anxious that his appetite failed him (as Lizze told me that he did not eat much of anything for 2 or 3 days) and others state that he started before daylight the day after enlisting and went to Dr. Hunts and got a certificate of Disability which he presented to the surgeon at Concord at his examination and got off. He is fool enough to think that folks are satisfied with his patriotism therefore he <u>noses around</u> more than ever. I gave you the facts & leave you to judge for yourself in regard to his patriotism. The President has ordered a draft for 500,000 men to take place on the 10ᵗʰ of March and all that have enlisted and been drafted previous to the first of March to be deducted. Matters here this Winter are about the same as usual. A Dancing school has been held and is now finished. They had a party at the closing night. Temperence Meetings come off occasionally with spicy debates by W. H. Haynes, <u>the fool,</u> and others. I have not looked over the list of Marriages in town lately but I guess the list is a rather short one. In fact so short that it cannot be seen. Smith Jones and Juliet Johnson's marriage I suppose you knew about. My sheet warns me and I must close. Hope this will find you all well.*

    F. U. Moore

Richmond Prison, located on Belle Isle, Virginia, at one time housed 10,000 Union prisoners and was a place from which few escaped. The U.S. Sanitary Commission paid a visit there and reported that the men were starving and crowded into tents, fifteen men to a tent. By March, 1864, the prisoners were transferred to the prison in Andersonville, Georgia.[11]

The February draft call of 500,000 men was shortly followed with another draft of 200,000 in March. These were the last draft calls of the war.

A list of thirty-three townsmen who paid money in 1864 for the purpose of filling the quota by buying men to serve from the town of Sudbury can be found in Appendix H.

Knoxville
Feb 19th/64

My Dear Father

I will try and answer your letter which I received a few days ago. it was dated Jan 24th I was very glad to hear from you Albert and I have not received many letters until within a few days we have received letters from Francis and Mary and mother we were very glad to hear from you all and shall answer them just as fast as we get a chance. It is pretty cold here now to write but we can get on the sunny side of the building and keep quite comfortable

Everything is quiet here now but I don't expect it will remain so much longer for it is getting to be about time to make a move in some direction and I understand that Gen Grant is in town so I expect something is going to be done we have all confidence in Gen Grant. The rebs have got to have a pretty large army to whip us now and I don't believe they can get men enough together to take Knoxville now it is a pretty strong fortified place. I should hate to charge one the works if they were full of "Johnies"

We expected to be on our way North before this time but old Regts reenlisting have taken so many out of this department that we have got to wait until more troops arrive here before we start

I understand that the President has called for 200,000 more troops I guess he means to have something accomplished this summer and I guess he will need them all for there is going to be some hard fighting and we want men enough to whip them if we gain two or three large victories it will about end the fighting we don't want the Rebels to gain a single victory this summer. I wouldn't care if the President called for every man north, every good able-bodied man I mean leave the rest to raise the crops but then that would be a little foolish after all, for it would take 12 months to organize them.

I don't suppose there is much doing anywhere just now, only enlisting, had Sudbury raised its quota yet, if not how many have they got and who are they. I heard that Uncle Thomas enlisted and the surgeon wouldn't accept him where are all the young men where is that model family (the Willis family) and a number of others that I can mention. Just think of those that have enlisted from Sudbury <u>Centre</u> and see how many there is outside of the Curtis Moore grandchildren[12] (grandfather Moore I mean) there is only three and one of them is discharged

How are you all getting along at home now how do you get along this winter. I had some money to send home but I could not get a chance to send it so I loaned it until next payday at the 1ˢᵗ of March they will owe us 4 months pay. We are getting half rations yet, and growing fat at that. I weighed 172 a few days ago I must think of closing for it is so cold my fingers are getting stiff

Give my love to all the folks and friends write soon
From your son
George

P.S. you will find enclosed some peas that I want you to plant this spring and save the seed next fall

George clarified which Curtis Moore he meant (Grandfather Curtis Moore, Uriah's father) as he also had an uncle named Curtis Moore (youngest brother of Uriah). There were eight grandsons in the Civil War: John, Albert, George, and Alfred Moore, Rufus Hurlbut, and Spencer, Curtis, and Henry Smith.

The Uncle Thomas referred to in the letter was the husband of Uriah's sister, Mary, and father of Rufus Hurlbut. Another cousin, Curtis Smith, was the son of Joseph and Olive Moore Smith. Charles and Mary Parmenter had several sons, and their son, Albert ,was one of the Sudbury conscripts in the draft. Albert's brother, Edwin, went as his substitute and was mustered into the Eighteenth Regiment in August 1863. He was mortally wounded at the Battle of Bottom Bridge, Virginia, and died on June 9, 1864. As for Bent, no Sudbury soldier by that name could be found in the list of Civil War soldiers, but in *Hudson's History* there are four men with the name Bent who furnished a substitute or paid commutation money.

On February 24 the regiment marched nineteen miles back toward Strawberry Plains after receiving news that Longstreet had advanced toward that town with pontoon boats. Orders were issued to be ready for a fifteen day march "with shelter tent and blanket roll only, one hundred rounds of cartridges per man, and five days rations."[13] The country was flooded with freezing cold wind and rain "like the old north-easters at home."[14]

The first page of the following letter to George is missing but its contents indicate that it was written around this time.

to go down and buy the men...Charle Thompson and your Uncle Thomas were the commity that man that you herd had enlisted but your Uncle Thomas was so frightened for fear of the draft would come that he went to a Phisition to be examined previous to this last move but before they bought the men they were five or six vollentured from Town Curtis Smith C Parmenter son[15] Thomas Bent son[16] one or two from the Powder Mills and one dark man cant call the name and bought 9 in Boston Forhenors to fill the quota for the 300,000 and paid one hund dolls apiece for them three of them the Government would not except so Sudbury lost $300 dolls out of that move so now they hold a Town meeting this afternoon have got an article in the warent to see if the Town will refund the money back to those individuals that subscribed money to buy those men so they got a vote to refund the money by laying a tax on the Town for that so you may see the businesses is controlled by that party which used to stile themselves Republicans you may call them as you please and what you please I was mistaken in the amount raised it was $1500 so the Election of our Town officers at March Meeting was controlled by that Party which your Uncle Thomas was elected as one of the Selectmen and for one of the Overseers of the Poor that Parker Fairbank by the same party as big a Rebel as goes on two legs very pleasant wether for March not much frost in the ground no snow those pees you sent me I will plant as soon as the frost is out wrote to Albert last week John wont enlist will write the rest next time write soon we are all well hope this will find you well
  From your Father

A Poor House located in North Sudbury housed paupers from the town as well as those who wandered in. The farm was run by a warden, and the residents were expected to work in exchange for their room and board. Some were let out to work for others. The three Overseers of the Poor, elected by the Selectmen, were responsible for keeping the accounts of the expenditures for the Poor House. Several funds had been set up in town specifically designed to serve the poor and needy. The industrious poor did not receive assistance from the town.[17]

George received the following letter from his twelve-year-old brother, James Edgar.

Dear Brother

   How do you do we are all well and hope you are the same they say the opper school is not a going to keep moch longer. Mr Parminter keeps the opper school and Mrs Abby young keeps the lower school I wish you wood rite to me as soon as you can and tell me what is a going on out there it snowed last satorday all day bot not hard enough to be very deep. our school finshed last week of Friday after noon and the opper school finished last week of Friday after noon have rote all i can think of now so good by from your loving Brother

   James E. Moore

The march to Morristown was the last duty for the Thirty-fifth at the front in East Tennessee, and on March 13 they parted from the Fourth and Twenty-third Corps and headed into Kentucky.

> Our tried and true companions of the winter of hardship; they remained to follow Longstreet towards the Virginia line, then to join General Sherman in the campaign in Atlanta; we, by the long route over the mountains marched to face Longstreet again in the Wilderness Campaign. [18]

The men who were able to march headed over the mountain route, while the sick, which included Albert, went on the cars by way of Chattanooga and Nashville. Marching through the snowstorms and freezing rain, the regiment crossed the mountains into Kentucky and arrived twelve days later on March 25.

March 16, 1864

Dear Brother

 Having a little spare time today. I will try and answer your letter which I received a while ago. Albert wrote that you was on the move and that he having a sore foot was left behind. also William Bowen. He said that you might be going to Richmond but did not know for certain if that was the destination, he would like to be in at the taking. I am anxious to hear all about the movement. There is nothing in the papers that I can find in regard to the exact situation of affairs in your Department.

 I received a letter from John dated March 9th at Culpepper Court House, Va. He is in the City yet, but expects to be moving soon. He says that he does not get letters very often. Says he saddled a mule the other day and went up to the regiment and drew a pair of pants, shoes and drawers and got my letter to him. Had a long talk with Spencer and he and Spencer concluded not to reenlist. George Smith and Mortimer Johnson have reenlisted and expect to come home in a few days on 35 days furlough. He says not many of the 13th or 12th are reenlisting but most of the Potomac Army are reenlisting. Some Regiments are just returning from their furlough. Gen Meade is being overhauled for something or other done at Gettysburg.

 Perhaps you have heard of Kilpatricks great Raid to Richmond lately. The object of the Expedition was to release Union Prisoners at Richmond and do all the damage they could there and also on the route. It seems that they accomplished everything they set out for excepting to release the Prisoners. They reached the City and took the outer fortifications but the Expedition being <u>betrayed</u> by a negro beforehand. The Rebels were prepared to defend the City and send for reinforcements and repulsed the Federals. Sherman has also been making a grand Raid down in Alabama and the Rebel papers are groaning in consequence. He destroyed many Millions of property, took Thousands of prisoners and brought them in and also lots of provisions. John thinks that Lee is reinforced by a part of Longstreets army. There is no news from other quarters at present.

 The Draft has been postponed for the present. High authorities note that men are volunteering as fast as they can be provided for or fitted out. About 2000 per day it is estimated are enlisting on the average at the North. When the Draft does come it will not exempt anybody unless they are mentally or physically disabled. The family are as well as usual.

 Harriet writes that she likes it at South Framingham first rate. She and the Brigham girls are at work there on bonnets. Emily Smith is alive *yet but is very low. The Doctor (Libby of Boston) thinks that he can cure her and if she gets well of course he will get the credit of the cure by the family. The small Pox scare here in town is about over I think. Not but one case in town that I have heard of. Father imagined that we had been exposed, but after <u>dieting</u> on <u>poultry</u> for a while and also put down the <u>pills</u> he has finally concluded that we shant have the disease I guess. Alfred thought that we had been exposed but the time for the appearance has expired and we have got around home again. He has been at work at Horace Parmenters[19] lately. The March Meeting came off resulting in the election of all the Republican Candidates for Town Officers (or who were nominated by those who call themselves Republicans) J. S. Hunt Town Clerk,- T .P. Hurlbut, Charles Hunt and Walter Rogers, Selectmen - T. A. Jones,Treasurer and Collector - T. A. Jones, James Moore and John H. Dakin, Assessors - James Moore, T.B. Battles and J.P. Fairbanks, Overseers of Poor.*

I shall be obliged to close
F. U. Moore

When Francis says that Meade was being overhauled, he may have been saying that President Lincoln was dissatisfied with the manner in which General Meade commanded the troops at Gettysburg. Lincoln felt that Meade had not attacked Lee when he had the opportunity, moving so slowly that he gave Lee time to escape and missed the opportunity to end the war.[20]

General Kilpatrick planned to liberate the Union prisoners at Libby Prison in Richmond by breaking down the door. Colonel Dahlgren was second in command and took five hundred troops, including the First Vermont, preceding the regiment. Kilpatrick discovered the strength of the Confederates, and, when he failed to hear from Colonel Dahlgren, he abandoned the idea and moved on to join Butler at Yorktown. Dahlgren, not knowing this, continued and was led astray by a guide "either through treachery or stupidity" and arrived at a river he was unable to cross. When he did reach the city, he discovered a much larger force than expected, and while withdrawing in the very bad weather, he became separated from his men and was ambushed and killed.[21]

Seven-strand straw braids used in the manufacture of hats were braided at home by local women and their children from pipe grass harvested along the sides of the Sudbury River. The braids were traded for goods at Hunt's Store at 2 cents a yard.[22] The Temperance Movement was fairly active in town during the Civil War but not until 1871 did the town vote against the sale of hard cider and ale.[23] Spencer Smith, a cousin of the Moore brothers, and Ed Moulton, a shoemaker from Marlborough, Massachusetts, enlisted on March 30, 1864, in the Fifty-ninth Regiment, Company I. James Moore is the father of John Herschel Moore of the Thirty-second Regiment.

Letter from Father, April 3, 1864, Sudbury Historical Society,
Photograph by Chuck Zimmer

Sudbury
April 3ed 1864

Dear George
    I have not received a letter from you cince one dated Feb 19th one that you sent those pees in have wrote to you cince but I will write now cince I have heard the good news by the way of Albert I received a letter from him last night dated March 22ed he wrote that you had left that department for the North and it was the opinion that they would come to Anapalas M.D I suposde you have arived at that place or on your journey drawing close on to that place when you get to Anapalas I hope you can get a furlow to come home before you start on that expedition if you cannot or see no prospects of geting a furlow and a going to stop there

a short time or long enough for me to come out there write to me and let me know and I will try and get a pass to come and see you for I want to see you very much Spencer Smith wrote home last week that he had a good mind to reenlist I hope John wont think of it if I was in his place after they had been so much said and done from Sudbury to get them to reenlist and the course that they have taken here in Sudbury to raise their men of late rather than to reenlist now I would go into the Regt if they compeled me to and into the ranks first when you get to Maryland I wish you would write to John and advise him not to reenlist Alfred had enlisted and was excepted and sworn in to the service and Ed Molton has enlisted I understand that our quota is all filled the largest portion of them were Forenors that they bought Alfred went down to Reedville last Wensday to enlist and has not been home cince he has been so bewitched about going out South that he has not been worth much to me this winter so I have not got my wod near closed up so I have not commenced farming any yet some of the farmers have commenced plowing frost all out of the ground the month of March has been very pleasant till within a few days have had a very servear Northeast storme with rain hail and snow the snow on Friday last was about 4 inch in debth so they sledded logs to Mill some sleighs out fair today ground still covered with snow and pretty cold have hired that Daniel Moore place this year for the same rent intend to have Charles go out to work this season but have not found any place for him yet Alfred might have had twenty dolls or more per month for eight Month on a farm this season Charles does not seem to be very ruged he cant seem to labor much is unwell every now and then a day I keep the white face horse yet and one Cow Keep the Chaise and Sleigh and have one horse hay wageon and a horse cart the price of articles of Consumption are very high beef stake out of the Cart 16cts per lb butter from 50 to 75 cts per lb Chese 20cts sugar 15 to 20 Molases 65 to $1.00 per gal flower is the cheapest article from 8 to 12 dolls per brl Corn and Rye $1.50 per bush white beens $3.00 per bush lard 16cts hay 25 to 35 dolls per ton potatoes $1.25 per bush and all kinds of cloth Boots and shoes as high accordingly John sent us home ten dollars last week Mary is to work at Camb-Port yet Hattie is in the straw business at South Framingham my sheet is about full so I will close and write the rest next time write soon we are all well and I hope this will find you well

*   From your Father*

Alfred Moore enlisted in the Fifty-ninth Regiment Massachusetts Volunteers.

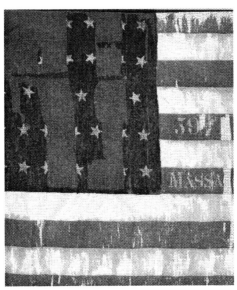

First National Flag, Fifty-ninth Regiment Massachusetts Volunteers (Fourth Veterans) in Civil War, 1987.213 issued April 26, 1864 (Eaton to Ord Dept same date) Received by Sergeant-at-Arms, Nov 21, 1864. Courtesy of the Commonwealth of Massachusetts Art Commission

First State Color Fifty-ninth Regiment Massachusetts Volunteers (Fourth Veterans) Issued April 26, 1864, (Eaton to Ord Dept same date).Received by Sergeant-at-Arms Nov. 21, 1864, 1987.208. Courtesy of the Commonwealth of Massachusetts Art Commission

Baltimore Md
April 7, 1864

Dear Father
    This is the first opportunity I have had to write for a long time and
I expect to have to leave this before I get half through but I will try and
write a few lines We arrived here last night stopped in the Barracks on
Eutaw street expect to leave here today for Anapolis, don't know where
we are going from there probably with Burnside wherever he goes. I
hope so at least for I had rather be under him than any other Gen'l I
know of I suppose you know that we were going to leave Tenn. sometime
ago. We marched all the way from Morristown to Nicholasville
Kentucky (223 miles in 14 days) took the cars at Nicholasville for
Covington crossed the river into Cincinnati took the cars here for
Columbus stopped there about 1 hr started again for Pittsburgh Penn
changed cars here got a collation, started again for Harrisburg got a
collation there stopped there about 3 hours started again for Baltimore
and here we are all right an ready for another start Al having a lame
foot got a chance to go from Knoxville to Cincinnati on the cars he
went around by Chattanooga Nashville and Louisville all those that
were not able to march went that way I saw William Bailey at Knoxville
he had just arrived there as the 9th corps was ordered away. he is on
the sick list yet & guess he always will be. all the rest of the Sudbury
boys are all right. That is all there is here Mr Garfield and Eli Wallis
I don't know anything about not having seen them for 6 or 8 months
Eli has not been to the Regt since he had his furlough don't expect he
will be with us again unless he is obliged to be Mr. Garfield has been
pretty sick don't know whether he has got well yet or not. Rufus is with
us and tough as you find them William Bowen is all right his foot is
all well now Harry Hall is all right he is taking care of the Horses at
Headquarters Al is all right except his foot which will trouble him if we
have a long march I am well as I wish to be and have been ever since I
left Mississippi we have seen some pretty hard times, but we have had
good health which is worth more than anything especially out here have
been in one of the healthiest places I ever was in if we only got enough
to eat I would like to stay in East Tenn it is as good union place as a
great many Northern States and better than some. I hope the Northern
people will do something to help them. I know if they could see the
condition they are in they would and they are not to blame for what
the state has done, and the State would never of gone out of the Union
if the Government had sent the arms and means to find themselves

they asked for. Tenn is worth a dozen Kentucky's I don't think much of Kentucky the people I mean it is a good state if only it had good people in it. There are some good Union people in it but then the most of them don't care which side they are on it is not so in Tenn there is no half way people there they are either Union Or Rebels and are a very few rebels there now

Our Colonel is in command of our Brigade he says he will try and get the 35th a chance to go home on a furlough but I hardly think he will succeed. I must close now excuse this letter for I wrote it in a hurry. I am almost ashamed to send it for it is blotted so but I can't stop to write another tell the rest I will write to them when I get to Annapolis

> *Good morning*
> *George*

Because mail was slow and often lost, both soldiers and families looked for a direct route, or for a friend who was traveling, to hand-carry the letters.

Sudbury
April 10th 1864

Dear George

Your letter of the 7th I received last night and was glad to here from you and know that you have all arived safe your long march over the Mountains must have been teactious I received a letter from Albert dated the 22ed of March he wrote the Regt had just left for the North I have wrote to you cince you left for the North and wrote to have you write to John as soon as you arived in Maryland and advise him not to reenlist I wrote to you about the course Sudbury took to raise thier men to fill their quota and the doings at March Meeting and who they selected for their Town officers the party that have stiled themselves Republicans selected and elected for one of their oversears of the Poor that Rebel Parker Fairbank so you may gess the other officers of the Town and the names of some of those that Volenteerd from Sudbury Alfred has enlisted and was Mustered in or sworn in a week ago Friday and went to Camp at Readvill and got a furlow last Thursday for five days he is at home with a bad Cold and a sore foot is not able to go back to Camp is a gont to try to get his furlow extended for a few days think he will be able to go in a few days he goes in the 59th Regt of Infentry which they expect to brake Camp about the 15th or 20th for Anapolis M.D. to join Burnsides Army so you may see each other I wrote to you wishing you to write to me as soon after you got to Maryland as you could assertain wether they was any prospect of you getting a furlow to come home if they was not any I would try and get a pass to come out there if you thought that you should stay there time enouth for me to get out there and see you for I want to see you all very much Curtis Smith has enlisted and is going in the same Company with Alfred and Henry Smith is a lieutenant of the same Company half past three Oclock wind Northeast snowing quite hard... the month of March very pleasant April has been very rough so far cold wether I have not done any farming as yet...have not got my wood closed up yet not much news just now in my last letter I wrote to you I gave the enormous high prices of articles of consumption an a most everything is very high Recd a letter from John dated March the 20th he was well he sent home 20 dolls in Money have got some new Neighbors in the Centre of the Town this spring have in that old George Moore house Old Taylor and in that little house on the Common Old Garison Mary is at Camb-Port yet Hatty in the straw business at South Framingham wee are all well hope this will find you well please answer

From your Father

The Second Division of the IX Corps covered one hundred and seventy miles in the next eleven days, over treacherous mountain passes and muddy roads, to reach the railroad station at Nicholasville, Kentucky, on April 1, retracing the route taken south just a year before. Six days later, traveling by rail and steamboat they arrived at Annapolis. There they learned that there were twenty thousand troops forming four divisions plus a regiment of cavalry, intended for the Ninth Corps with General Burnside in command. The regiment was rejoined by the men who were unable to march over the mountains. Albert and Rufus were now sent to convalescent camp and the regiment set up in their previous campground. The contrast between the appearance of the old, ragged and smoke stained tents, and the clean quarters of the new troops, was apparent. The destination of the combined troops was still unknown to the soldiers. Friends came to visit because it was near the city. The Thirty-fifth was assigned to the First Brigade of the First Division along with other Massachusetts regiments, including the Fifty-ninth Massachusetts. Colonel Carruth was made Commander of the Brigade. John Moore of the Thirteenth Massachusetts Regiment was with the supply wagon train traveling with the corps. All four Moore brothers were part of this campaign.

On April 23 the men awoke to reveille at 2:30 am and started on their march when Uriah Moore and John Morse's father arrived. George and John Morse got a pass for 24 hours to visit. The Fifty-ninth Massachusetts arrived nine days later on May 2, and George had another reunion, this time with his brother, Alfred, and another Sudbury boy, Ed Moulton.

General Grant was determined to concentrate his forces against Lee continuously and constantly, not allowing him to escape. As the corps marched, they passed towns and battlefields that many had seen before, including Warrenton Junction, Manassas Junction, and Bull Run. On May 5, Company D, including George Moore, was detailed to guard the ammunition train, and Albert was detailed to the Brigade commissary. This meant that George and Albert, as well as John, would escape the fighting except when John was delivering ammunition. Now the regiment and the ammunition train were traveling parallel to the fighting troops. As the regiment neared the Rapidan River, musket fire and the booming of cannons could be heard. Battle sounds raged around them for the next three and a half months. Company D would not rejoin the regiment until the end of June.[24]

Sudbury
May 8th 1864

Dear George
I write you a few lines now as I promised I would in Alberts Letter after so long a time but they is not much news a sturing here now except war news I wrote to Albert in a day or two after I arrived home got home the next day after I left you all right found the folks all well such a happy meeting it seeme as though I never expearanced so pleasant and happy a time as I did wile out here with you boys it seemes to me like a dream coming out here and seeing you the time seemed so short while with you I hope the time will soon come when I shall see you all at home safe and sound and the Rebellion put down and every Man free white and Black it was reported a few days ago that Meads whole force had crossed the River he was a falling back and was reported in the papers yesterday that a battle had commenced on the front it is reported that Burnsides Army is put in reserve I hope you wont be needed to the front I wrote to John cince I saw you at the time I wrote to Albert but it is reported that all communication is cut off from the front so I don't know as John has received my letter if so we shall not get any more letters at present and you wont be likely to get this but if you do please answer soon and let me know where you are and if you were well wee received a letter from Alfred last Monday he wrote on Saturday before that they arrived at Alexandria the day before all right but had not seen you boys I suppose you have seen Alfred before this time
Sudbury has got to draft after all the last men they bought was eight and paid one hund and fifty dolls a piece and have lost six of them so they have lost nine hund dolls
Emely Smith died last Monday and was buried last Wensday they thought her better till within a day or two before her death I will close now and write more next time wee are all well hope this will find you well

From your Father

Canisters filled with minie balls exploded creating terrible showers of missiles whistling overhead. Deadly cannon fire was heard at the front of the wagon trains, day after day, as the corps proceeded toward Fredericksburg. The men camped near the same battlefield where they had fought the December 1862 Battle of Fredericksburg. Horse drawn black hearse-like ambulances carrying wounded from the front passed by, along with 3,000 captured Confederates. Men guarding the wagon train were anxious to be at the front and know what was going on. General Grant did not stop to rest after the North Anna engagement. By May 15, George was still waiting to hear from Alfred, and on May 17, the regiment headed towards Spotsylvania and met the Thirteenth Massachusetts Regiment (John Moore's) just as they had prior to the Battles of South Mountain and Fredericksburg. The Thirty-fifth was at the front in the battle, and when George was sent to the front bringing rations he saw some of the wounded of the Thirty-fifth.[25]

Fredericksburg Virginia: View from Across the Rappahannock River. 165-SB-30
Photograph by Timothy H. O'Sullivan, National Archives, Washington, D.C.

Fredericksburg Va
May 16 1864

Dear Mother
I suppose you are all anxious to hear from us and having an opportunity I thought I would write a few lines to let you know that we are all safe and well, all except Alfred I have not seen or heard from him for sometime the last I heard he was wounded in the hand slightly and went to the Hospital I guess he is all right. John is with the wagon train

*working at his old job of saddler I saw him yesterday Albert is detailed
at the Brigade Commissary's so he wont have to go into battle William
Bowen is detailed also Eli Willis also Harry Hall. Rufus is sick and has
been sent to the Hospital so there is nobody left in the company from
Sudbury but me and Mr. Bailey George & Spencer Smith were all right
yesterday. Saw Gardner Darling[26] a few days ago he is with the train.
this Reg't has not been in the battles yet we have been guarding the
train but I expect we will be ordered to the front everyday the front is
10 miles from here the army of the Potomac has seen some pretty hard
fighting since they came in this month but we have whipped the Rebels so
far we have taken a large number of prisoners we hear Butler & Smith
are doing big things but you know more than we do about it but I must
close for I want to send you this by Capt Lyons who is going home give
my love to all hope this will find you all well excuse this for I wrote in a
hurry*

From your loving son

George

A series of confrontations, collectively known as the Battle of the
Wilderness, began on May 4. The Fifty-ninth Regiment Massachusetts
Volunteers (Alfred Moore's regiment) was now part of General Grant's
Army, and on May 6, only ten days after it left Massachusetts, it was
engaged in the Battle of the Wilderness. It was here at the North Anna
River that Alfred Moore was severely wounded. (The regiment engagement
on May 6 was listed at the Plank Road, but Alfred Moore's government
records state that he was injured at the North Anna River on May 6). The
Fifty-ninth lost twelve men, with twenty-seven wounded, and five missing.
News reached George that his brother had been wounded in his hand and
George wrote home that he thought Alfred would be all right. However,
Alfred was more seriously wounded, having sustained a contusion in his
side, and he was sent to a field hospital and then to U. S. General Hospital,
"Satterlee," in Philadelphia, Pennsylvania. He was still listed as "in
hospital" as late as February 28, 1865. Alfred was later transferred out of
the Fifty-ninth Regiment to the VRC 9 (Veterans Reserve Corps A series
of confrontations, collectively known as the Battle of the Wilderness,
began on May 4. The Fifty-ninth Regiment Massachusetts Volunteers
(Alfred Moore's regiment) was now part of General Grant's Army, and on
May 6, only ten days after it left Massachusetts, it was engaged in the Battle
of the Wilderness. It was here at the North Anna River that Alfred Moore

was severely wounded. (The regiment engagement on May 6 was listed at the Plank Road, but Alfred Moore's government records state that he was injured at the North Anna River on May 6). The Fifty-ninth lost 12 men, with 27 wounded, and 5 missing. News reached George that his brother had been wounded in his hand and George wrote home that he thought Alfred would be all right. However, Alfred was more seriously wounded, having sustained a contusion in his side, and he was sent to a field hospital and then to U. S. General Hospital, "Satterlee," in Philadelphia, Pennsylvania. He was still listed as "in hospital" as late as February 28, 1865. Alfred was later transferred out of the Fifty-ninth Regiment to the VRC 9 (Veterans Reserve Corps).[27] He did not return home until September of 1865.

The soldiers from Sudbury kept in touch with other soldiers from town, and then saw that this information reached home.

Alfred M. Moore, Fifty-ninth Regiment Massachusetts Volunteers Infantry. U.S. Army Heritage and Education Center RG985-CWP155.25 Carlisle, Pennsylvania

Because General Burnside held a superior rank over General Meade, the regiment was now permanently part of the army of the Potomac. The Thirty-fifth Regiment had been appointed Engineering Corps for the First Division and was placed under the orders of Major James St. Clair Morton, chief engineer of the IX Corps. This detail duty, difficult and often perilous, lasted until the first of September.[28] Usually, engineering regiments are exempt from battlefield duty, but withdrawing the regiment from the battlefield would have weakened the attack, so the men took part in all the battles as well as performing their engineering duties. One day, the regiment was within one hundred yards of the enemy's entrenchments and they lay down in the field as enemy shots whizzed over their heads for more than three hours.

> While lying thus, a man in the uniform of a staff officer came along the line with a solid shot in hand inquiring for a certain battery: turning to the front he disappeared through the line, which let him pass, not suspecting his

intention, until he pulled out a white handkerchief and sprang into the Confederate entrenchment, much to the chagrin of those who watched the performance,...spy, deserter, or Confederate officer caught in our lines.[29]

Trenches were dug, allowing the men to travel unseen to and from the picket and front lines. In late May skirmishes resulted in heavy loss of life. A number of soldiers in the regiment were taken prisoner and several of these men spent the remainder of their service as prisoners of war. By mid-June the regiment was advancing towards the city of Petersburg.

The following letter is to George from Francis:

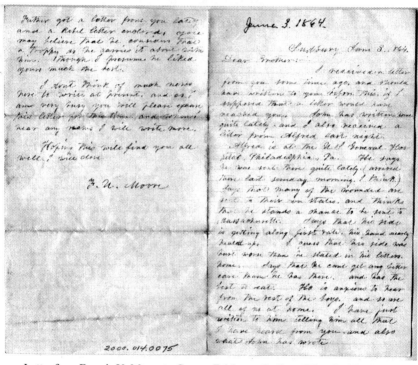

Letter from Francis U. Moore to George F. Moore, Sudbury Historical Society, Photograph by Chuck Zimmer

Sudbury
June 3, 1864

Dear Brother

    I received a letter from you some time ago and should have written to you before this if I supposed that a letter would have reached you. John has written home quite lately and I also received a letter from Alfred last night.

    Alfred is at the U. S. General Hospital, Philadelphia, Pa.[30] He says he was sent there quite lately (arrived there last Sunday morning I think) Says that many of the wounded are sent to there own states and thinks that he stands a chance to be sent to Massachusetts. Says that his side is getting along first rate, his hand nearly healed up. I guess that his side was much worse than he stated in his letters home. Says that he cant get any better care than he has there and has the best to eat. He is anxious to hear from the rest of the boys and so are all of us at home. I have just written to him telling him all that I have heard from you and also what John has wrote. According to all accounts the Sudbury boys are all right up to May 25th with the exception of Charles Haynes[31] in the 13th Regiment who is wounded. John says that he saw you and Albert lately and he has also seen Edward Moulton who was in the rear, sick and continues to get no better Moulton is now in the Hospital (forgot the name of the Hospital)

    Says the soldiers have great confidence in Grant and I think everybody has at present. I should like to send you some papers if I thought they would reach you so you could read all about the news better than I could write it. However I will state that folks have great confidence in the army of the Potomac. Sherman is gaining victories over the Rebels in Georgia. Butler is doing well on the south of Richmond and Fort Sumter is undergoing another pounding.

    As you perhaps have not heard of the particulars of the late Draft here I will state that six men were drafted in Sudbury to make up the deficiencies from the Town

    The three first were Uncle Thomas, Jonas A. Hunt and Sam Bent and they paid commutation. The other three were not required to appear as three men were bought for the quota since the Draft was made. The examining board said that Tom, Jonas, and Sam were the best conscripts that had appeared before them for a long time

    Another Draft is expected about the first of July so to keep Grants army full up to its present numbers.

The folks at home are all as well as usual. Pleasant weather and prospects of good crops and also abundant of fruit here.

Charles is at Lewis Taylors at Cochituate. He went over June 1ˢᵗ to work for him at 15 Dollars a month to work in the beer shop, principally washing bottles, don't know whether he will get to be chief bottle washer or not.

I have been pretty busy for 4 or 5 weeks carriage painting. Father has been Teaming some lately, his planting is rather late. Harriet is now at home.

Ambrose Page[32] is getting better he says and is anxious to get well and join his Regiment again . Alfred says he wants to go to Richmond with the rest. Father got a letter from you lately and a Rebel letter enclosed, you may believe that he considers that a trophy as he carries it about with him though I presume he liked yours much the best.

I dont think of much news here to write at present and as I am very busy you will please excuse this letter for this time and when I hear any news I will write more.

Hoping this will find you all well, I will close
F. U. Moore

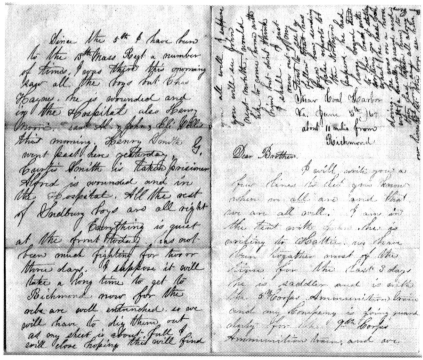

Letter to Francis from George June 5, 1864. Sudbury Historical Society

Near Cold Harbor Va
June 5/64
About 10 miles from Richmond

Dear Brother

I will write you a few lines to let you know where we all are and that we are all well. I am in the tent with John he is writing to Hattie we have been together most of the time for the last 3 days he is saddler and is with the 5ᵗʰ Corps Ammunition train and my Company is doing guard duty for the 9ᵗʰ Corps Ammunition train and we are camped close together we are about 2 or 3 miles from the front don't have much to do except guard duty nights. Al and Eli are Brigade Butchers they are at Brigade Headquarters so I have not seen them for sometime but I heard from them today they are all right. Harry Hall[33] is at Brigade Headquarters also Rufus is in the Hospital at Washington or near there sick. I have not heard from him since he left us. William Bailey and myself are with the Company

I saw Henry Moore day before yesterday he is wounded through the arm but has no broken bones he said he left all of Sudbury Boys in the 13ᵗʰ all right. Mr Capin is all right Henry and Curtis Smith were all right last I heard from them Ed Moulton[34] is in the Hospital he is not able to march on account of that rupture that he was troubled with before he left home.

June 8, 1864

I had to quit writing the other day for the "Johnies" made a charge on our lines and some of their shot came too near for our comfort, but they got drove back after about 10 minutes fighting and lost a large number of men

Since the 5ᵗʰ I have been to the 13ᵗʰ Regt a number of times. I was there this morning saw all the boys but Chas Haynes, he is wounded and in the Hospital also Henry Moore[35]. Saw Al and John, Eli Willis[36] this morning Henry Smith went past here yesterday Curtis Smith is taken prisoner Alfred is wounded and in the Hospital all the rest of Sudbury boys are all right. Everything is quiet at the front today. has not been much fighting for two or three days. I suppose it will take a long time to get to Richmond now for the rebs are well entrenched, so we will have to dig them out as my sheet is about full I will close hoping this will find you all well I suppose you will see John next-month would like to come home with him but don't think I shall. I just run out of my tent to see a fellow that has been sending false reports to the Northern papers. he had a large board tied to his back with writing on it stating what he had been doing. he was on a horse with a Cavalry guard and they had taken him to the front and all along the lines to let the boys see him

From George

In George's letter of June 5 he wrote that he thought that his cousin, Curtis Smith, was alright, but by the end of his letter on June 8, he had learned that Curtis had been taken prisoner. Curtis Smith was at Andersonville Prison in Georgia and died there of starvation October 19, 1864. Curtis was at Andersonville at the time this photo was taken.

Issuing Rations at Andersonville Prison, Georgia, August 17, 1864. Photograph by A. J. Riddle 165-A-445 Courtesy of National Archives, Washington, D.C.

The Thirty-fifth Regiment continued to advance towards the James River. Captain Hudson was appointed Engineering Officer of the Division. The engineering regiment was now repairing roads and building rafts for the artillery to cross. They also constructed bridges, with one pontoon bridge extending for 2,200 feet. They cut roads through the thick underbrush of the woods for the troops and artillery trains to travel. On June 15, 1864, the regiment crossed the river, which was by now filled with fleets of transports and steam tugs. The regiments that crossed were greatly reduced in numbers from their former full ranks. By June 16 the regiment was within two miles of the city of Petersburg. The engineers continued building bridges, cutting the roads, burying the dead, and making gabions, (a cylindrical wicker basket used to reinforce earthworks or to replace them). For two months the infantry was in two lines of trenches, with the pickets in the front exchanging positions with the men in the back every three days. Field guns and cannon were used as needed, with sharp-shooters keeping watch for the enemy. In the Battle at Cold Harbor, the battlefield was strewn with dead horses (forty horses to an acre,) trees full of holes, and the enemy lying where they fell.[37] On June 18 the corps suffered heavy causalities. The Union lost their opportunity to capture Petersburg without a siege.[38] Company D, which had been detached to guard the ammunition trains since May 5, returned to the regiment on June 25.

Making Gabions. from the Civil War. Mathew Brady Collection. (Army) Exact Date Shot Unknown NARA File #111-B-4859, Washington, D. C.

The following letter is from Francis to George.

Friday July 1, 1864

Dear Brother
     *Your Letter dated June 5ᵗʰ came to hand a while ago and I was glad
to hear from you. I received one from Albert dated 19ᵗʰ and received one
from Alfred last night dated 25ᵗʰ. Albert wrote but little news, but I see by
the papers that there has been hard fighting before Petersburg. I am glad
that all of you can see each other occasionally. Alfred writes that his side
is better and for the past week has felt pretty comfortable. He is in the
U. S. General Hospital, Philadelphia,, Pa. and has the best care and the
best to eat. He says the doctor thinks he had better stay with him a while
longer and he wants him to write for him for 3 years if he will, but Alford
says he told him he was a poor writer and thought he should decline the
offer, although thinks it would be a good thing for him and I think so too,
don't you? He says that he has not got paid off yet, and therefore ordered
some of his bounty endorsed to him to buy boots etc as he wants to go to
a picnic on the 4ᵗʰ if the doctor is willing.*
     *Henry Moore and Charles Haynes have arrived home on a furlough.
I spoke with Henry Moore last evening. He said he saw you boys just
before leaving, about June 3d. His furlough extends 30 days, so I suppose
the regiment will be mustered out by that time. Mr. Lovell is at home
on a furlough as he has been wounded. He is with his wife at E. Stones
who now lives on the Wm Smith Place near Assabet. Rufus Hurlbut is in
Hospital at Washington I believe and is rather slim, having a slow fever
etc so he writes to his folks. Edwin Parmenter has been killed I hear. He
went out last summer as substitute for his brother who was drafted.*
     *The three men who were drafted from Sudbury under the last call
have paid their commutation by $100 cash out of their own pockets
and the balance out of the fund raised last winter. The men were Tom
Hurlbut, J.S. Hunt and Sam Bent (perhaps this is no news to you).*
     *Congress has now abolished the commutation clause and therefore
every able bodied man who is drafted must serve or provide a substitute.
The enrolled men in town are raising money by subscription to procure
men to fill the quota in anticipation of a draft to take place soon.*
     *George Smith has lost a foot I am pained to hear. He writes to his folks
as though he was in good spirits however. There is a story going the rounds
here in which Ed Moulton is figured badly . That when his Regiment first
formed line of battle in face of the enemy, he took his gun and turned back
to the enemy and went to the rear. The commanding officer ordered 3 or*

*4 men to fire on him but did not have the effect to stop him. Unless <u>you</u>
<u>contradict</u> this story folks will be compelled to give some credit to it.*

*The ladies in Sudbury are at work on articles to send to soldiers
hospitals. A Levee is to be held in the Town Hall on the 4th of July, the
proceeds to go to the Sanitary Commission I believe. We are having a little
sprinkle of rain this morning. The first for many weeks vegetation is drying
up. Haying is coming on immediately. Strawberries are scarce on account
of the dry ground. They fetch 30 to 40 cts per box. I continue at the
carriage painting yet. Charles it likes well (at Lewis Taylors-Cochituate)
he says. Father has gone to Boston today and taken Edgar and Ellen with
him but it is so dusty on the road that a ride is not very pleasant.*

Hope this will find you well

F. U. M.

The letter below is George's reply:

Near Petersburg, Va.
July 3rd/64

Dear Brother
*I received your letter sometime ago and should have answered it
before this but we have been so busy that I could not get time to write.*

*My company is with the Regt. now. we joined them last week and
have worked every night this week and all night to. so we have to
sleep daytimes. I am getting used to it so I don't mind it as much as
I did at first we are building a Fort out in an open field and we have
to work nights for the Rebels can see us in the daytime they keep up
a firing all night but they cannot see us. so if any of us get hit it will
be a chance shot. I believe there has but two fellows be wounded
since we commenced. my company was the first to commence the Fort
Capt. Hudson had charge of the work and he said he wanted Co. D
to commence it. we had to lay down to dig and then the Rebel bullets
passed pretty near our person, but every man staid where he was put to
work and they soon got a place dug deep enough to protect their person.
when a bullet came very near us the boys would say "a miss is as good
as a mile" and keep to work. none of the company have been hit as yet.
we have got the Fort nearly done guess we can finish it tonight. there is
going to be placed within it 6 32 pound guns and they want to get them
in tonight so as to celebrate the 4th tomorrow morning. I think they can
shell the city from this Fort. we have got batteries planted where they*

can destroy the city at any time but Gen. Grant don't want to destroy it and I don't think he will be obliged to.

I think we will be in possession of it within 30 days. the army is growing larger every day now for the Conscripts and recruits are arriving. it was reported yesterday that the 19th corps had arrived here from Gen. Banks department don't know whether it is so or not, there is not much firing today, guess they are getting ready for tomorrow's work. 12 days more and I expect John will start for home, and all the rest of the boys except George Smith and M Johnson. I should think they would feel bad to see the other boys leave. I know I should if I were in their place. the last I heard from the 13th boys they were all right. I see John every few days. we have received letters from Allie, and Rufus within a few days they are getting along well. So the town bought substitutes for those drafted men well I don't care much what they do for it don't concern me. Only I think they had ought to make poor Everett's 300 up to him. I think if I had been in uncle Thomas place I would of come out anyway after volunteering but then he can do as he pleases and other folks can think what they please.

The boys are all right that are with the company and all the rest as far as I know. Write soon and write all the news give my love to all inquiring friends. Tell me all about the big time that you have tomorrow in the Town Hall.

Tell Father I will write to him next.

From, George

P.S. I have just heard that George Smith was wounded in the right leg. don't know how bad.

In a second letter to his brother, Francis, George describes how he is doing.

Camp Near Petersburg, Va
July 17th 1864

Dear Brother

I will now try and answer your letter which I received sometime ago, and was very glad to hear from you. I do not get much time to write for our Regt. is detailed as Engineers for the 1st division 9th corps and we have to work most every day. This is the first day we have had to ourselves for most a month. part of the time we have had to work nights but I am satisfied with the work as long as we don't have to go into the Rifle pits and lay in the hot sun. We have had some pretty hot weather, but the worst trouble with us is the water that we get here is not fit to drink and it is pretty scarce at that. but I suppose there will be plenty when it rains, we have not had any rain of any consequence for two or three months and it is awful dusty.

Our forces are not doing much just at present but you may expect news in a few days. I think this army will make a move in some direction before this week is out. I see by the papers that Gen'l Sherman is doing great things in Georgia. I hope he will keep on and drive the Rebs into the Gulf of Mexico.

The Rebels have made quite a big raid into Maryland. but they did not quite get Washington this time and if they get back to Richmond all right they will be lucky and don't think Grant is at all troubled about it I suppose the Johnies thought they could make Grant leave this place. but they did not succeed. Grant sent one Corps (the 6th) from here and I understand they arrived at Washington just at the right time.

Mr. Bailey has gone to the Hospital again sick. so I am the only Sudbury boy in the company now. I don't know what ailed Bailey he has not got constitution strong enough for this kind of business. He has been sick or away most of the time since we left home. I shall be glad when Rufus gets back here. I believe the boys are all well I suppose you will see the boys from the 13th soon but I must close. love to all, write soon, and tell me what kind of a time they had the 4th

from George.

Francis replied with the following letter.

Sunday
July 17, 1864

Dear Brother
Your letter dated 3d, I have received, also received one last night from Albert and a few days ago got one from Alfred and John.

The 13th Regiment has not arrived home yet or had not reached Mass Wednesday. Arrangements are being made in Boston, and also in Sudbury to give the public reception on their arrival home.

Alfred writes that he is getting along pretty well. Says that he has escaped a good deal of hard fighting but <u>not</u> a good deal of hard pain.

I am glad to learn that letters have lately been received both ways by Alfred and you boys. He wrote me a while ago to give you his address so that there would be no delay in his getting your letters. Therefore I will give it now.

U. S. General Hospital
Ward E
Philadelphia, Pa

   The 4ᵗʰ of July passed off with considerable éclat in Sudbury. The day was usual in by the clanging of bells interspersed with a few powder guns and five (——) torpedoes etc (which two can cost <u>money</u> this year) The Levee³⁹ Held in the Town Hall from 10 O'clock AM all day. The proceeds to go for the benefit of sick and wounded soldiers was a decided success. I was unavoidably prevented from being present. Therefore cannot give you a very particular account of the proceedings. The folks about all went and they expressed themselves as having had a good time. The day was a fine one. Rather dusty but a cool breeze.

   Some of the committee of arrangements were in favor of holding the fair in a grove and applied to P. Willis for permission to use the one on his land but he refused it, as he did not sympathize with the <u>object</u> of the Fair.

   There was a large turnout of the people of Town and also some from out of town at the Hall. The admission was free to all. The articles on sale were mostly eatables, refreshments, confectionary etc. A few speeches were had and songs by the Methodist choir. Picnics were also held in other parts of town. Assabet had one I think. Therefore there was some riding for those that wished to visit them all. I suppose it was quite a contrast to the 4ᵗʰ with you. I understand that the Richmond papers say that the "Union Salute" on the 4ᵗʰ near Petersburg knocked over quite a number of Rebels.

   I suppose that you have heard of the Rebel raid into Maryland lately, with all sorts of wild rumors flying about. The President called for 5000 men from Massachusetts and also men from other states to serve 100 days to repel invasion and the call is generally responded to. A number of Regiments are now organizing in Massachusetts with some of the old Regiments as a nucleus and Readville Camp is being put in Military trim in all haste. In Boston full companies have been trained in the space of 2 or 3 days. The latest news from Washington is that the Rebels are retreating and have probably recrossed the Potomac. Fears are now entertained that they will escape without being cut off. Their object seems to be plunder and supplies, scare the people, and perhaps to draw Grant away from Petersburg, but Grant understands the game I guess and it looks as though he meant that the <u>home guards</u> should repel invasion as he probably knew beforehand all about the movements of the Rebels. Don't think of any more news of importance now. We are having <u>very</u> dry weather here. Had but one shower of rain for two months or more. Nothing has been accomplished in Sudbury *yet in regard to the next quota. Yesterday the enrolled men of town had an opportunity to present claims of exemption on account of Alienage, Overage, non residents & Physical Disability. Between 20 & 30 names were stricken from the roll as the result. Have not learned the names of those exempted. 2 or 3 only have I heard the names of that got exempted. L. S. Jones Physical Disability (Dr Johnson done the business for him) Ed Hunt Loss of teeth, J. L. Willis had two teeth too many. I must close. Hope this will find you well.*

    F. U. M

John Moore's Regiment, the Thirteenth had been involved in many difficult battles since they left Massachusetts on July 30, 1861. Their three years in the army was coming to an end. They left City Point, Virginia, by steamer on July 15, 1864, traveling past Fortress Monroe, and up the Potomac where they marched down Pennsylvania Avenue to their quarters for the night. The following day they traveled by rail to Baltimore, Philadelphia, and New York.

> The Thirteenth Massachusetts Volunteers arrived in the city yesterday from the front with ranks shattered and decimated, and covered with the smoke and dust of the battles they have been through. It has participated in the battles under General George McClellan's command and those of his successor, General Grant. The Thirteenth has recruited, since its departure, up to fourteen hundred and forty men, and now return with but two hundred and sixty-five men and seventeen officers. The regiment, or what there is left of it, looks well and hearty. **From the *New York World*, July 21, 1864**.

The 13th Massachusetts Regiment marching
down Broadway.

Thirteenth Regiment Massachusetts Volunteers marching down Broadway in
New York. Picture from the Charles H. Roundy Diary. Courtesy of the U.S. Army
Military Institute, Carlisle, Pennsylvania

When the troops arrived in Boston on July 22, the local newspapers
heralded their return.

> On July 22 the regiment arrived in Boston, and was
> escorted from the station by the Germania Band a force
> of police, and proceeded directly to Boylston Hall where
> they disencumbered themselves of their equipments and
> then marched back to the United States Hotel, where they
> partook of a bountiful breakfast. Thence they returned to
> Boylston Hall. The regiment after a procession through
> the streets arrived at Faneuil Hall decorated with a banner,
> "Welcome Home Thirteenth." "The ladies in the hall threw
> bouquets and kisses and waved their delicate kerchiefs at the
> noble veterans as they filed into the hall and took their places
> around the tables." **From** The Boston Herald **July 22, 1864**.

On August 1 the troops assembled on Boston Common and were mustered out. John Moore did not re-enlist. Subsequently, however, John remained connected to wartime work joining the Christian Commission. The men who did re-enlist were transferred to the Thirty-ninth Regiment. The Thirteenth Regiment lost eighty men during their three years and left 136 men in the hospital.

Thirteenth Regiment Massachusetts Volunteers Presentation National 1987.410 Presented by Hogg, Brown & Taylor Company, Made by Thomas Savory. Courtesy of the Commonwealth of Massachusetts Art Commission

near Petersburg Va.
July 24, 1864

My Dear Brother,
I received your letter yesterday morning, and one from Hattie last night and was glad to hear from you both shall write Father this afternoon as Sunday is the only day I have to write we work every other day in the week from 6 ½ A.M. til 6 P.M. but by doing this we get rid

of fighting unless we are attacked by the Rebels while at work on the fortifications

It has been awful dusty here till within a few days, we had a little rain a few days ago so it is pretty good traveling now there is not much doing here now, but we expect there will be a move made soon there is a rumor in camp today that Lt. Col. King is trying to get this Reg't home or to Boston he is on duty there and he wants the Reg't there but John can tell you what a <u>rumor is</u> in the army, and how much confidence we place in one. There is pretty good news from Sherman's Department I hope he will be successful and drive the Johnies into the gulf of Mexico or somewhere out of the United States.

I suppose John is at home now. I wish I could come home too, but I don't suppose I can for about 1 year more. well I am willing to stop that length of time and I hope they will not need anyone after that time. I hope this war will be over by that time, but hardly think it will for the "Johnies" are a stubborn set, as John or any of the veterans can tell you.

Did Old Sudbury give the boys a reception if so, tell me all about it for I suppose it would be a grand affair, I hope they gave them one for I think they deserve one if anyone does for they were the first to go to war, and went without bounty, is the town going to give them 7 dollars a month as they promised to. but I must close.

Remember me to all the boys
Write soon From George
P.S. tell John to write to us and tell us all the news.

The following poem *Our Veteran Volunteers* was preprinted on the stationary that George used for the previous letter.

OUR VETERAN VOLUNTEERS

—ooo—

By G. P. Hardwick, cor. F st. and N. J. Ave., Washington, D. C.

—ooo—

Air.—*Hoist up our Flag, and long may she wave.*

Now, Union Boys, come near me and listen while I sing
About your recent victories, which make the valleys ring,
At Gettysburg you whipped the Rebs, and show'd to them most clear
They couldn't stand the shot and shell of the Veteran Volunteer.

CHORUS.—Shout, boys, shout, and cheer, boys, cheer,
　　　　Sport your colors on your hat, my Veteran Volunteer;
　　　　Hoist up our Flag and long may she wave
　　　　Over the Union, the Home of the Brave.

Next day it was a glorious 4th, the Western Mountains ring
That Pemberton to U. S. Grant was then surrendering.
Jeff Davis looses Vicksburg with all the men and store,
And Banks soon took Port Hudson and fifteen thousand more.

Now where's the famous Johnson, who, a few months ago,
With his hundred thousand men the Veterans was to show,
He'd march right into Vicksburg, and soon the Yankees clear,
And save the rebel garrison from the Veteran Volunteer.

Why, he's running back to Davis to tell him he's a fool
To think the Southern Chivalry can live upon a mule;
For U. S. Grant and Banks have stole the Texas steers
To feed the Union Army and the Veteran Volunteers.

Let Davis send the news to Mason and Slidell
To help his cause in England, and Sunny France as well,
If they make a Duke of him and Marquis of his friends,
He will have to hurry up before Secession ends.

Now give three cheers, my boys, the Mississippi's clear,
You've whipped the Rebel Gray Backs with the Veteran Volunteer.
Now Banks has Corpus Christi, the Stars and Stripes must shine;
You have shown the Texan Rebels they cannot come to time.

Entered according to act of Congress, in the year 1863, by G. P. Hardwick, in the
Clerk's Office of the District Court for the District of Columbia.

The Adjutant General's report stated that George F. Moore was wounded and missing on July 30, before the battle at Petersburg, Virginia. However, George's diary contradicts this. His entry for Saturday, July 30 states:

> Pleasant and hot...turned out this morning about 2 am... joined the division...went to the front...blew up the Reb fort...division made a charge...took two lines of troops but had to abandon them...fell back to our old positions... lost heavy

The mid-summer climate in the steamy South was hard on the northerners accustomed to more moderate summer weather. In the North the newspapers circulated discouraging accounts of the war. "Those were laborious days, and trying to the soul and body of man. After the tremendous exertions of the campaign we seemed to be little nearer to the end."[40] The Forty-eighth Pennsylvania, made up of many coal miners, dug an underground tunnel that extended beneath Pegram's Salient, a small fort. On July 30, Burnside's IX Corps exploded the mine beneath the Salient. The blowing up of the Salient was successful; however, it created a crater so large and deep that the Union soldiers became caught in it as they advanced. The ensuing confusion allowed the Confederates time to counterattack, resulting in the heaviest single day casualties of the war. "The carnage became terrible past description...few expected to survive until night or get back to our lines, so completely was the space swept by the shower of missiles."[41] According to George Moore's diary of July 31, 1864, "General Grant sent in a flag of truce today to bury his dead and the Johnnies wouldn't let him." On August 1, George writes in his diary "the Rebs gave Burnside the privilege of burying his killed...they would not accept of a flag of truce from Grant...my Regt buried all the dead in our division." The loss to the Thirty-fifth was one officer and eleven men killed in battle or died from wounds, and thirty-five wounded. General Burnside was relieved of his duties for his role in the debacle.[42]

Landing Supplies at the Wharf at City Point Virginia in 1864, 111-B-152.
Photograph courtesy of the National Archives, Washington, D.C.

Sudbury
Aug 9, 1864

Dear Brother
  *Yours of July 24ᵗʰ I received some time ago and would have written
to you before now it I had felt able, but have been unwell therefore
you will please excuse the delay. The folks have received letters from
you all since the late terrible fight near Petersburg, and are thankful
that you escaped without a wound. It seems hard to have to give up
the entrenchments after working so hard to get possession of them and
Petersburg almost within grasp also. However I suppose that it is only
a <u>delay</u> and that the getting possession of the City is only a question
of time and must be accomplished by the loss of many men. I wrote to
Albert on the 29ᵗʰ of July giving him the particulars of John's arrival
home and the Reception of the 13ᵗʰ at Boston and also the two Companys
F & J at Marlboro and that Sudbury was going to give the boys a
Reception the next day. You have written to the folks, some of them , that
Albert had received a letter giving all the particulars of the Reception on*

that day, therefore it will be no news to you now and I will say nothing about it, only that I had a pretty good time.

John is enjoying his freedom tip top I think. He has not been the rounds yet, although he is off almost every day somewhere. The regiment has not been paid off yet, owing to the officers not having the rolls ready. I suppose that the officers are in <u>no</u> <u>hurry</u> as long as their pay goes on just the same.

I went down to Boston the day that the men of the 13th were mustered out of service, and they appeared to be well pleased with the arrangements.

Alfred wrote that a fellow who occupied a bed near his in the Hospital at Philadelphia, could tell all about his case, and if I would be at Boston when the 20th Regiment were there I might find him. Therefore I went and went on the day that the regiment was mustered out of service and found the man on the common. He told me that Alfreds case was a very bad one, said that his side was hurt near the lower ribs and was pressed in the surface black and blue. He raised blood for two months after the hurt and still continues to raise some blood. The man was of opinion that Alfred would get his discharge. John thinks of going out to see him and have a talk with him as soon as he gets his money for service. The Town will probably have a meeting soon and pay the boys that sum to make up their pay to 20 Dollars per month.

The quota of Sudbury under the last call of the President for 500,000 has not been filled yet and not much prospect of filling it. The enrolled men of town have subscribed the sum of about 4000 Dollars to buy the men with and I understand that the selectmens combined efforts have procured 3 men so far. 18 men are required to fill the quota.

We are having hot and dry weather here as usual. Don't think of much news to write. The latest from the south says that Admiral Farragut has destroyed some of the Rebel fleet near Mobile and he has passed the fort at the entrance of the harbour. I will close with the hope that this will find you all well.

F.U. Moore

Sudbury
August 14th 1864

Dear George
I received your letter of the 6th a few days ago and was very glad to hear from you and to know that you got out of that teriable fight the

*30th of July safe and all right it was reported in the papers that you was
missing but I received a letter from Albert before that report came out
that you had come in all right so that paper report did not harm me at
all that (——)and blowing up of that fort must have been great work
the explosion must have been a great sight to see Im sorry that you was
not successful in accomplishing the work that you undertook but don't
let this dishearten you for I think that you will subdue them before long
only want the men and enough of them to do it with which the North are
to work pretty busy in raising them and sending them forward they has
several of the Towns have Volenteerd enough to fill there quota for wee
begin to see the evil of buying those Forignors to fill up the quota or
to answer the call of the President I hope practice will cease in buying
men to send into the field Sudbury has been to work a raising money by
subscription to buy men enough to fill the quota they went to Boston and
bought 9 as I heard and 6 of them was rejected only 3 excepted and they
have been to Boston once or twice cince and have not got one as they
report that they cant buy any more so if they don't volunteer they will
have to stand the draf if so hope the right ones will get drafted it was
reported in the paper the Rebs have been retaeliating on that blow up by
trying to blow up one of our forts but it did not amount to much I see by
the account that Sherman is a doing well and the account that Mobille
has Surenderd to our forces and other points that they were a doing a
good thing your letter was very interesting giving all of the particulars
of the Battle on the 30th and describing the tunnel and explosion and the
charge (——) but it must be a savage looking sight*

 *Had a letter from Alfred last night he is a getting along well John
is at home a waiting for his pay soon as he gets it he is going out to see
Alfred very warm and growing wether for the crops now write soon and
give me the account of the Rebels explosion we are all well hope this will
find you well*

From your Father

On August 15, the Thirty-fifth Regiment, now under the command of
General Julius White, received orders to march. They moved toward the
Weldon Railroad in the direction of Petersburg. On August 16, George wrote
in his diary "not very well today" and three days later he was sent down to
stay with Albert until he got better. In his diary George wrote that he was
so weak they put his knapsack on the back of one of the cattle. On August
22, Corporal Lawrence Qualters, a friend from Waltham, Massachusetts,
also of Company D, took George to the First Division IX Corps Hospital

at City Point. The record states that the patient, on arrival, was assumed to be George F. Moore, suggesting that possibly George was not conscious. Hospital records list "debility."[43] From City Point he was sent to Grant Hospital in Richmond, Virginia.[44] George's absence from the regiment meant he missed the battle at the Weldon Railroad from August 18-21.

The Battle at the Weldon Railroad was the second assault by the Union on the railroad. The Union successfully destroyed miles of track while under constant attack from the Confederates. As a result the Confederates were forced to carry their supplies thirty miles by wagon. The Battle at Poplar Springs Church was part of a simultaneous attack against the western and eastern flank of Lee's army. During this attack, one of the IX Corps brigades was forced to surrender.

George was feeling well enough to write to Albert back at the Thirty-fifth Regiment from the division hospital at City Point. George had been suffering from typhoid fever.

City Point
August 30th

Dear Brother,
I arrived here last Saturday, it is a very good place here but I shall be glad when I get out of it when I left the Hospital at the front I had to walk to division Hospital where Doctor Snow is. I was all the afternoon (from the time we started) and all night getting down there I was so sick when I got there I could hardly sit up. The next day we were sent down here. I lost your Rubber Blanket on the way so the first chance you get you draw one and have it charged to me. I cannot write much today I am growing dizzy already. when you write home tell the folks how I am and where I am tell them I will answer their letters as soon as I can give my respects to Morse and all the rest of the boys tell Qualters I hope I shall have a chance to help him sometime for what he done for me but hope he never will be in my condition. If you get a chance to send my letters by anybody here but don't send them by mail for I may leave here anytime. I must close for I am awful dizzy. Write soon
From George
If you write me and send by mail direct to 1st *division 9*[th] *Corps Hospital, Ward 9, tent 5 City Point, Va.*

U.S. Military R. R. City Point Va. Field Hospital. 111-B-462. Mathew Brady
Photographs of the Civil War Era: Personalities and Scenes; National Archives,
Washington D.C.

Sudbury
Sept 13ᵗʰ 1864

Dear George
*Your letter dated the 10ᵗʰ came this evening and we were very glad
to hear from you. I received a letter from Albert last evening stating that
you had left City Point and he had not heard where you had gone, but
expected he should hear soon. I wrote to you after I heard you was sick,
but you did not get my letter, for Albert wrote that he had got it, and
should send it to you as soon as he knows where you are.*

*John has been to see Alfred and came home last Saturday. It is too
bad he didn't know you was there at that time how glad you would have
been to see each other. But perhaps you will see some of us soon. I hope
you are where you will have good care and will soon be getting well.
Alfreds Doctor told John that he would get Ally a furlough soon, and I
hope you can get one, and both come home together.*

*John says Alfred has been a great suffer since he was hurt but he
is much better now. I had no idea he was hurt so bad as he was, for he*

always wrote as though he was quite comfortable. I fear he will never be very healthy again, but I am thankful that his life is spared.

Francis is in New York if he is not on his way home. I have been writing a few lines to him this evening to let him know about your being there so he would call and see you if my letter reaches him soon enough.

He has been at Dansville, Livingston C., New York. I don't expect he will stay there long and he may leave before my letter gets there.

It is getting late so I will bid you good night
M H Moore

Uriah and Mary Moore went to visit George in the Hospital in Philadelphia before he returned to his regiment. The large Union Hospital was built near a rail line to facilitate quick transport of the injured to the hospital and then back to their regiments.

On September 30, with Major Hudson in command, the regiment marched down Poplar Spring Church Road, and before they reached Peebles Farm, with skirmishing all around, they found themselves in a grove overlooking Petersburg, in plain view of the enemy. That evening they were surprised when a Confederate battalion came up behind them as well as beside them. The men couldn't fire behind them for fear of firing at their own men. The enemy that had been to their front now was positioned to their right and behind them. Some men were so startled they failed to move quickly enough and were immediately captured, while others got lost in the darkness. Some recruits fired into their own lines. The following day, on October 1, when the regiment regrouped, 10 had been killed, 15 were wounded,

Lieutenant John N. Morse Company D, Thirty-fifth Regiment Massachusetts Volunteers. Sudbury Historical Society

and 163 were missing. In spite of these losses, the battle was a Union victory.[45]

On October 3, George returned to the regiment to find old members gone. His cousin, Rufus Hurlbut, and friend John Morse, who were injured at the Battle of Poplar Springs Church, were now in the hospital. Rufus had been injured in the head and was in danger of being left on the battlefield when his friend, Lieutenant John Morse, who had been injured in the leg, refused to be carried off the field unless they also took his friend, Rufus. Rufus eventually returned to the regiment and served out the remainder of the war. John Morse's injuries, a ball that had to be extracted from his leg, would prevent him from returning to the regiment. He received an honorable discharge January 18, 1865.[46]

The Germans and French had now joined the regiment as paid recruits. The officers and men felt that they could not depend on them, primarily because the new recruits could not speak English. It would take the new men time to learn the language and their soldierly duties. Communication became difficult in battle. George Moore rarely complained of his life in the army and the difficulties he faced every day. He was generally optimistic, but he was not optimistic about the reliability of the new soldiers.

Near Petersburg, Va.
Oct. 4th/64

My Dear Mother
I am with my Company again as you will see by the heading of this I arrived here last night.

Oct. 6th
I had just got to writing the other day and the Johnies attacked our picket line and drove in the picket, and I had to leave my writing and go into the pits, I was in the tent with Mr. Campbell, (of Wayland) he packed up our things and had just gone out of the tent as a shot from the Reb Battery passed through it about 2 feet from the ground I had been out about 3 minutes I thought that was a good reception for my first day yesterday I was on duty all day so I did not get a chance to write today everything is quiet not a shot is to be heard When I arrived here I found my Company pretty well broke up. most of the old members are gone Rufus, John Morse, E. Bracket[47] and Byrnes[48] were wounded in this last battle and 7 of the other old members were taken prisoners, and one new recruit my Regt. lost 187 killed wounded and missing the Duch have just

spoiled the Regt. the officers can't depend oppon them anywhere The
Adjt. Gen'l said after the fight that the 35ᵗʰ once could be depended upon
anywhere but now they could not trust the Duch Regt. (I didn't hear him
say so but the boys told me he said so) I don't know but what they will
get so they will do well after awhile our Regt. has had a good name and I
hope they won't spoil it entirely, Rufus was wounded in the head I guess
he will get along all right or as well as can be expected John Morse got
an ugly wound in the leg he has got to have pretty good care to come out
of it E. Bracket (of Waltham) lost his foot.

I am pretty well now but not so well as I used to be. but I shall be in
a few days I did not see Francis or did not go to N York to see Mr. Gerry,
for I did not stop in the hospital but a few days after you left me, but I
stoped long enough Have not any news but what you have seen in the
papers I will close now as my sheet is about full Give my love to all and
write soon.

The mail has just come in and I have got 3 letters for Albert, one
from you and one from Father

George

Francis Moore, George's oldest brother, who was in poor health, had
been living at "Our Home" in Dansville in New York, since August 17.
"Our Home" offered the water cure, using mineral-rich waters of the
area and hydrotherapy, including showers, wet sheet wrappings, and
mineral-rich spring water. The diet put an emphasis on fresh vegetables,
unprocessed grains, and fruit. No red meat, sugar, coffee, tea, or alcohol,
was allowed.[49]

"Our Home" Dansville
Livingston Co
New York
Oct 9, 1864

Dear Brother
I suppose that you have heard through letters from the folks of my
being out here. I was sorry to hear of your being sick but a letter from
Albert a short time ago states that you are getting better.

I expected to be able to leave here about Oct 1ˢᵗ and call and see
you, but as I shall be obliged to stay here a while longer, I am deprived
of that pleasure. Hope you will keep up good spirits. John perhaps

will come and see you. I have not received any letters from home for a fortnight.

I would like to have you out here with me. The <u>social</u> atmosphere here would be a grand thing for you.

I came out here about Aug 17*th* and have been in this institution about 7 weeks now. I came here to get the benefit of this "water cure" to hear the lectures by Dr. Jackson before the institution and to learn all I can. There are now about 150 persons here male and female. We have dances here in Liberty Hall about once a week. Have lectures three times a week. Conventions once a fortnight.

We have games and other healthy recreations and in fact it is a grand place here for anybody to come and stay awhile whether sick or well. If it was possible to get him here I would like to have Father come and stay here a year. He would learn to look on life in an entirely a different manner from what he does now. The last I heard from home the folks were all well as usual. Alfred was getting along first rate. John had been to see him.

We don't get any Massachusetts papers here therefore I do not hear what is going on there. New York papers we get. The War news seems to be very encouraging. When Albert wrote he said that matters near Petersburg remained about the same, but I see by the Paper that Grant is moving.

I have written to about all of the folks since I have been here. You will please excuse this short letter as it is against the advice of the doctors that I congest my brain by writing at all. We have a good deal of cloudy weather here during a month back with cold rains. This morning the Hills are quite white with <u>snow</u>. I room in a club room here called "Canada" with 6 others and all are first rate fellows, three of them have been in the army and came here to get cured of wounds and sickness got in the army. Dr. Jackson gives us a sermon this afternoon in the Hall. I tell you he is <u>bully</u> in almost anything.

I will close hoping that this will find you well.

Francis

"Our Home on the Hillside", Dansville, N.Y. Property of the Town of North Dansville, N.Y. Courtesy of Quentin Masolotte, North Dansville Town Historian

Sudbury
Oct 23, 1864

Dear George

I received your letter a few days ago and was very glad to hear that your health is so much improved.

We should have been very happy to see you at home, but I did not much expect you, for I could see when I was there that you had no hopes of getting a furlough yourself.

Well you have commenced the last year of your term of service, and the time will soon get away, then I hope we will see you come home a free man, so you can stay as long as you please, without a furlough. Three years seems a long time when we look forward, but when John came home he looked so little changed, I could not realize that he had been gone so long, and had passed through so much hardship and danger and hope you will all come home as healthy as he is. Alfred has not got his furlough yet, but writes that he expects to come home soon. Perhaps he will be here by Thanksgiving. Francis has sent for some of his everyday clothes, so I expect he has found some work where he is, and will stay awhile longer. Your Father has called to see John Morse since he came home and we hear from him quite often. He is doing well. I am glad he is at home. It must be a great comfort to his Mother, to have the care of him herself. Perhaps he would have had good care at the Hospital, but then his folks could not know how he is getting along from day to day, as they can now. I wish all soldiers would be at home when they are sick.

The boys have not got that money yet which the town promised them when they went to War, but I think they will get it. It will be decided at the November Meeting. Some say the town can get rid of paying it if they choose, while others say they are obliged to pay it, but if they don't pay it, I shall think Sudbury is a meaner town than I ever believed it to be.

I expect there is not much doubt that Mr. Lincoln will be reelected, and I think it ought to be a cause of gratitude and thanksgiving throughout the Country. It seems as though a change in the administration at this critical time, would be the greatest calamity that could befall us. I hope and trust that all our troubles will be over for the best, and we shall soon have peace instead of war.

We took the Cars for home the evening after we left you, and arrived at South Framingham about daylight. We hired a team at the center of town and reached home about 9Oclock. I took cold the last night we rode in the cars and was half sick for a few days, but I soon got over it and am well now.

Mary has been sick lately but is better now. She is hoping to be able to go back to Mary Browns in a day or two. The rest of us are well as usual, and I hope these few lines will find you in good health and spirits. I don't think of much news to write so I will bid you good bye for this time.

Mary H Moore

The subject of payment for the Sudbury soldiers was still a recurring theme for the Moore family. By October, John Moore and the other members of the Wadsworth Rifle Guards, who had mustered out in July, had still not received the money they were promised by the town of Sudbury.

Sudbury
Oct 30th 1864

Dear George
I will write a few lines to you I have written twice to you cince have receive a letter from you I wrote soon after I got home and directed my letter to the Hospital but I suppose you had left before it got there I

wrote again as soon as I heard that you had left for the Regt I received a News Paper last Knight I suppose it was from you by the writing on the Paper the Weekley National Republican Washington D.C. I received a letter from Albert dated the 15th and have wrote to him cince and have received one from Alford cince I was out there dated the 18th Hattie received one from Albert last evening stating that you was detailed am glad of that she also received one from Alfred he is pretty comfortable now and feeling pretty well he thinks he shall be to home at Thanks Giving I wish I could meet you all at Thanksgiving I saw it reported in yesterdays paper that the Patomac Army had made a forward Move the Reports seem to be chearing from all sources now in regard to the coming of the Presidential Election there is a great many here North that would have voted for McCleland three months ago that wont vote for him now a grand Union Demonstration and torchlight Procession in Boston next Friday Evening Nov the 4th it is very still in Sudbury not but a little said about the Election here not any movement made by the People of Sudbury Albert stated that you had received a letter from John Morse I went to see him the second day after he came home to Wayland he spoke of seeing you the day before he left for home he was as comfortably as could be expected we were all to home now but you three Boys that were in the service and Francis will Close not much news write soon and let me know all about this move we are all well hope this will find you well and success in all your undertakings

From Your Father

The government decided to make an example of men who accepted the bounty of $500 and then either tried to escape before reaching their regiment, or, once they joined, doing little or no work. The Thirty-fifth Regiment witnessed the first execution of one such deserter in October 1864. One of the muskets of the firing squad was loaded with a blank cartridge so no one in the firing squad could be sure whether he had fired the fatal shot.[50]

General Rosecrans had issued Order No. 3 in November 1862 requiring two men from each company to be detailed as an Engineering Corps attached to the regiment called the Brigade Pioneers. These twenty men would be half-laborers and half-mechanics and would move in advance of the army. To be selected for the Brigade was a compliment to the soldier. In the following letter, George tells his mother that he has been selected to be one of the Brigade Pioneers.

Near Poplar Grove, Va
Nov. 3rd/64

My Dear Mother,

I received your letter a number of days ago and was very glad to hear from you. I wrote to Mary yesterday and calculated to write to you, but did not get time so I will improve this opportunity. It is a stormy day today. It was the same yesterday and it is pretty cold. I would like to be in some house sitting by a good fire, but we make ourselves pretty comfortable. We build our houses after the Tenn style that is of logs plastered with mud. Chimney's built of wood, plastered inside with mud which is as good as mortar

I suppose you have heard of our late move long before this. I don't know what it was made for but suppose to find out how things were we did not have much fighting my Division did not get engaged at all. only a little skirmishing on the retreat which my Brigade covered the 2nd corps done some fighting and took quite a number of prisoners We are in our old camps where we started from and think we shall stop here till after Elections at least, There is nothing going on here for excitement Once in a while we hear firing down front of Petersburg. but in front of us the pickets are as friendly as neighbors. we can see the "Johnies" from our camps. Their batteries can throw shell into our camps. one year ago we couldn't lay in this way and not get shelled. the Pickets exchange papers every day and there is considerable conversation between them. some of the Rebels desert and come into our lines every night sometime 3 or 4 together come into our Brigade and I don't know how many come in on the rest of the line. Gen. Grant says they average a whole Regt. per day

I received a letter from Father this morning stating that Al wrote that I had got a detail. but I suppose you don't know what kind of one it is so I will tell you. It is in Brigade Pioneers. it is the same as my Regt. was doing in front of Beltensburg only they were Division Pioneers. it does not keep me from going into battle but I don't have any picket or skirmish duty to do or don't have to drill. when we go on a march I go in front of Brigade. don't have much of anything to do now. do not have any work to do myself being a Corp'l and have charge of a squad. I am as well as ever now but I was not well when I left the Hospital. but I stoped there as long as I wanted to.

I will close now hoping to hear from you again soon.

George

Camp Near Poplar Grove Ch Va.
Nov 8th, 1864

Dear Father,
I received your letter a few days ago and was glad to hear from you. You stated you received a paper from me. I wrote a letter to you the day before I sent the paper. don't see why you didn't get that to. I sent you that paper because it had a speech from one of our Gen'ls in it and I thought it was a pretty good thing. What do you think of it .it gives Buchanen some pretty rough hits.

This is Election day. I suppose there is considerable excitement in the northern cities. how is it in the city of Sudbury. I suppose the Republicans carry the day there. I used to think all they cared for was to see which party carried the day. but I begin to understand such things now. but I don't think much of party. I would vote for the man that I thought was best fitted for office. let him belong to what party he would. Tell me what Sudbury done about paying the Boys their money for I am very anxious to know. I suppose Mr. Andrews will be Gov. think I shall try for that office next Fall.

There is not much war news this time to write. we some expected the "Johnies" would shell us today so as to stop the soldiers voting. but they are quiet as _lambs_ for all I can see, and I hope they will keep so.

There is a rumor that the 9th Corps is going to leave this Department. I don't know whether there is anything in the rumor but am inclined to think there is for I don't think Burnside is to remain idle much longer and wherever he goes his Corps goes with him. I had rather be under him than any Gen'l in the army. I always feel safer when he has command I don't know what makes me only I know if he gets us into a bad fix he will stay with us till he get us out. You wanted me to tell you all about the late move which I am unable to do as my Division did not get engaged in it at all. I didn't see a Reb only a prisoner. I don't think it was made with the intension of doing any more than to find out about Lee's position on our left. and I guess the 2nd Corps found it out for they had some pretty hard fighting. The Negro Division was engaged for a short time and behaved well.

I received a letter from Hattie this morning stating Alley had got home. I am glad of it and hope he won't have to come back again. I must close now. give my love to all. write soon and write all the news.

George

On November 8, 1864, the election would decide whether the people in the North would elect the "peace party" under McClellan to end the war. A vote for Abraham Lincoln was a vote to continue the war. *The Thirty-fifth Regimental History* states that none of the Massachusetts soldiers voted in the election. The vote in the country and in the army was to continue the war whatever the cost. The army vote was over seventy percent for Lincoln, even though his opponent was General George McClellan. Desertions in the Confederate ranks began as soon as the vote was announced, but the Union soldiers still expected severe fighting ahead.[51]

Camp near Poplar Grove Va.
Nov.19th 64

Dear Father,
    I have forgotten whether I have answered your last letter or not. so I will write a few lines today as it is stormy and we have nothing to do. it has been trying to storm for sometime and now it has got at it I guess it will last a while.
    There is no news of importance to write today. we have had a quiet time of it since the late move on the left. and everything looks like stoping here for sometime to come. the boys have got their log houses built and are comfortable as need be. I am now sitting in front of a fireplace with a nice fire in it and my tent is loged up and plastered with "sacred soil of "VA", which leaves mortar in the shades
    Albert has moved up close to our camp so we are near each other again. he received 5 letters yesterday and they were all from home but one. we had been waiting for letters for sometime and didn't find out what we wanted to after all. we want to know whether the Town is going to pay the boys that money or not, or whether they took a vote on it or not. I think if they don't pay then they are a meaner set than I ever believed them to be. I know it is hard times there North for money, but if they had begun to see the hardship those boys have seen there would be some reason to back out of their bargain. I don't think any of those boys would have staid at home if the town hadn't offered that pay, but if the town don't pay it and there comes another call for men it will have a bad influence. and I think they will have hard work to get the men. there is men yet in the North willing to come out here. but they want those that <u>don't</u> come to back them and do by them as they agree to. a soldier has enough <u>sometimes</u> to discourage him without having those at home try to do it. if there is anyone that don't think those boys deserve that money they had ought to enlist for 3 years and <u>try soldering</u> a little, or

*let them enlist for one year and come into the army of the Potomac. I think
one such Campaign as they have had this summer would satisfy them.*

*I suppose we shall have some good news from Sherman in a few
days. he is probably making a bold move somewhere but I don't think he
is going towards Charleston or Mobile. I think he is either coming this
way or going to Woods rear.*

*I must think of closing as my sheet is about full give my love to all friends.
write as soon as you get time and don't forget to tell us about that pay*

*I am going to write to Ellen and Edgar and send it with this, if I get
time. I wrote to Mary yesterday and Hattie the day before.*

From George

The regiment delayed celebrating Thanksgiving for two days, waiting
for the boxes of fruit, vegetables, turkeys, and pies, gifts from Boston
merchants, to arrive.

*Sudbury
Dec 4th 1864*

Dear George

*I received yours of the 19th sometime ago and was glad to hear that you
were well and had got a comfatible house and a fireplace it so you can be
warm in a cold day hope you can stay where you are for some time and enjoy
your huse if it is a good location I received a letter from Albert dated the 15th
he wrote that he had been sick with a cold hope he is better I wrote to him
soon after the Presidential Election and gave him the Votes of this Town and
District and this State excuse me for not answering your letter before and I
will try and write oftonor have been very much engaged a hauling my wood
to market it sells very high and I shall make a good thing out of it*

*I think I have two letters ahead of you now never mind I shall keep a
writing as oftoner as I can and want you to write as often as you can as to
that Money that Town agreed to pay the Soldiers of the 13th Regt or those
that went out from Sudbury the thing has been called up before the Town
twice the first time the Town chose a Commity to investigate the matter and
report to the November Meeting this Commity reports at that meeting but
their report was not made out understandingly so the Town instructed them
Commity to make out the sum total and report to some future Meeting there
is a going to be a speshall Meeting called I think they will get their money*

*Your Aunt Olive received a letter from a Soldier that had been in
Richmond Prison for about nine months..received this letter last Thursday*

night he wrote from Anapalus Maryland he has been exchanged he was a Mass man he wrote that Curtis Smith died in Richmond Prison on the 19th of October this man was the only survivor out of 22 that was taken prisona out of his company he did not give any particulars about him but if they wished he would write the partickulars your Aunt wrote write back to him to have him write her the particulars for she wanted to no the worst of it this is the hardest stroke to your Aunt that she ever met with put all her former troubles together I dread to have her get the particulars this man was with Curtis when he died it was his last request to this man that he should write to his Mother if he should ever have a chance must close hoping I shall have better news to write next time

we are all well and all at home but you three boys & Francis received a letter from Alfred cince he got back he is all right hope this will find you well write soon

from Your Father

In July of 1864, the captured Union enlisted men were transferred from Richmond Prison to Andersonville Prison in Georgia while their officers were transferred to Libby Prison. Andersonville Prison records list a man named Curtis Smith who died on October 24, 1864. There are sixty-five men on record who died on this date, whose graves are numbered 11375 to 11417. All are named but one. Number 11417 is marked as unknown. It may, or may not, be Curtis Smith. The letter from Father to George on December 4, 1864, states that Curtis died at Richmond Prison on October 19, 1864, which contradicts the Andersonville records.

Near Petersburg, Va
Dec. 18th /64

Dear Mother,
I received your welcome letter yesterday and was very glad to hear from you. I have received letters from you all lately, and I believe I have answered them all.
There is not much news of importance to write from this quarter, but I suppose you have news from other sources to make up for this, we were awakened this morning by the report of Artillery firing. the first shots I thought the rebs had marched in but I listened to hear the shell pass over but not hearing any I came to the conclusion that the guns were loaded with powder only, so I turned out to hear the news. for I knew they were firing a salute for some reason. it was for Thomas' victory over Hood.

I have seen no accounts of the Battle yet but suppose it was a pretty large victory. there is a rumor in camp tonight that Sherman has captured Savannah. I hope it is so, and I hope we may be secure at every point. I don't think there will be much going on in this vicinity until Spring now. we are all in Winter quarters and I hope we may remain so until cold wether is over. I don't think it would be of much use to advance here now for the rebels have largest Army here and they are strongly entrenched. and also they have a pretty smart Gen to command them. but if we hold what we have got and destroy their Railroads and communications with the South as much as possible and let us have victories at other points. this Rebellion will soon play out. and I don't care how soon. I hope it will be over by the time I come home that is by next August.

I wrote to John to send us a box he mentioned it in his letter so I suppose it is on the way or will be soon. I think it will come right through now as we are all in camp and there is no movement on foot.

I suppose you all had a good time when Alley was at home. I wish I could have been there to but I don't care much now for if I had been I should be having the blues now. I don't think I shall apply for a furlough this Winter, my time will be out next Summer and then I can have as long furlough as I wish.

When you write let me know whether the town has paid the boys that money or not or whether they are going to. I can't believe the town will cheat them out of it. I think they will pay them. if they don't I would like to give them a piece of my mind but I hope it is all right and they will have no trouble about it.

I got into an argument with a New Yorker (citizen) a few days ago about this war. He was a McClellan man. and I talked to him pretty hard and he got so mad he could hardly say anything. then I laughed at him and told him he was a fair example of the whole party. didn't intend to hurt his feelings but was bound to tell him what I thought. he got over it in a few days and speaks to me the same as before but I don't like the look of him a bit. he has as long a face as a mule but I guess I must close as my sheet is about full

Give my love to all inquiring friends. write again soon and tell me all the news. all the boys are well. I hope this will find you the same.

From your son George

Sudbury
Dec 23ed 1864

Dear George
I received your letter of the 18th this evening and was very glad to hear from you. I think you have improved your time pretty well lately.

We have all received a letter from you within a few days, except Mary. It is very pleasant to hear from you so often and I hope you will be situated so you can write whenever you please, this winter.

We sent a box to Boston last Wednesday to be sent on to you and Albert, which you will probably get before you receive this letter. You want to know whether the town is going to pay the boys that money. Well I don't know how it will be decided but I guess they will get a part of it if not the whole. There is to be a town meeting, a week from Monday, to see what the town will do about it. I hope they will get every cent of it.

Does Francis write to you or Albert lately? We have not got a letter from him for a long time. I begin to feel anxious about him. I wrote to him some time ago, but have received no answer. I had a letter from Alfred a few days ago. He don't appear to know what they intend to do with him, But I shouldn't be surprised if they should discharge him by and by.

John and Spencer are chopping wood for your Father now, but I don't think they feel contented as they would if the war was over. They often talk as though they wanted to get into business away off from here, but perhaps they will feel better if they get that money. If they don't get it I shant blame them for wanting to leave town.

All three of the girls are at home now, but I expect Hattie will go into a straw shop before long. I hate to have her go away, but the times are hard and she must do something to earn her clothes. When Ellen has done going to school, I suppose she will have to go out to work then I shall be all alone, but I must not complain while the children lives are all special and I can enjoy the hope of seeing them all together once more. The papers seem to be full of good news lately, and I hope we shall soon hear that the war is over.

It is getting late so I will close. Give my love to Albert and write soon.
Mary H Moore

Near Petersburg, Va
Dec 30th/64

My Dear Mother,
"I wish you all a happy new year." And may it prove to be a happy new year to our Government. May it bring peace to our once happy land. and may it bring us a plenty of presants like the one Gen'l Sherman gave us for Christmas. I suppose it will be the last year of our stay in the army and I hope it will be the last year anybody will be obliged to stay in the army and I think it will be (hole in paper) looks encouraging (hole in paper) And I think when the men last called for get into the field we shall have men enough to go ahead with. but still I

*don't think it would have been a bad plan if the President had called for
500,000 more the sooner that we have them the sooner the war will be
over the most of the Rebel Army is in front of us. as Sherman's Campaign
proves. he marched through from one side of the Confederacy to the
opposite side without losing a gun or wagon. he lost a few men but they
were probably straglers. and then to top off with he captures a city with
150 guns a large amount of cotton and government property. (hole in
paper) Jeff Davis didn't dare to send any men of (hole in paper) here to
stop him for (hole in paper) takes all the men he (hole in paper) got here
to hold these lines. and they are deserting every day. the Pickets are only
3 or 4 rods apart here and they are nearly as friendly as though they all
belong to one side. their pickets told our boys not to get together in a
bunch for they had orders to fire if they saw them the other evening when
our boy cheering over Thomas' victory the Rebels wanted to know what
the news was, our boys told them Hood had gotten another whiping, they
said "if Hood gets a few more whipings there won't be much left of him."*

*We have not received that box yet. the express does (hole in paper)
come through only once in 5 or 6 days and I suppose (hole in paper) did
not get to (hole in paper) Washington enough to come on the last boat so
it will probably come next time which will be tomorrow or the next day.*

*I do not hear anything from Francis but I guess he is all right he
said in his last letter that the Doctor didn't want him to write letters.*

*When you write tell me what they done at the town meeting about
paying the boys, and write all the news. Give my love to all the folks and
all enquiring friends and accept a share for yourself.*

From your son

George

In the letter above, George mentions the distance between the pickets
showing how very close they were to one another. A rod is only sixteen
and a half feet.

Although Confederate desertions continued, soldiers loyal to General Lee
stayed with him and the Union knew that there were still battles to come.

The eventful year (1864) closed cold and blustering, and New Year's
Day opened revealing the country white with a light fall of snow, which,
however, was gone before night.[52]

1. Committee of the regimental Association, *History of the Thirty-Fifth Massachusetts Volunteers, 1862-1865,* (Boston: Mills, Knight & Co., 1884), 199-201.

2. Col. Samuel Leonard, Bolton, MA, age 36, mustered in as Colonel, July 16, 1861, Thirteenth Massachusetts Volunteers, wounded at Gettysburg.

3. Alfred S. Hudson, *History of Sudbury, Massachusetts 1838-1889* (Salem, MA: Higginson Book Co.) 502.

4. George F. Moore Diary, 1864, January-February.

5. Private Eli Willis, Sudbury, MA, enlisted in Massachusetts Thirty-fifth Infantry Co. D, Aug 16, 1862, mustered out June 9, 1865, Alexandria, VA.

6. Private Curtis Smith, Sudbury, MA, son of Joseph and Olive (Moore) Smith, 59th Regiment, Co. C, cousin of George Moore.

7. Private George Harry Hall, Sudbury, MA age 22, enlisted Aug 16, 1862 in 35th Regiment, Co. D, mustered out June 9, 1865, Alexandria, VA.

8. Hudson, *History of Sudbury, Massachusetts,* 524.

9. George Moore Diary 1864, February 26, 1864.

10. Levi Goodenough, M.D., country physician, Univ. of Vermont Medical School., practiced for over 56 years in Sudbury, Hudson, *History of Sudbury, Massachusetts,* 603-604.

11. Robert H. Kellogg, *Life and Death in Rebel Prisons,* (Hartford, Conn: Wiley, Waterman & Eaton, 1866).

12. Curtis Moore's grandchildren: John Moore, Albert Moore, George Moore, Alfred Moore, Rufus Hurlbut, Curtis Smith, Spencer Smith.

13. Committee of the regimental Association, *History of the Thirty-fifth Regiment,* 209.

14. Ibid., 209-210.

15. Son of Charles Parmenter, Edwin, 20, went as his brother, Albert's, substitute. Eighteenth Regt. Aug. 1863, mortally wounded at Battle of Bottom Bridge, VA, died June 9, 1864, Ancestry.com.

16. No soldier from Sudbury named Bent was found in the list of Civil War soldiers, however there were four listed in Hudson's *History of Sudbury, Massachusetts,* who furnished a substitute or paid commutation money. 564.

17. Hudson, *History of Sudbury, Massachusetts,* 483, 533, 683.

18. Committee of the regimental Association, *History of the Thirty-fifth Regiment,* 211-212.

19. Horace Parmenter was a shoemaker.

20. Roy P. Baster, editor,*"The Collected Works of Abraham Lincoln"* http://www. civilwarhome.com/lincolnmeadletter.http

21. George G. Benedict, *Vermont in the Civil War, 1861-5*, (Free Press Association, Burlington, 1888). 627-33, http://www.vermontcivilwar.org/battles/ Kilpatricksraid.php.

22. Hudson, *History of Sudbury, Massachusetts*, 488.

23. Sudbury Chamber of Commerce, http//www.sudbury.org/townof.html.

24. Committee of the regimental Association, *History of the Thirty-Fifth*, 214-225.

25. Committee of the regimental Association, *History of the Thirty-Fifth*, 227-231.

26. Gardner H. Darling, Pvt., 30 years old, Sixteenth Regiment, Co. H, watchmaker.

27. Office of the Adjutant General, Massachusetts National Guard Museum & Archives, Worcester, MA, records of Alfred Moore, Fifty-ninth Regiment, Mass Volunteers.

28. Committee of the regimental Association, *History of the Thirty-Fifth*, 250.

29. Ibid., 234.

30. U. S. General Hospital, called Satterlee (1862-1865) was one of the largest Union Army hospitals of the Civil War.

31. Charles Haynes, Thirteenth Regiment Massachusetts Volunteers, Co. F, member of the Wadsworth Rifle Guards, farmer.

32. Private Ambrose Miranda Page, Wayland, MA (1842-1909) Thirty-fifth Regiment Massachusetts Volunteers, Co. D, Full Lieutenant Aug 25,1864, mustered out Sep 9, 1864, Commissioned an officer Co. C, Mass 4th Heavy Artillery, mustered out Jun 17, 1865.

33. George Harry Hall, Thirty-fifth Regiment Massachusetts Volunteers Co. D, shoemaker.

34. Edward Moulton, it is believed, was a member of the Fifty-ninth Regiment Massachusetts Volunteers, Co. I, who was mustered in April 2, 1864, transferred to Company 4th United States Veterans Reserve Corps on March 15, 1865, and mustered out September 12, 1864, N.Y., shoemaker.

35. Henry Moore, Thirteenth Regiment Massachusetts Volunteers, Co. H, Wadsworth Rifle Guards, carpenter.

36. Eli Willis, Thirty-fifth Regiment Massachusetts Volunteers, Co. D, shoemaker.

37. Ibid., 243-246.

38. Ibid., 261.

[39.] Levee is a reception held to celebrate a special occasion or honor a specific individual.

[40.] Committee of the regimental Association, *History of the Thirty-Fifth*, 263.

[41.] Ibid., 271.

[42.] Ibid.

[43.] Adjutant Generals Records, Adjutant Generals Office, Worcester, Massachusetts, record of George F. Moore, Thirty-fifth Regiment, Massachusetts Volunteers.

[44.] Ibid.

[45.] Committee of the regimental Association, *History of the Thirty-Fifth*, 293-299.

[46.] *The Town of Wayland in the Civil War of 1861-1865 as Represented in the army and Navy of the American Union*, (Wayland: 1871) 364. Conversations with Rufus Hurlbut's Great Granddaughter.

[47.] Corporal Edward J. Brackett, Waltham, MA, Thirty-fifth Regiment Mass Vol, Co. D, lost his foot.

[48.] Corporal Daniel J. Byrnes, 23, Roxbury, MA, Thirty-fifth Regiment Mass Vol., Co. D, lithographer.

[49.] http//www.dansville.lib.ny.us/history.html, (accessed 12 Dec 2010).

[50.] Committee of the regimental Association, *History of the Thirty-Fifth*, 360.

[51.] Ibid., 308.

[52.] Ibid., 318.

1865

I don't know what I should do if couldn't write. There is a great many in the army that cannot. I have written a letter this evening for a young fellow to his wife.

Letter from George to his mother May 5, 1865

Early in 1865 the Thirty-fifth Regiment was in Petersburg, Virginia, located 400 yards behind Fort Sedgwick, in a forest that had been reduced to stumps. In anticipation of remaining for the winter, a regular camp was laid out supervised by Colonel Carruth. Small earthen hut buildings with mud and stick chimneys, were constructed. Breastworks were erected in front of the entrenchments, and picket lines were strengthened with gabions. The Confederate pickets lay only 300 yards beyond the Union picket line. A freezing snow storm, followed by heavy rain flooded the rifle pits with icy slush, leaving the men sometimes ankle deep in frigid water. The duty of the regiment was to be ready for an attack, to furnish a detail of men for picket duty, and to act as an alarm guard at the breastworks. The old flags carried onto the battlefields had become so tattered that new regimental and national flags were requisitioned. Both the old and new flags were marked with the names of battles in which the Thirty-fifth had fought. These flags now reside at the State House in Boston.

Each day Confederate deserters arrived in camp saying the war would end soon. News of Sherman's victories as he proceeded north increased hope that this was so.[1] "One deserter declared that the end of the war was very near: he hoped that we would 'hang Jeff Davis, but let Bob Lee off, for he was a good fellow.'"[2] At night the enemy would fire bullets over, and on one occasion sent over 100 bombshells in an evening. This action wounded very few.

An attempt at peace was made at the end of January when, under a flag of truce, a group of Confederates passed through the lines and met with President Lincoln at City Point. This attempt failed.[3]

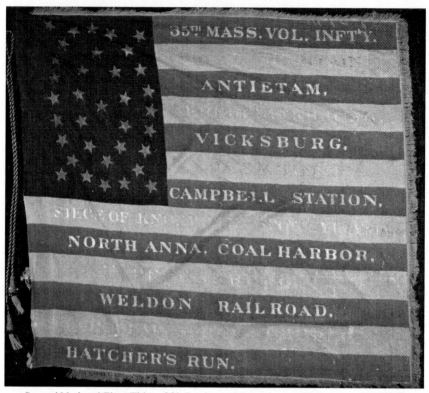

Second National Flag, Thirty-fifth Regiment Massachusetts Volunteers, 1987.168
Issued by the Federal QM December 20, 1864, lettered for Grand Review. Courtesy
of the Commonwealth of Massachusetts Art Commission.

The following is a letter to George from his father.

Sudbury
*Feb 5*th *1865*

Dear George
    *I received yours of Jan 16*th *sometime ago and was very glad to here from you and to know that you were well It is a snowing to day but not very cold this is the fifty eighth day cince the snow first come and have had good sleighing all of the time cince the snow come all of the way to Boston Monday Jan 9*th *commenced Sleding the remainder of my dry*

*wood to Watertown one load to Camb Port with the horse on my new
horse sled that I built this winter double runners shod with spring steel
which I have taken about eighty dolls for what wood I have sledded
cince the above date beside choping and getting up fire wood enough to
burn and sledded some logs to Moors Mills and have let my sled three
times to carry hay down for 50cts a time and have got about five cords
of wood more to carry off have sold all of my lumber that I shall have on
this lot that I bought this Winter which I think I shall have about twelve
thousand feet about three thousand of it Chestnut and Oak lumber which
I have for that thirty dolls per thousand at the Mills think I shall have
from 30 to one hund cord of wood on this lot which I paid about 250
dolls for the whole not much news to write seems to be a good deal of
exciting news about the peace Commishomers in the newspapers of late
but I don't think much of those reports but I hope they wont have to be
any more fighting done they talk pretty strong of building another large
Factory at Asabet and another Meeting house up there Mr Harriman
the carpenter that lives up there has offered John two dolls per day and
board to work for him as a carpenter had a letter from Francis not long
cince he wrote he was getting better had got downstairs he thinks of
coming home as soon as he is able to come Gen Butter arrived in Lowell
last Saturday he made a speech before the People of Lowell and it was a
very satisfactory speech Edward Everett was buried with great honors
the Emancipation proclamation news was announced by the ringing of
Bells and the firing of Cannon in Boston and other large places except
Sudbury the Collector has not paid that money over to the boys yet
according as he reports they wont get but about one hund dolls a pice
so you may Judge what some of the people of Sudbury are or how they
feel I think the whole sum could be collected of the town Mary is to work
at a Mr Tarbells at Marlborough Feltonville Village do suppose you're
a having a great time with your fiddle now we are all well hope this will
find you well write often*

From your Father

Edward Everett (1794-1865) was a strong supporter of the President and the
Union. He gave the speech before President Lincoln gave his at Gettysburg.
He spoke for two hours while President Lincoln's Gettysburg Address
lasted only a matter of minutes. During his life, Everett was a Senator, U.S.
Congressman, Minister to the Court of St. James, President of Harvard
University, an orator, and student and friend of Daniel Webster.

On January 1, 1863, under his war powers act, President Lincoln issued the Emancipation Proclamation, an executive order which granted freedom to slaves in states that had seceded from the Union, leaving the states along the border that were friendly to the north, still with slaves. Following the Emancipation Proclamation, a constitutional amendment to the Thirteenth Amendment was made, which was passed by the Senate on April 8, 1864, and by the House on January 31, 1865. On December 6, 1865, the Thirteenth Amendment was ratified, abolishing slavery.

The "Copperheads" were mostly Northern Democrats who opposed the Civil War and wanted peace, blaming the abolitionists for the war. Their name derived from the practice of cutting the likeness of Lady Liberty from the copper penny and wearing it as a pin.

Camp Mead Petersburg Va.
Feb. 12, 1865

Dear Father,
    I received your letter yesterday and was very glad to hear from you. we have not received letters from home lately. Johns are the last before yours. and we received his last week. Mary has written to us lately. also Alfred. I am glad to hear that Francis is getting better. hope he will be able to go home soon. wonder if he thinks as much of cold water as he did before. better live in an ice house and have done with it.
    We are having very pleasant wither lately. and it has not been very cold for the Season. We have not had very much snow this winter but have had plenty rain. and expect to have a great deal more soon for it is the Season for rain now. I suppose you have heard long before this that the army of the Potomac has moved. and you have seen the papers and known of the particulars better than I do for my Division did not move only one div. of the 9th corps moved (the 3rd), the 1st & 2nd were left to hold the lines in front of Petersburg. a thing we were very willing to do for we knew, we should not get into any Battles. the fighting was done mostly by the 5th & 2nd Corps. and the Cavalry done some pretty good fighting. and I believe part of the 6th Corps was engaged. I don't think there was much gained, although I don't know what they tried to do
    I suppose they moved more to keep Lee from reinforcing Hardee than anything else. and I'm thinking Hardee needs a few more men to stop Sherman but it will not do for Lee to send them from here.
    There has been a great talk about peace. but I guess that question is settled now. and I guess they will have to let Messrs. Grant, Sherman

& Co. be peace Commissioners a little while longer I don't believe this war is over yet. although I think this Summer will end it if the North will only send men enough to settle it, and send good men. they had better let the draft take affect and not buy any more men. take Gen'l Butler's advice , he says a large portion of the bought men are good for nothing and he speaks the truth, for they buy anything. I don't mean to say they are all poor soldiers for there is some good men among them. there is some in my own Company, but then so many of the substitutes are bounty jumpers that they don't know who to trust. let the draft take who it will. and we are pretty sure to get good men. I would not like to see men come out here that are not able, but I would like to see those that are able come out. I mean those that are able to do duty in the field. and there are some in every place yet. I don't <u>know</u> how it would be but I <u>think</u> it would be a good thing if the President would call for all the able bodied men between 20 & 40. let them come out for one year. and I am thinking we would not need them any longer. but I suppose our leaders know what is best. and I am willing to trust them. all but one. and that is Meade. I have not much confidence in him and his Army has not either. I was in hopes they would give us Sheridan this summer, but perhaps he could not handle a large army but he has proved that he can a smaller one I see by the papers that Gen'l Burnside is not blamed for the disaster on the 30th of July last and his corps never blamed him. I believe Burnside is one of the most patriotic Genl's we have. and I don't think he would do a wrong thing by his Country. all I wish is that we were under him now

So the boys are not likely to get their money now or not all of it I am sorry they are not but if I was one of them I would not say anything about it let it go for these men that did not pay will think of it some future time and I'm thinking they will wish they had paid they deserve to have their names published I shall rather go without a cent if I was one of those boys than to take my place among one of those that did not pay. They keep my fiddle going most of the time there is some good players in my Regt. guess I will close now for my sheet is about full.

Give my love to all enquiring friends. Please write again soon and write all the news from <u>old</u> Sudbury.

Good night.

George

There was tremendous loyalty among the troops for General Ambrose Burnside. George wrote that he would rather fight under Burnside than any other general.

Camp near Petersburg
Feb 24, 1865

My Dear Mother

   I received your letter this morning and I was very glad to hear from you and to hear that you were all well. I received a letter from Mary and Charlie this morning and shall write them as soon as possible

   I have just witnessed the firing of a shotted salute in honor of the fall of Wilmington. I wonder what the "Johnnies" thought was coming when they heard the shells flying through the air but I guess they have got used to hearing salutes fired for it is an everyday occurrence here or nearly everyday seems as though we were having Victories at all points now and we are having Victory here though we don't have to fight for now but we are getting Rebels fast as any Army 14 rebs came in our Brigade last night and 18 to the 2ed Brigade. there was 9 men and one Sergt came in last night out of one company they were out of the 2ed South Carolina Regt. they said that they had no hopes of peace now and they said they knew they had to give up sometime and they thought they might as well come over here and get rid of this summers Campaign. they say Lee has to keep a picket line in the rear of the army to keep the men from going home. I think that will make a good Army to fight this summer. the only good men they have got are Virginians and some of them desert now Wilmington and Charlestown are taken. Sherman will have a large Army for Gilmore and Schofield can join him although I don't see as he needs them for he seems to go where he pleases (or where he don't please) now all that I am afraid of is that he will be too bold but I guess he is pretty prudent. I remember when he took command of the army of the Cumberland some people thought he was crazy even some of his Gen'ls thought so and I guess South Carolina and Georgia think he has made a crazy mess of them. I think this summer will close the war but there has got to be some hard fighting first but the men will have some heart to fight when they know the end is so near.

   What is John doing that keeps him so busy that he cannot write I suppose he is away most of the time, well never mind he will catch it when I get hold of him again if he don't write pretty soon I am glad to hear that Francis is getting better hope he will be able to come home soon guess he got enough of <u>cold water</u> this time I think if he could have some <u>hard tack</u> and <u>salt horse</u> he would soon get well I tell you there is nothing like it think I shall live on it when I get home.

But I must close give my love to all friends tell Charlie I will write him tonight if I get time write again as soon as you can and tell the rest to write

From your affectionate son
George

As the men continued to keep watch for any signs that the enemy was leaving Petersburg, Colonel Wild, their old commander, sent them a football for some recreation.

Camp near Petersburg
March 5, 1865

Dear Father
I have nothing to do this evening so I am going to write you a few lines if I can think of anything to make it interesting for we do not have much news or changes to write about here for everything is as quiet as can be but probably will not remain so much longer for it is getting near the season of active operations and they are liable to commence anytime now

We have had considerable rain lately and the roads are in a bad condition for a move now especially for Artillery but then we can move without that but I don't know as there is any such calculations at present

We had a report here yesterday that Gen'l Sherman had fought a battle with Lee and that (Sherman) whipped him. I <u>hope</u> he did for I don't want our Gen'ls to get defeated now and especially Sherman for some think he is rash and going to far and think when the rebs make a stand they will be able to whip him but I hope he will show them that he is able to carry out what he undertakes. I should not be surprised if Sherman flanked Grant and got into Richmond first and to Washington in 1869 as our next President. I understand that Sudbury has been quite a lively place this winter I suppose it was partly on account of the sleighing for I hear you have had good sleighing every day this Winter. Would like a good sleighride but shall have to wait till next Winter but I don't care if I get one then. So John talks of coming out this way soon I would like to see him or <u>any other</u> man. I owe him a letter but suppose there is no use in writing to him if he is coming out here so I guess I will wait til I hear from him again. I suppose the boys have not got their money from the town yet and I suppose they never will get it all but there is one

good thing we all know who did not pay it and my opinion is they will be
ashamed of it sometime

    There is a report that the Johnies have dug under one of our forts
but I don't believe it is so but it may be if it is they will find the yanks
prepared for them for once for if it is true our officers know it before
this time for there has been plenty deserters into our lines lately and our
Officers are keeping a good watch of the rebs now

    But I must close for now for it is bed time give my love to all the folks
write soon and write all the news from the City of Sudbury

    From your son

    George

On March 7, 1865, the regiment exchanged living quarters with the Forty-eighth Pennsylvania for the rest of the month, moving from one side of the fort to the other. They were now living in the section nicknamed Fort Hell. The new quarters were underground earthen hovels, so damp, gloomy, and wretched, that the soldiers were more comfortable outside the huts than inside. The purpose of burrowing the huts into the ground was to bomb-proof (really bullet-proof, for they would not stop unexploded shells) their shelter.

> The roofs were made of logs and earth, in rainy weather moist and dripping and making the interior dark and dismal...making on the whole about as chill and gloomy a tomb as one could well wish to be buried in. Rain turned these rat holes into dripping baths, which continued to drip long after the weather above ground had cleared. After a few days' trial of underground life most of the officers pitched tents in the rear of the mounds of their bomb-proofs, and occupied them, except when an uncommonly severe mortar shelling made the security from flying pieces compensate for the descent into Avernus.[4] (Greek, entrance to the underworld)

Pickets were so close to each other that false information was spread by both sides to encourage desertions. "The North offered the price of a stand of arms to each Confederate who brought his musket with him and the Confederates offered an open road to Europe through Mexico for foreign substitutes."[5] Near the end of March the men slept with their shoes on to be on the alert.

Quarters of the Men in Fort Sedgwick, Known as Fort Hell.
Photograph by Timothy H. O'Sullivan, 1865, Smithsonian American Art Museum,
Museum purchase from the Charles Isaacs Collection made possible in part by the
Luisita L. and Franz H. Denhausen Endowment

Sudbury
March 13th 1865

Dear George

I received yours of the 5th and was glad to here from you and to know that you were well and were having so easey time now I returned this Morning from a visit out to see Francis your Mother went out with me found him dangerously sick with the Brain fever saw him last Friday in the afternoon he did not know us the next morning he had his reason and then he knew us but he did not ask any question wee got out to him Friday about 4 of the Oclock P.M. and I started from their Dansvill for home about 6 of the Oclock in the afternoon and his simtons looked more encouraging that day than the day before had a slite hope of him a geling up again left your Mother with him she is going to stay with him a few days Alfred returned to Parmenters to day the Town voted at the March Meeting to have all of the names reported that don't pay the tax that is assets on them for to raise the sum of money that they agreed to pay the Boys will close for I am so sleepy have rode in the Carrs two

*knights agoing after you have read this hand it to Albert for him to read
all well hope these few short lines will find you well*
                                        Your Father

Early on March 25, the men were awakened to the sounds of picket firing and
could hear cannon fire in the distance. During the night a group of Confederates
came into the picket line pretending to surrender, bringing their weapons to
be traded for money. Under this pretense they were able to capture the men
on picket and take prisoners of the sleeping men. Field guns from the forts
opened fire and at daybreak the soldiers could see that the attack which had
threatened the Union forces had been turned back at Fort Stedman, about two
miles from the regiment. The Union artillery, with General Hartranft and the
Pennsylvanians, saved the day and took 2000 prisoners. Lee had been stopped.[6]
"This brilliant recovery of Fort Stedman has always been considered by the
army as the happy beginning of the triumphant ending of the war."[7]

*Camp Near Petersburg, Va
March 26 1865*

Dear Father,
    *I have some news to write so I take this opportunity to write it.
we awoke this morning with the music of Artilery ringing in our ears.
we soon got out of bed and got well woke up and soon came to the
conclusion there was some fighting going on and not far from us either.
pretty soon the news came that the Johnies had taken Fort Stedman and
battery II. that is on the right of these lines in front of Petersburg and in
the 1st Division of this Corps.*
    *Well after waiting two or three hours in camp I came to the conclusion
that this (the 2nd Div.) would not be called upon. so I got permission to
go down near the battlefield. pretty soon the news came that our boys had
taken the Fort back again, so I and one of my comrades started for the
field. and we found that our fellows had been having a pretty hard fight.
the rebels took them by surprise. they told our Pickets not to fire for they
were coming into our lines to give themselves up. so our boys did not fire
for the rebs had been coming in there of late. but there was enough to take
the picket line come this time. and they took it and then charged on the fort
and took that while the boys were in bed. the fort did not have a chance
to use their Artilery before the rebs had it. they took most of the men in
it prisoners. but a great many got away again. then they took battery II.
but it had no guns. they then advanced up in the rear of our line and got*

the rear of Fort Haskul. but the boys in this fort were awake and were ready for them. the Artilery did good execution and soon checked the rebs. by this time the 3rd Division got to the field of action. they formed and charged the rebs and got their line broke. and sent them scattering back to Fort Stedman but our boys had got started and was bound to have the fort again. so they kept on to the fort and soon had the rebs out of it and drove them back to their own lines again. our boys cut off a large number and took them prisoners. our lines are the same now on the right as they were yesterday. I think our loss was very slight compared with the rebs. Think 700 will cover our loss in killed, wounded, and prisoners but I think the rebs lost 2500. among the wounded is Lt. Henry Smith. I saw him as they took him off the field. he was wounded in the ankle. I don't know whether any bones are broken but hope not. he was sitting up in the streacher when I saw him. He will get over his wound without losing his foot I think although I cannot tell if the bones are broken he will lose it but I don't think they were he was cheerful when I saw him and if he keeps so he will get along. Well while I am writing this they are fighting on the left. Don't know what the result is but think while the rebs were fighting down here our 5th and 2nd Corps advanced and took some of their works on the left perhaps the Southside R.R. at any rate they are doing something will write again when I find out what it is. I wrote this to let you know about Henry. You can tell aunt Olive if she has not heard already. will put this right in the mail and it will start today give my love to all. write soon and tell us how Francis is getting along.

From your son.

George

At the end of March, General Sherman, arrived in the rear of Fort Sedgwick with large columns of cavalry to regroup. One day the men of the regiment observed a man in gray, with patches that resembled Confederate flags sewn onto his clothing, run from the Confederate lines towards the Union pickets, quickly identifying himself as a Union scout for General Sherman. He informed the pickets that he had traveled through the Confederate lines from the valley below with information which he then produced from the heel of his shoe. He was sent off to the cavalry with this information. The Confederates had been fooled by this Union spy.

On March 29, General Sherman organized an assault by the entire division, and all were in the line of battle when it was called off because of poor weather. Two days later the soldiers were awakened, and in the darkness, the Third Division and part of the First Division gathered in front of the Thirty-fifth's fort and removed any gabions or obstructions in front. The Pioneer Brigade (including those of the Thirty-fifth) found they were to be in the front of the columns of cavalry and soldiers, to break up the Confederate obstructions as the army advanced. The soldiers, both Confederate and Union, were up and awake now and artillery rifle fire began to light up the night sky. The Thirty-fifth, situated in the front of Fort Sedgwick, was under heavy mortar attack. Several men were killed. At 4 AM cheers from the front lines indicated success. General Hartranft captured the Confederate artillery and over 600 prisoners. The Thirty-Fifth was now delivering ammunition to individual soldiers in the front lines, a very dangerous job. This was the first time that they had used Spencer repeating rifles during the war. The Spencer rifles were breach loaded with cartridge clips that could be rapidly replaced, enabling the soldier to fire rounds one after another. By early afternoon reinforcements were called for. The Sixty-first and Twenty-first Massachusetts plus a regiment of Zouaves[8] responded. The assault was successful and five Corps completely surrounded Petersburg, (II, V, IV, XXIV, XXV Corps) "… cutting the Confederate Army in half."[9] On April 2, when Lee saw that his lines were broken irreparably and he could no longer remain he informed President Davis that Richmond and Petersburg must be evacuated that night."[10]

Depot of the U.S. Military Railroads, City Point, Virginia 1864,
showing the engine "President" #111-B-4860.
Photograph courtesy of National Archives, Washington D.C.

On April 3, Richmond fell to the Union troops. As the division proceeded down the Plank Road they met President Lincoln, Secretary Steward, and Admiral Porter, who had come on horseback from City Point. The troops cheered the dignitaries who had come to meet them. The war was not yet over and the army continued to march alongside the trains still following Lee. The men expected more difficult fighting ahead. However, Generals Sheridan and Ord had already surprised Lee and had him surrounded. On April 9, 1865, at Appomattox Courthouse, General Lee surrendered to General Grant. Colonel Carruth read the official announcement to great cheers and elation.[11]

General Ulysses S. Grant, Union Army: engraving from Pictorial History of the Great Civil War, 1878

General Robert E. Lee, Confederate Army, engraving from Pictorial History of the Great Civil War 1878

Sudbury
April 13th 1865

Dear George
Your Mother received a letter from you last night stating that the Sudbury Boys were all right this letter was dated the 6th inst Was very ankcious to here frorm you and Albert and to know that the Sudbury Boys came out of the last great and Glorious struggle all right the greatest excitement ever was known I think prevaiting here in Mass. About this time when the news came on Monday that Lee had serendred with all his forces people seemed to run mad with joy Bells rung Cannon a firing Steem whissels a whisiling in all directions where they was an Engine dinner Bells rung and horns blown and all sorts of noises that could be made and the stars and stripes thrown to the trees where ever there was any to be had but there was a very sad and melloncaly affair happened in Marlborough on Monday caused by the firing of a selute that afternoon to Capt. Whitcum while he was a Charging a gun it went of and blown both of his armes of and is feared both of his eyes are put out and burned him otherwise he was a living yesterday but little hopes of his recovery I wrote to you and Albert the day that your Mother got home from New York giving the particulars of her journey home stating that she was detained on the way some two weeks on account of the great freashets at that time a washing the railroad bridges awy so she had to leave poor Francis and bury him away out in Weslton New York but your Mother got home all right and well she was very fortunate in falling in with friendly people on the way home that twenty five dolls that you sent home came in a time that done us more good than a hundred dolls at some times for it helpt pay part of the sum that we had to borrow to go out there with we are all well hoping this will find you and Albert well write us ofton as you can

Your Father

P.S Hattie recd a letter from John night before last writing from Richmond he is to work for the Christian Commission driving a teem

Francis Uriah Moore died at the age of thirty-one, on March 15, 1865, while still at "Our Home on the Hill" in Dansville, New York. The cause of death was never mentioned, only that he suffered from "brain fever." Eventually his body was returned to Sudbury and was buried in the family plot at Wadsworth Cemetery.

A group from the Young Men's Christian Association formed the Christian Commission in the fall of 1861 to care for the soldiers' spiritual needs as well as to distribute supplies such as bandages to the battlefields, hospitals, and prisons. Among their members was the poet, Walt Whitman, who helped care for the wounded in hospitals. John Moore joined the Commission after he mustered out of the regiment and drove wagons that transported injured men from the battlefields for the rest of the war.[12]

General Ambrose Burnside resigned from the Union Army on April 15, 1865, after having never been recalled to duty following the Battle at the Crater (part of the Siege of Petersburg) in August 1864.

Sudbury
April 30th 1865

Dear George
I believe I havnt answered the last letter I received from you as I ought to have done before now, for that letter did a great deal of good. It contained the first tidings about the Sudbury boys after the late Battles, and relieved a great many anxious hearts. I hope we shall not hear of any more battles to feel anxious about. The Rebs have surrendered, but it seems they are not quite satisfied. They want to destroy our government some way. How dreadful it seems to think such a dear good man as President Lincoln should lose his life by the hands of an assassin. When we first heard of his death, almost every one felt as though our Country was undone, but we feel differently now. It was wrong to place so much dependence upon one man, for Mr Lincoln was only an instrument in the hands of God to carry out this great work which has been accomplished, and his death reminds us that we must look above this world for help in these days of trial. I think there are not many men, if any, who are equal in all respects to Mr. Lincoln, yet it seems as though his heart was too tender to punish treason as it deserves, and perhaps that is why he was relieved from such a painful duty, and a sterner man put in his place. The Rebs will see their mistake in having his life destroyed, if they have not seen it already, but I suppose they intended to murder all our great men, and we ought to be very thankful they did not succeed in carrying out that plan.
People hardly know what to think about General Sherman since his agreement with Jonston, some think he is deficient in judgment, and others think he is a traitor, but perhaps he will be able to explain his conduct so it will be better understood than it is now. It is reported in the

papers, that the 9ᵗʰ Corps have been ordered to Washington, and some think the 35ᵗʰ will be discharged soon. How rejoiced we should be to see you at home, but I hardly dare to expect you till your term of service expires, for it seems as though they would want a large army till affairs are settled. They will certainly need a strong guard at Washington.

Rufus wrote to his folks that he had seen John so I expect you have seen him too. He expected to find you as soon as he got out there, but he kept writing home that he had not seen you and sometimes that he didn't know where you was. I guess he felt pleased enough when he did see you. I hope he will make out well there for he is in debt and I want to have him get able to square up with every one he owes. If the town had done what they agreed to do, he would have paid his debts before he left home, but if he is well and has good luck he can soon be independent again. I received a letter from Alfred a few days ago. He writes that he is well as ever he was, but I fear he will find himself mistaken when he takes hold of hard work.

Mary has gone to Mary Browns and Hattie, Charley, Ellen and Edgar are at home. It seems sad to think poor Francis can never come home again. I little thought when he went away, he was going there to die. I could see his health had failed some, but thought he might live a number of years, but did not expect he would ever enjoy good health. He suffered very much with a distressing feeling in his head which sometimes made me fear he would lose his reason if he didn't get help, but his sufferings are ended now, and I hope he is better off than to be here. It was hard to part with him, but God knows what is best and we must try and be reconciled to His will. Although I have passed through a great trial yet I have much to be thankful for, and I hope I shall prize the blessings I enjoy.

We are having quite an early spring. The cherry trees are in bloom and other things are as forward as they were the last of may last year, but I suppose the season is much earlier where you are than it is here. I don't think of much news to write this time that will be interesting to you so I will bid you good night. Please write soon and let us know where you are.

From your loving Mother

Mary H Moore

On April 14, 1865, President Lincoln met with General Grant who had arrived in Washington from City Point the previous day. The President invited the General and Mrs. Grant to attend the theatre that evening with him and his wife, but the Grants declined, saying they were on their way to visit their sons. Partway through the first act, the President and Mrs. Lincoln arrived to "Hail to the Chief". In the middle of Act III John Wilkes Booth shot the President at point blank range, then jumped from the presidential box to the stage where he fell and escaped. Lincoln was carried to a tailor's house across the street where he died the next morning. Only hours later, Andrew Johnson was sworn into office. John Wilkes Booth was found on April 26 and shot to death. Booth's co-conspirators had also planned to kill Vice President Andrew Johnson and Secretary of State William Seward at the same time. No attempt was made on Johnson, and William Seward recovered from a stabbing. The co-conspirators were arrested, tried, and hanged.

On April 16 the assassination was reported to the horror of the citizens and the army. Orders were given to keep the regiment in camp and under arms to prevent any disturbance. The Thirty-fifth Regiment marched back towards Petersburg on April 22, and two days later to City Point. From there they took a steamer, passing Newport News and Fortress Munroe, landing in Alexandria, Virginia on April 28. For the next few weeks the soldiers were garrisoned near the Mount Vernon Road with Lieutenant Colonel Hudson in command of the regiment.

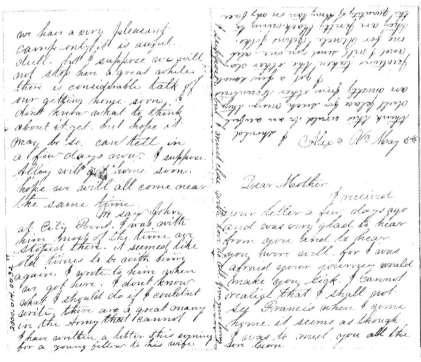

Letter from George to his Mother on May 5, 1865. Sudbury Historical Society

Alex. Va.
May 5, 1865

Dear Mother,

I received your letter a few days ago and was very glad to hear from you and to hear you were well. for I was afraid your journey would make you sick. I cannot realize that I shall not see Francis when I come home. it seems as though I was to meet you all the same as I left you but I know we shall miss him when we come to see the things that belong to him and not see him around.

How things have changed since I wrote to you last. then we had just taken Petersburg and Richmond and were following up Lees demoralized Army. Then we felt confident of an easy Victory, but little expected to capture the whole of his army and it was hard to make us believe it was so till we had it officially announced from Grant. then the army was wild with joy. but in the midst of our rejoicing came the news of the murder of Mr. Lincoln. then you had ought to have seen the difference. I think if the boys could have got hold of Booth about that time he would have fared hard. but I am glad now he met his death in the way he did for I think it saved a great deal of trouble. It seems that Jeff Davis is conserned in the murder. also a great many other leading men of the Confederacy that was. I hope they will catch all those men and I think there is a prospect of it now. We are in camp about 1 mile from Alexandria we have a very pleasant camp, only it is awful dull, but I suppose we will not stop here a great while. There is considerable talk of our getting home soon. I don't know what to think about it yet but hope it may be so, can tell in a few days now. I suppose Alley will get home soon. hope we will all come near the same time.

We saw John at City Point. I was with him most of the time we stoped there. it seemed like old times to be with him again. I wrote to him when we got here. I don't know what I should do if I couldn't write. There are a great many in the army that cannot. I have written a letter this evening for a young fellow to his wife. I should think this would be an awful dull place for such men. they are mostly from other Countries. I got a few small pictures taken the other day and I will send you one. also one for Uncle John's folks, they are pretty black owing to the quantity of Army tan on my face, I suppose, but I must close. with love to all

from your loving son
George

During the Civil War, about eighty-five percent of the soldiers were able to read and write and the men spent much of their spare time in camp writing friends and families. The unprecedented number of letters written helped document the war from the soldier's point of view.

Drawings of Jefferson Davis by Charles H. Moore located at the First Parish Church Belfry Tower, Sudbury, Massachusetts

Sudbury
May 7ᵗʰ 1865

Dear George
I received your long and interesting letter of April the 12ᵗʰ from Farmville Va and was very happy to know that you came out of the last campaign all right and the last fighting you will experience I hope received your letter sometime ago but have wrote one and directed it to Albert cince I received your last one which I intended for both of you and have received one from Albert dated April 18th which was a long and a equally interesting one hope you will excuse me for not writeing oftoner for I have been quite out of health for a few week and have not been able to labor for a few dayes past have been a handling wood and timber and doing my planting have overdone and taken Cold and got my stomeac week which I must rest awhile and then I shall fetch up again by taking a few Beandreth pills you know some of the Farmers here have

*got most through with their planting have got my corn planted and part
of my potatoes the Spring is very forward although it has been quite cool
for a few days past I have got pees Corn potatoes cucumbers cabbedge
and lettice up the appletrees beginning to bossom good feed for the
Cattle now people that own pastures in the Country have drove of their
Cattle to the pastures the Coperheads here among us have to keep pretty
wist now cince the Assasination of the President have been some tared
& fethered and booted and compeld them to acknowledge the stars and
stripes and out over there doors and some have come forword and have
made an appoliga for the centiments that they expressed it was reumored
in the papers last knight that they had got old Jef If they havenot I think
they will get him those news paper that I sent you and Albert the first
weekly Journal that I sent out had Reverend Ward Beeches speech
in that he delivered at the raising of the flag on Fort Sumpter in that
speech he gives my sentiments precisely in reference to the cause of this
Rebelion want you should read it must close for I feel pretty tired By
saying that I understand that you were encamped at Alexandria waiting
for further orders I suppose to be relieved from service in a few weeks
according to the accounts in the papers and then you will all be to home
with us again I hope a safe Return must excuse this short letter for this
time write soon hope this will find you both well*

   from Your Father

The Reverend Henry Ward Beecher, brother of Harriet Beecher Stow, was
a powerful orator who was sent by Lincoln to Great Britain to convince
them to remain neutral during the Civil War.

*Alexandria Va
May 12*

*Dear Father
    I received your letter yesterday and was very glad to hear from you.
I also received a letter from Charlie. I don't have much to do now so I
have plenty of time to write only I don't get letters enough to answer.
    We are in camp near Alexandria about 1 mile from the city. I
believe you visited the place once but it probably looks different than
it did then. I guess it was quite a nice place once. I wish I could have
seen Richmond, they say it was a Splendid City once. Petersburg was*

a splendid city not a very large one though, but there was some very handsome buildings in it and a great many of them had been injured by our shells. The inhabitants were very poorly off for everything. a great many of the _first families_ were glad to ask the _Yankees_ for bread. the first day we went through they kept in their houses. I heard some of them say they never were so surprised as they were to see our Army go through the place in such good order. they expected we were going to rob and burn the whole place. the women seemed to have just two suits of clothes one very nice one that they wore Sundays the next day we would see the same ones dressed in a dirty ragged dress and no hooks. there were a very few that dressed well. they were daughters of some of the men that had made money by blockade running or some office in the Confederacy where they were paid with gold and every place I have been in is in the same condition. some places they are worse off. I don't know what they are going to do for food this summer. They have no money and the Farmers have no seed to put in the ground. I pity those that were forced into the Rebellion but the others I haven't much pity for. It is hard for anyone but they made their own bed took their choice and they have got to take its reward. I think the South has learned a lesson in this war that they will not easily forget. I see by the papers that some of the delegates of the Christian Commission visited Genl Lee and expressed themselves foolishly. The North will see what some of their delegates in both Christian and Sanitary Commission are sometime. I have no doubt but what that thing was got up in good faith but they have been imposed upon by a set of brainless milk and water chaps that couldn't make a living at home. both Societies are the same. but the Sanitary has done a good deal more good than the other, especially around our Hospitals but the Christian Commission may have done some good in some places but such a set as I saw at City Point where John was enough to make anyone disgusted and I supposed they were the ones that went to see Lee. You see what John says about some of them when he gets home. I don't mean to condemn the societie for this. It is some of the delegates I am writing about. I think both are a good thing if properly managed.

  I stopped with John most of the time while I was at City Point and had a good time. There is considerable talk of our getting home soon. I don't know whether there is any truth in it or not but then I should think they would commence to send troops home soon if they are going to send any before their time is out for everyday they keep us here idle it costs just as much as it did to keep us through the winter...it is adding just as much to our war dept. and that is plenty large enough without any addition. especially to keep men in idleness but perhaps they haven't got

*through with us yet. They probably know best so we must wait patiently
we are doing well enough I guess I shall have to close soon for it is
almost time for the mail to go out. I will write to Charlie tonight or in the
morning. Give my love to all. write again as soon as you get a chance for
you may not have a chance to write much more before I see you all*

    From your affectionate son
    G. F. Moore
    Tomorrow is my birthday

What began as an impromptu torchlight procession on May 12 by one
regiment soon spread to others, and in the following letter George describes
this very moving scene:

The following letter is most likely written to George's brother, John.

Alexandria Va
May 14/65

Dear Brother
    *I received your letter a few days ago and was very glad to hear from
you. I meant to have answered it yesterday but Rufus wanted me to go to
Mt. Vernon with him so I went. Mt. Vernon was Gen'l Washington's place.
it was worth going to see. it is about six miles from here. we walked down.
I suppose it was considered a splendid place in its day an in fact it is as
handsome place as there is around here now I went through the House
and Gardens also to Washington's tomb. I guess nearly the whole of our
Corps has been there. I have some Magnolia leaves from the tree that
Washington planted near his house. I will send one in this. tell Mother to
put it with the other things we have sent home. I think she said she had a
number of things that we have sent perhaps if she keeps them we may tell
something interesting about them when we get home.*
    *I saw one of the grandest illuminations a few nights ago that I ever
saw in my life. there are two Divisions of our Corps camped here together
and they all illuminated their tents by setting a candle on top of each end
of the tent and there are nearly 12000 men and a candle to each man and
they are in camp on a side hill so we could see the whole camp. it was a
splendid sight. then the regiment turned out with their guns with a candle
stuck in the muzzle of them. they marched all around the Camp and the
Regts were from different States and as they went by a Mass camp they*

would cheer for that Regt and Mass boys would go by their camps and give them a cheer and so with other States. it was a pleasant night and not a breath of wind stirring so the candles burned first-rate.

There is considerable talk of our getting home soon but I don't know whether to think so or not. we may get home before our time is out but not for some time yet we are going to have a review today so I have not time to write much more. Yesterday was my birthday. 23 years old . think of it. shall be an old batch soon. Al comes pretty near don't he I laugh at him about it. I will now close. give my love to all. write soon and tell me all that is going on in town

From your brother
George

Grand Review of Union Troops, May 23-24, 1865, Looking Down Pennsylvania Avenue. Artwork by James E. Taylor, July 1, 1888, #111-BA-69. Courtesy of the National Archives, Washington D. C.

On May 22 the Thirty-fifth marched to Washington with the rest of the IX Corps to join the entire Army of the Potomac for the Presidential review:

> The number of muskets in the ranks, next morning, was three hundred and eighteen. Colonel Carruth commanded the brigade. Lieutenant-Colonel Hudson commanded the

regiment. Column was formed before ten o'clock in the morning of the twenty-third, and, at noon, with orders to keep closed up very compactly which while it gave the appearance of solidity forfeited all freedom of motion the march in review was commenced: by the imposing capital where upon the east portico, the school children were gathered and sang patriotic songs; down the broad Pennsylvania Avenue our thoughts wandering back the while to that sunny afternoon in August 1862, when, with full ranks and unbounded enthusiasm, we took the first steps in the rough march of years which was to end here; on by the Treasury Building, the throngs of happy faces and plaudits of the people; by the White House, where the President and all the government officers, civil and military, were looking on, and were saluted with cheers and shouldered arms; and so to Georgetown and across the Potomac.[13]

The Thirty-fifth Regiment was mustered out on June 9, and the following day they said their good-byes to old friends, and started toward home by ferry and rail, through Philadelphia and New York. The Seventh Rhode Island (their comrades from Jackson, Mississippi) invited them to join them in a celebration to be held in Providence. On arriving in Providence aboard the steamboat, *Oceanus*, the regiment "marched past the home of General Burnside where our beloved leader sat on the porch to welcome us."[14] Taking the cars, the regiment reached Readville, Massachusetts, and set up tents to wait until they were paid off. Stopping at Readville was a disappointment for the men who had looked forward to the opportunity to march together into Boston Common to surrender their colors at the State House in front of friends and families. But on June 27 the men were paid off, and returned home to some grand local celebrations.

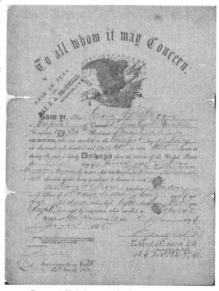

George F. Moore discharge papers.
Sudbury Historical Society

1. Committee of the regimental Association, *History of the Thirty-Fifth Massachusetts Volunteers, 1862-1865,* (Boston: Mills, Knight & Co., 1884), 310-316.

2. Ibid.

3. Ibid., 319.

4. Ibid., 322.

5. Ibid., 321-324.

6. Ibid., 325-326.

7. Ibid., 327.

8. Zouaves were soldiers who had adopted the colorful and exotic designs of uniforms worn in the 1800s by the North African troops employed by the French colonials. There were Zouaves on both sides.

9. Committee of the regimental Association, *History of the Thirty-Fifth Massachusetts*, 392.

10. Ibid., 393.

11. Ibid., 392-393.

12. United States Christian Commission, *History of the USCC*, (usccgettysburg.org/history), (accessed 10 Nov. 2010).

13. Committee of the regimental Association, *History of the Thirty-Fifth Massachusetts*, 403-404.

14. Ibid., 407.

George F. Moore

1863 Diary

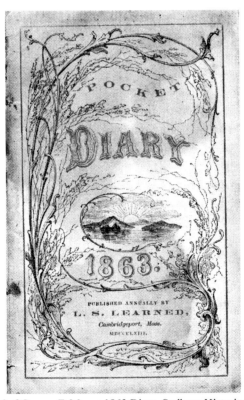

Inner leaf of George F. Moore 1863 Diary, Sudbury Historical Society

Thursday, January 1, 1863

Pleasant & cool.....Our officers had a high time last night.....the Band Played after 12 o'clock until most morning.....Camp near Falmouth

Friday 2

Pleasant & cool.....received a letter from John

Saturday 3

Pleasant & warm.....went to the 32ed Regt and to Falmouth.....had a good time

Sunday, January 4, 1863

Pleasant with warm south wind.....wrote to John.....went on inspection

Monday 5

Warm and Pleasant.....Grand Review by Gen. Burnside of Sickels Division near our camp

Tuesday 6

Cloudy with a little rain.....Grand review by Burnside of our— the 9th Army Corps.....a splendid sight

Wednesday, January 7, 1863

Cold and freezing.....the Regt is on picket opposite Fredericksburg.....Eli's chimney caught fire had a great time putting it out

Thursday 8

Cold.....did not thaw any today.....Had a piece of cake that came from Wayland to W. L. Parker.....Regt came off picket about 12 o'clock

Friday 9

Cold.....had an auction and division drill.....the Wayland boys sold Parkers box and contents at auction and sent the money to his wife

Saturday, January 10, 1863

Stormy day.....rained all day.....Albert was on guard.....I had nothing to do.....received a letter from Francis and C.J.G.

Sunday 11

Cloudy and cold.....Nothing to do today.....Wrote to Francis.....one month ago today was the Massacre of Fredericksburg

Monday 12

Pleasant and warm.....Nothing in particular happened today.....tonight the boys had a great time because it was warm.....wrote one letter to CJG (Clara J. Gerry, born 1846, daughter of Charles Gerry)

Tuesday, January 13, 1863

Pleasant and warm.....John came.....we had a tip top time.....he went back about 5 o'clock.....he is about eight miles from us

Wednesday 14

Cloudy & warm.....our Regt is on picket opposite Fredericksburg.....four months ago was the Battle at South Mountain

Thursday 15

Cloudy with a great wind.....some of the tents blew down.....Regt came off picket about 12 o'clock.....funeral of a private of Company E.....Brigade Band attended.....two months ago the fight at Sulphur Springs

Friday, January 16, 1863

Cold and freezing.....funeral of a private of Company A.....ordered to be ready to march tomorrow at 7 o'clock.....3 days rations in our haversack

Saturday 17

Cold.....rained last night.....no movement yet.....received a letter from Geo Smith and one from M A J.....Battle of Antietam was four months ago today

Sunday 18

Cold & freezing all day.....no movement yet but expect to move tomorrow at an early hour

Monday 19

*Cold & Cloudy.....Went on duty for the first time since the battle.....had a game of ball.....wrote to W J Forsyth.....no movement yet (*John Forsyth, Sudbury, Sixteenth Regiment, Company H, promoted to Sergeant, killed at Gettysburg)

Tuesday 20

Cold & Cloudy with rain this evening.....funeral of another private of Company A.....he shot himself accidentally this morning and the doctor gave him so much Chloroform that it killed him.....a great movement of troops.....but not us yet.....wrote to Laura

Wednesday 21

Cold Northeast storm.....went on picket.....awful muddy.....a private of Company B fell down a bank 30 or 40 feet into the river.....nothing found but his cap and his gun

Thursday, January 22, 1863

Cold and Stormy.....stood picket 6 hours last night like to froze.....Came off picket about 12 o'clock.....Received a letter from Mary

Friday 23

*Warm and Cloudy.....Burnside stuck in the mud.....troops all went back to camp.....Saw John driving team.....Cleaned out Brigade salter.....3 men wounded.....received a letter from C.J.G. (*salter: a place where a person treats meat with salt)

Saturday 24

Pleasant this morning.....Cloudy this afternoon.....we built us a fireplace..... officers got drunk last night.....troops going back to Camp today

Sunday, January 25, 1863

Pleasant today.....found the body of the fellow that was drowned

Monday 26

Cloudy morning.....went on guard around camp.....funeral of the private that was drowned.....Pleasant afternoon

Tuesday 27

Rainy.....came of guard at nine O'clock.....went on picket.....slept in Maj Lacy's House of the rebel army

Wednesday, January 28, 1863

Commenced snowing about 5 O'clock this morning.....came off picket about 9..... snowed all day.....received a letter from father, Luther Thomas..... driving rain

Thursday 29

Snowed all night.....the snow is about 6 inches deep.....it has cleared off warm and the snow is melting

Friday 30

Pleasant & warm.....the snow and mud is knee deep.....received a letter from Francis and CJG.....wrote to CJG.....Gen'l Hooker took Command today

Saturday, January 31, 1863

Cloudy & warm.....snow is melting.....wrote to father

Sunday, February 1

Cloudy & warm..... snow most all gone.....~~received a letter from Charles~~

Monday 2

Pleasant but cool.....rained a little last night.....went on Battalion drill..... wrote to Mary

Tuesday, February 3, 1863

Cold & squally.....received a letter from Charley.....went on picket

Wednesday 4

Cold & fair.....the ground froze up solid.....stood six hours on picket.last night death of another private of Company A

Thursday 5

Cold & snowing.....part of the Company was on picket

Friday, February 6, 1863

Pleasant.....snow all gone.....mud about 3 inches deep.....wrote to CJG

Saturday 7

Pleasant & warm.....Cold last night.....mud about the same as yesterday..... Washing day.....orders to move

Sunday 8

Pleasant & warm.....mud about 6 inches deep.....orders to move tomorrow morning.....going on transport

Monday, February 9, 1863

Pleasant & warm.....left camp.....took the cars at Falmouth Station for Aquia Creek.....Arrived there about noon.....went abord the Steamer Louisiana..... lay in channel.....start in the morning

Tuesday 10

Pleasant & warm.....started this morning at daybreak.....had a first rate ride.....Regiments aboard 5-1 PX 21MV & 35 MV.....passed 3 Gunboats

Wednesday 11

Cloudy with a little rain.....warm.....anchored last night at 12 ½ Oclock off Fortress Munroe.....left about 7 this morning for Newport News.....arrived there about 2.....pitched camp.....saw a Monitor wreck of Cumberland

Thursday, February 12, 1863

Pleasant & warm.....went down town and down on the beach.....had a good time.....wrote to Francis

Friday 13

Pleasant & cool.....on guard.....had a Brigade guard mount.....received our box

Saturday 14

Pleasant.....wrote to Francis.....came off guard.....raining this evening

Sunday, February 15, 1863

Pleasant & warm.....rainy last night.....went on inspection.....wrote to Hattie.....received a letter from Mother

Monday 16

Pleasant & warm.....went on drill twice today.....received a letter from Laura and a paper from Mary Young

Tuesday 17

Stormy.....wrote to mother.....nothing to do

Wednesday, February 18, 1863

Stormy.....wrote to CJG.....nothing to do but help the cook

Thursday 19

Cloudy & warm.....received new winter tents.....received a letter from CJG

Friday 20

Pleasant & warm.....moved into our new tents Eli Garfield Albert Sherman and I in one tent.....received a paper from CJG

Saturday, February 21, 1863

Pleasant & warm in the morning.....Cold before night.....built a tent for Capt Dolan.....Albert on guard.....Colonel Curruth and Adjutant just returned (Dennis Dolan of Boston Captain of Company D)

Sunday 22

Snow storm last night.....Al had the teeth ache and I stood guard for him..... Washingtons birthday

Monday 23

Cold & rainy.....Colonel Curruth took command.....Leut Hudson in command of Company.....received a letter from Mary & Lou

Tuesday, February 24, 1863

Pleasant & warm.....Had a Brigade drill.....Adjutant Wales acting Major on Gen staff

Wednesday 25

Pleasant & warm.....Had a review by Gen Smith of the 9th Army Corps..... quite a number of ladies present.....the first I have seen for a long time (Major General William F. Smith succeeded General Sedgwick for a very short time)

Thursday 26

Pleasant this morning.....raining this afternoon.....Had a battalion drill..... wrote to Addie Tower and CJG.....funeral of private of Co. P

Friday, February 27, 1863

Pleasant.....Albert and I on guard.....had a game of ball.....there was a dance here in front of our Regt.....no ladies present

Saturday 28

Cloudy with a little rain.....mustered in for our pay.....the Government owes us for four month

Sunday, March 1

Pleasant and warm.....wrote to MAJ.....the Chaplain preached his farewell sermon and is going home

Monday, March 2, 1863

Pleasant & warm.....went on Brigade drill.....had a game of ball

Tuesday 3

Pleasant & warm.....had a game of ball in the morning.....went on Brigade drill in the afternoon then drilled with the Bayonet

Wednesday 4

Cloudy & Cold.....not much drilling today.....received a letter from father

Thursday, March 5, 1863

Pleasant but Cold.....funeral for a private of Company F.....Damon of this camp died this morning.....received a letter from father last night (Private Zachariah Damon of Weymouth died 3-5-1863, at Newport News)

Friday 6

Pleasant but cold.....no duty to do.....excused from guard by the Adjutant General.....Funeral of Damon

Saturday 7

Cloudy but warm.....nothing to do today.....washing day.....Received four letters.....one from Francis Clara Powers W J Forsyth & CJG (Clara Powers, seventeen year old daughter of Abijah and Delia Powers)

Sunday, March 8, 1863

Pleasant & warm.....went on inspection.....wrote to Mary

Monday 9

Pleasant in the afternoon Cloudy morning.....had an inspection by the Inspector General.....wrote to CJG

Tuesday 10

Cold Northeast storm today.....nothing to do.....wrote to father

Wednesday, March 11, 1863

Stormy morning.....pleasant afternoon.....played Ball

Thursday 12

Pleasant & cold.....had a drill.....played Ball.....wrote to Francis & Charles.....Received a letter from Addie Tower & CJG.....Campbell went home on a furlough

Friday 13

Pleasant & cold.....movements of troops.....received a letter from Hattie..... had two drills......John Wheeler went home on a furlough

Saturday, March 14, 1863

Pleasant & cold.....nothing to do today but wash.....part of this Brigade gone into barracks

Sunday 15

Cloudy & cold.....Albert and I are on guard

Monday 16

Cloudy & rainy.....Came off guard.....went on Battalion drill this afternoon

Tuesday, March 17, 1863

Pleasant & warm.....had two Battalion drills today.....had a game of ball..... Wrote to CJG, Rufus & Bill got their box.....orders to be ready to start at a moments notice

Wednesday 18

Stormy afternoon.....went on a pass to Fortress Munroe

Thursday 19

Stormy & cold.....wrote to Laura.....received a letter from Hattie and Ellen

Friday, March 20, 1863

Snowstorm.....snow about 4 in deep and still snowing.....part of the Regt on picket.....Albert sick

Saturday 21

Still snowing.....snow about 8 inches deep.....Cold & Freezing.....wrote to cousin Lucretia (Lucretia Smith, twenty-five year old daughter of Joseph and Olive Moore Smith (sister of Uriah))

Sunday 22

Weather moderated.....raining this morning.....cleared off about 9 oclock and warm.....went on a pass to Fortress Munroe.....wrote to C. A. Powers

Monday, March 23, 1863

Pleasant & warm.....nothing to do this forenoon.....drill this afternoon..... Received a letter from CJG.....Capt Dolan got his discharge

Tuesday 24

Pleasant & warm.....wrote to Hattie and Ellen

Wednesday 25

Cloudy & warm.....went down to the fort.....Capt Dolan went home today

Thursday, March 26, 1863

Pleasant & warm.....Mr. Campbell came back today.....brought a package for me.....Received a letter from Allie Mary Charlie and Father.....struck tent and are ready to move.....going aboard boat tonight

Friday 27

Pleasant & warm.....Left Newport News last night.....reached Baltimore about 2 oclock today went aboard the cars about 6 PM

Saturday 28

*Stormy on board the cars.....stoped at Mifflin and got some hot coffee.....
stoped at Altoona about 8 oclock last night and got some hot coffee*

Sunday, March 29, 1863

*Stormy.....arrived at Pittsburg.....had a good breakfast.....went aboard the
cars bound for Cincinnati*

Monday 30

*Cloudy.....rode all day .....*arrived at Cincinnati about 9 oclock last night.....
took supper crossed the river into Covington Ky about three this morning.....
lay in the street.....wrote to father

Tuesday 31

*Cloudy..... arrived at Cincinnati about 9 oclock last night.....took supper.....
crossed the river in Covington Ky about 9 this morning.....lay in street.....
wrote to Father*

Wednesday, April 1, 1863

*Pleasant.....took the cars for Paris.....arrived here about 7 PM.....Colonel
Clark in command of Brigade.....Ferrero in command of division* (Lieutenant
Colonel Charles S. Clark of the Twenty-first Massachusetts in command of
the Seconed Brigade, IX Corps)

Thursday 2

*Pleasant.....slept in the Baptist church last night.....played on the organ.....
wrote to CJG*

Friday 3

*Cold and cloudy.....started for Mt Sterling about 8 this morning.....arrived
within a mile of the town.....went into camp about 7 PM*

Saturday, April 4, 1863

*Pleasant and cool.....broke camp.....marched through the town of Mt
Sterling.....Camped about a mile the other side.....Al and me on guard*

Sunday 5

*Pleasant and warm.....came off guard.....a lot of citizens in camp today.....
both ladies & gentlemen.....part of the Regt went to town to meeting*

Monday 6

*Pleasant & cool.....Ferrero took command today.....had a lot of work to do
today*

Tuesday, April 7, 1863

Pleasant and warm.....went on drill.....nothing else to do

Wednesday 8

*Pleasant & warm.....on guard.....Maj King came to the Regt today.....brought
us some U.S. colours*

Thursday 9

*Pleasant & warm.....came off guard.....received a letter from Laura and
CJG*
    Friday, April 10, 1863
*Pleasant & warm.....nothing to eat today.....Mustered in to the service to
see how many men we have going to fill up with conscripts*

Saturday 11

*Pleasant & warm.....nothing to eat but one ration of fresh meat.....nothing
to do.....Al on picket.....wrote to Alfred*

Sunday 12

Pleasant.....Went on picket.....got some rations last night

Monday, April 13, 1863

Pleasant and warm.....wrote to CJG.....came off picket

Tuesday 14

*Cloudy forenoon.....rainy afternoon.....nothing to do..... Paymaster in
camp.....Pay rolls come*

Wednesday 15

Cloudy & warm.....signed the pay rolls

Thursday, April 16, 1863

Cloudy & warm.....went on picket.....got a letter from Francis and M A Jones.....had a good supper at a Gentlemans house.....Gen Ferrero discharged.....Col Hartranft in command

Friday 17

Pleasant & hot.....came off picket about 12 o'clock last night.....started on a march about 3.....went about 19 miles.....went into camp about 9 PM at Winchester

Saturday 18

Pleasant and warm.....received a letter from CJG.....got four months pay

Sunday, April 19, 1863

Cloudy & rainy.....wrote to Mary.....Al and I sent home 60 dollars.....went on inspection

Monday 20

Pleasant & warm.....went to the town of winchester.....had a tip top time

Tuesday 21

Cloudy & warm.....got my picture taken.....wrote to Addie Tower.....sent her Als and Bills and my pictures

Wednesday, April 22, 1863

Pleasant and warm.....wrote to CJG.....went on two drills.....Al sent his and my picture to father.....I sent one to CJG

Thursday 23

Stormy.....nothing to do

Friday 24

Pleasant & warm.....went on two drills.....Played ball

Saturday, April 25, 1863

Pleasant & warm.....washing day.....nothing to do but go on dress parade

Sunday 26

Cloudy & cool.....a tip top day.....Al and me on guard.....Negro drill & dance

Monday 27

Pleasant & warm.....came off guard at 9AM.....nothing to do today.....wrote to Francis

Tuesday, April 28, 1863

Stormy.....nothing to do.....wrote to John William Forsyth and George Smith received a letter from CJG

Wednesday 29

Stormy.....nothing to do

Thursday 30

Pleasant & warm.....Fast day.....we were mustered in for two months pay..... had a review by Gen Sturgis.....lot of ladies present

Friday, May 1, 1863

Pleasant & warm.....went on drill.....had a drill this forenoon...nothing else to do

Saturday, 2

Pleasant & warm.....washing day.....no drilling today.....wrote to CJG

Sunday 3

Stormy forenoon.....went on picket.....had a thunder shower at night..... expect to move tomorrow

Monday, May 4, 1863

Stormy......came off picket about 11 oclock last night......started on a march about 9 oclock this morning......received a letter from father......went into camp about 5 PM......marched about 13 miles

Tuesday 5

Stormy......started on a march about 8 o'clock this morning......went through Lexington......camped about 5 PM......went about 13 miles

Wednesday 6

Pleasant & cool......marched about 17 miles......went into camp about 5 PM......raining......marched through Nicholasville

Thursday May 7, 1863

Stormy......started on a march about 9 Oclock this morning......went about 14 miles......went into camp about 5 PM......went through Bryantsville & Lancaster

Friday 8

Stormy......started this morning about 7....went through.......went into camp about 11 ½
.....marched about 10 miles

Saturday 9

Pleasant and warm......washing day......no marching......wrote Father and Charlie

Sunday, May 10, 1863

Pleasant & cool......started on a march about 8......went to Lancaster about 10 miles in 4 hours......received a letter from Mary

Monday 11

Pleasant & warm......went on drill and inspection

Tuesday 12

Pleasant & cool.....went on drill and inspection.....received a letter from Hattie and Addie Tower

Wednesday, May 13, 1863

Stormy.....nothing to do.....wrote to Mother Mary & Hattie.....My birthday and John Morse's.....received a letter from Francis

Thursday 14

Pleasant & cool.....went on drill.....Gen Sturgis came to see our dress parade.....received a letter from cousin Leu

Friday 15

Pleasant & cool....we......had two drills.....orders to be ready to march at a moments notice

Saturday, May 16, 1863

Pleasant & cool.....washing day.....nothing to do.....received a letter from CJG & George Smith.....no movement yet

Sunday 17

Pleasant & cool.....went on picket.....no movement yet

Monday 18

Pleasant & cool.....came off picket.....moved our camp

Tuesday, May 19, 1863

Pleasant and cool.....nothing to do today but clean up our camp.....wrote to CJG.....played on fiddle

Wednesday 20

Pleasant & warm.....wrote to Addie Tower.....had two drills.....played on fiddle.....Chas Reed came to the company

Thursday 21

Pleasant & warm.....had two drills.....Burns tied to a tree by the thumbs

Friday, May 22, 1863

Pleasant & warm.....went on two drills.....orders to march tomorrow

Saturday 23

Pleasant & warm.....started on a march about 7 oclock this morning.....went into camp about 4 Oclock PM.....marched about 10 miles

Sunday 24

Pleasant and warm.....lay in camp all day.....marching countermanded..... received a letter from John.....wrote to Francis

Monday, May 25, 1863

Pleasant and warm.....marched this morning about 8 AM.....went about 2 ½ miles.....went into camp.....stayed until 6 PM.....got orders to go further..... passed through Crab Orchard

Tuesday 26

Pleasant and warm.....marched last night at 7 PM.....went 10 miles.....passed through Stanford.....went into camp about 12 Oclock.....received a letter from CJG

Wednesday 27

Pleasant and cool.....nothing to do today.....wrote to George Smith.....some of our Regt on provost duty downtown

Thursday, May 28, 1863

Cloudy and cool.....had two drills.....one a Brigade drill.....wrote to CJG

Friday 29

Cloudy morning.....commenced storming about noon.....rained all the afternoon.....had a skirmish drill this morning

Saturday 30

Cloudy and cool.....went on picket.....had a good dinner

Sunday, May 31, 1863

Stormy.....came off picket about 10 oclock.....pleasant afternoon

Monday, June 1

Pleasant.....went on two drills.....received a letter from Mother & W J Forsyth

Tuesday 2

Pleasant cool.....went on two drills.....Gen Ferrero came into camp

Wednesday 3, 1863

*Pleasant & cool.....went on drill.....rained last night.....orders to be ready to move.....started about 5PM.....went through Lancaster 15 miles.....*went into camp about

Thursday 4

Pleasant.....started last night about 5 PM.....went about 15 miles.....went into camp about 12.....started this AM about 7.....went to Nicholasville.....took the cars for Covington

Friday 5

*Pleasant....*started this morning about 7 AM and marched......*arrived in Covington about 8 this morning.....crossed the river into Cincinnati.....took the cars about 6 PM*

Saturday, June 6, 1863

Pleasant.....rode all day.....got a white handkerchief last night at Laurenceburg, Ind and had dinner in this state

Sunday 7

Cloudy forenoon......stormy afternoon.....arrived here (Cairo) about 6 AM..... took supper last night at Centralia, Ill.....wrote to Mother

Monday 8

*Pleasant.....went aboard the transport Imperial bound for Memphis.....
received a letter from Mary, Allie and Addie Tower signed our pay rolls*

Tuesday, June 9, 1863

*Cloudy and rainy.....rode all day.....passed island No.10.....wrote to Mary
and Alfred.....got stuck this morning in the sand*

Wednesday 10

*Pleasant.....arrived at Memphis about 5 PM.....went into town.....got a
supper.....cooked 3 days rations.....paid off*

Thursday 11

*Pleasant.....went into town.....had a good time.....On guard aboard the
boat.....sent home 20 dollars for me and Al*

Friday, June 12, 1863

*Pleasant.....started down the river this morning.....stoped at Helena, Ark.....
came of guard at 9 AM*

Saturday 13

Pleasant & warm.....rode all day.....passed a number of gun boats

Sunday 14

*Pleasant and warm.....landed at youngs Point Louisiana within sight of
Vicksburg.....saw mortors shelling the city from the boats*

Monday, June 15, 1863

*Cloudy.....left camp.....marched about 4 miles below Vicksburg.....went
aboard the boats to cross the river.....got off again went back to our camp.....
wrote to John and Lu*

Tuesday 16

*Cloudy.....went abord the boat.....went up the Yazoo river.....stoped us about
18 mls.....slept abord the boat.....raining afternoon*

Wednesday 17

Stormy morning.....went ashore at snyders bluff.....marched about 15 miles.....went into camp.....went berrying on picket.....saw Gen Washburn (Major General Cadwallader C. Washburn led detachment of IX Corps)

Thursday, June 18, 1863

Pleasant.....picked about 6 qats blackberries.....came off picket about 1 PM.....Saw Gen Parks.....he is in comd of this corps (Major General John Parke, Chief of Staff under General Burnside for much of the war and then Commander after General Burnsides retirement).

Friday 19

Pleasant.....nothing to do today but clean up our camp.....Gen Potter headquarters near us (General Robert Brown Potter Commanded the Seconded Division of the IX Corps.)

Saturday 20

Pleasant.....Washing day.....the rebs tried to come out last night.....got drove back

Sunday, June 21, 1863

Pleasant & warm.....Cleaned our camp.....wrote a letter to Addie Tower.....
George Spring returned (Corporal George Spring, Waltham, Massachusetts, Thirty-fifth Regiment, Massachusetts, Company D)

Monday 22

Pleasant & warm.....went drill this morning.....nothing else to do but clean up camp.....orders to cook three days rations

Tuesday 23

Pleasant.....went out to dig rifle pits all day.....moved our camp

Wednesday, June 24, 1863

Pleasant & warm.....put up a tent.....nothing else to do

Thursday 25

*Pleasant & warm.....part of Regt diging trenches.....I have nothing to do.....
wrote to Ed Moulton & Bill Forsyth*

Friday 26

*Pleasant & warm.....nothing to do today.....went down to the landing with
Corpl Sherman* (Corporal Hiram G. Sherman, Waltham, Massachusetts,
Thirty-fifth, Massachusetts, Company D).

Saturday, June 27, 1863

Cloudy morning.....went to diging rifle pits.....dug all day

Sunday 28

*Pleasant & warm.....went on inspection.....wrote to Hattie.....nothing else
to do*

Monday 29

*Pleasant & warm.....went out to dig rifle pits.....went back to camp.....packed
up started on a march.....went about 7 miles*

Tuesday, June 30, 1863

*Pleasant & warm.....pitched our camp this morning.....saw Gen Sherman.....
Cleaned up our camp.....nothing else to do*

Wednesday, July 1

Pleasant & warm.....nothing to do today

Thursday 2

*Pleasant & warm.....Al left cook house.....had dress parade.....mustered
for two months pay.....death of Kiley of this company* (Henry Kiley of
Randolph, Massachusetts died at Mill Dale Mississippi)

Friday, July 3, 1863

*Pleasant & warm.....commenced cooking for Company.....rest to digging
rifle pits*

Saturday 4

Pleasant & warm.....Vicksburg surrendered.....received the first mail in Mississippi.....rcevd letters from Father, Francis, Hattie, Clara Powers, CJG & Capt Dolan.....started out on a march at 5 PM.....went into camp about 10 PM

Sunday 5

Pleasant & warm.....went into camp last night about 10 PM.....started this morning about 7 AM.....went about 3 miles.....went into camp

Monday, July 6, 1863

Pleasant & warm.....nothing to do.....received a letter from George Smith..... had a shower in the evening

Tuesday 7

Pleasant & warm.....wrote to father & CJG.....started on march about 1 PM..... cross the big Black.....went into camp at 12 PM.....had a thundershower..... got all wet

Wednesday 8

Pleasant & warm.....Lt Hawes QM killed by a tree falling on him yesterday..... started on a march at 5 ½ PM

Thursday, July 9, 1863

Pleasant & warm.....started to march about 8 AM.....went into camp about 8 PM.....buried a horse on the way

Friday 10

Pleasant & warm.....went into camp last night about 10 PM.....started this morning about 7 AM.....went into camp about 8 PM near Jackson

Saturday 11

Pleasant & warm.....slept with our arms last night.....broke camp about 9 AM.....formed line of battle came under the hill.....few shots passing over our heads.....volunteered to go on skirmish

Sunday, July 12, 1863

Cloudy morning with a little rain.....went on skirmish.....C. Wheeler & A. Webber were wounded.....10 wounded in Regt.....had a letter from Alfred last night

Monday 13

Cloudy.....came of skirmish about 3 AM.....lay in valley to support the skirmishes.....I was sent back to cook for the company

Tuesday 14

Cloudy.....Regt came back out of the field about 6 AM.....another Regt took their place.....Al and I are company cooks.....orders to move tomorrow

Wednesday July 15, 1863

Cloudy.....moved about ½ mile into camp.....stoped all day.....orders to be ready to move in the morning at 2 Oclock

Thursday 16

Pleasant.....Regt went to front about 2 AM.....had a little fight today..... Rufus birthday

Friday 17

Pleasant.....Marched into Jackson at daybreak.....our Regt first there.....took a lot of prisoners.....raised our flag on court house

Saturday, July 18, 1863

Cloudy.....went back to our old camp last night.....having a rest today

Sunday 19

Pleasant & warm.....not much to do today.....got orders to march at four oclock.....packed up got all ready then didnt go

Monday 20

Pleasant.....started on a march about 7 AM.....went about 20 miles.....passed by Clinton.....went into camp about 10 PM.....received a letter from CJG

Tuesday, July 21, 1863

Pleasant & warm.....started this morning about 4½ Oclock.....went about 18 miles.....went into camp near the Big Black.....passed through Brownsville

Wednesday 22

Pleasant & warm.....started about 4 PM.....crossed the Big Black.....had a big shower.....got wet through.....went into camp about 10 PM.....slept in a barn

Thursday 23

Pleasant & warm.....started about 4 AM.....arrived at our old camp at Milldale about 11 AM.....pitched tents.....probably stop here two or three days

Friday, July 24, 1863

Pleasant & warm.....not much to do today.....expect to go to Ky in a few days

Saturday 25

Pleasant & warm.....had to cook three days rations of meat last night..... cooked all night.....Sergt Hayes had a fit.....took us about a half an hour to bring him to

Sunday 26

Pleasant & warm.....nothing to do.....had a big shower

Monday, July 27, 1863

Pleasant & warm.....nothing to do today.....had a big shower.....wrote to CJG

Tuesday 28

Pleasant & warm.....not much to do today.....wrote to Marion & Geo Jones

Wednesday 29

Pleasant & warm.....not much to do today.....went down to landing.....got some flour

Thursday, July 30, 1863

Pleasant & warm.....not much to do today.....death and funeral of a private of company J

Friday 31

Pleasant & warm.....Regt on picket.....one year ago today that I enlisted

Saturday 1

Pleasant & warm.....Regt came off picket about 10 AM.....had a big shower

Sunday, August 2, 1863

Pleasant & cool.....not much to do today.....had a shower

Monday 3

Pleasant & warm.....nothing happened today.....First division going up the river.....considerable to do today.....Grant ordered Vicksburg & Jackson to be put on our Banners

Tuesday 4

Pleasant & cool.....not much to do today.....Wrote to Nellie Gerry.....troops going off every day

Wednesday 5

Pleasant & warm.....not much to do today.....wrote to Capt Dolan

Thursday 6

Cloudy & cool.....cooked 5 days rations.....went abord the transport Planet .....5 Regts aboard 51NY, 79N.Y. 45P.V. 11N.H. & 35 MVM

Friday 7

Pleasant & warm.....started last night about 9 oclock.....traveled on road all day

Saturday, August 8, 1863

Pleasant & warm.....road all day and all night last night.....passed Napolean this morning

Sunday 9

Pleasant & warm.....rode all night last night.....pass Helenor.....arrived at Memphis about 3 ½ PM.....went ashore.....cooked rations.....went into the city

Monday 10

Pleasant & warm.....started for Cairo about 11 AM.....passed Helenor..... wrote to Francis

Tuesday, August 11, 1863

Pleasant & warm.....rode all day.....passed New Madried and Island No 10

Wednesday 12

Pleasant & warm.....passed Columbus.....landed at Cairo about 8 AM..... cooked rations.....went aboard the cars about 5 PM

Thursday 13

Pleasant & warm.....stoped at Centralia.....took breakfast.....rode all day..... took supper at Vincennes

Friday, August 14, 1863

Pleasant & warm.....arrived at Cincinnati about 4 PM.....took dinner..... crossed the river into Covington.....went into camp about 8 PM

Saturday 15

Pleasant & warm.....not much to do today but clean up camp.....wrote to Hattie

Sunday 16

Pleasant & warm.....wrote to C. A. Powers.....orders to cook three days rations and move tomorrow at daylight.....had a shower

Monday, August 17, 1863

Pleasant & warm.....did not move today.....move tomorrow.....received a letter from CJG.....wrote to CJG

Tuesday 18

Pleasant & warm.....started on march this morning.....went about 16 mls..... passed through Latonia & Florence

Wednesday 19

Pleasant & warm.....started this morning about sunrise.....went 11 mls..... went through Walton & Crittenden

Thursday, August 20, 1863

Pleasant & warm.....started this morning about 5 oclock.....went 28 miles..... passed through Williamstown

Friday 21

Pleasant & warm.....started this morning at 9 Oclock.....went 12 miles..... went into camp about 1 PM

Saturday 22

Pleasant & warm.....started this morning about 9 Oclock.....went 21 miles..... went through Georgetown and Paris.....went into camp at Paris

Sunday, August 23, 1863

Pleasant.....Staid in camp all day today.....funeral of a private of Company H.....died yesterday.....Got trusted at a store in Paris

Monday 24

Pleasant.....started this morning at 6 oclock.....went through Lexington..... went into camp near Nicholasville

Tuesday 25

Stormy & cold.....started this morning at 6 oclock.....went through Nicholasville.....went into camp about 5 miles from Nicholasville

Wednesday, August 26, 1863

Pleasant —— today.....signed the pay roll

Thursday 27

Pleasant & cool.....not much to do today.....wrote to Mary.....received a letter from CJG John

Friday 28

Stormy.....nothing to do today

Saturday, August 29, 1863

Pleasant & cool.....nothing to do today.....went into town on a pass.....went to a concert

Sunday 30

Pleasant.....on guard.....wrote to Mary & CJG.....went on inspection

Monday 31

Pleasant.....came off guard about 9 AM.....were mustered for two months pay

Tuesday, September 1, 1863

Pleasant.....went on two drills.....received a letter from C.J.G.

Wednesday 2

Pleasant.....went on two drills.....nothing else to do.....went about 3 miles after some milk for breakfast

Thursday 3

Pleasant.....wrote to CJG.....Got promoted to Corpl

Friday, September 4, 1863

Pleasant.....received a letter from Geo Smith and Ed Molton *Dick and wrote to Mother & Ellen*

Saturday 5

Pleasant & warm.....nothing to do.....washing day.....signed our pay rolls..... got paid off

Sunday 6

Cloudy.....went to Nicholasville about 1 AM.....staid until about 12.....took the cars for Covington.....got there about 9 PM

Monday, September 7, 1863

Pleasant & warm.....went to Cov.....had a tip top time.....saw Alex and the rest of the boys.....got a pr pant & a shirt

Tuesday 8

Pleasant.....started for Lexington with Ambulances about 10 AM.....passed through Florence and Walton

Wednesday 9

Pleasant.....had a shower last night.....started this morning about 7 Oclock..... passed through Crittenden.....went into camp at Eagle Bridge

Thursday, September 10, 1863

Pleasant.....started this morning about 6 Oclock.....passed through Georgetown and Lexington.....went into camp at Lexington

Friday 11

Pleasant.....started this morning abo with the wagons about 7 arrived at our old camp.....Regt gone to Chraborchard

Saturday 12

Pleasant.....started this morning about 10 Oclock.....went into camp at Camp Dick Robinson

Sunday, September 13, 1863

Pleasant.....started this morning at 4 Oclock.....arrived at Craborchard at noon.....went to the Regt

Monday 14

Pleasant.....went on drill.....wrote to Addie Tower

Tuesday 15

Pleasant....went on drill.....wrote to Alfred and John

Wednesday, September 16, 1863

Pleasant.....moved camp.... wrote to.....received a letter from Francis..... went to town on a pass

Thursday 17

Pleasant & cool.....moved our camp about 80 rods.....part of Regt on provost duty down town

Friday 18

Pleasant & cold.....went on two drills.....went to town.....saw 2300 prisoners pass through from Cumberland Gap

Saturday, September 19, 1863

Pleasant & cold.....wrote to Francis.....no duty to do today

Sunday 20

Pleasant & cold.....had a heavy frost last night.....went on guard.....water frozen in the dippers

Monday 21

Pleasant & cool.....came of guard about 6 AM.....went on one drill.....saw a fellow from the 16th Indiana drill.....wrote to Francis

Tuesday, September 22, 1863

Pleasant.....went on drill.....nothing else to do today

Wednesday 23

Pleasant....got orders to go on fatigue.....marched about 10 miles.....went to work on the road

Thursday 24

Pleasant.....worked all this forenoon.....sent for part of the Regt to come back to camp.....expected a rebel raid

Friday, September 25, 1863

Pleasant.....started for camp about 6 AM.....worked most of the way..... arrived there about 3 PM

Saturday 26

Pleasant.....nothing to do today.....wrote to George Smith

Sunday 27

Pleasant.....nothing to do today but go on inspection.....received a letter from Addie Tower & mother

Monday, September 28, 1863

Pleasant.....went to town and went on inspection & dress parade

Tuesday 29

Pleasant.....went on drill.....got a letter from Marion A Jones

Wednesday 30

Pleasant.....nothing to do today.....received a letter from Capt Dolan..... orders to move

Thursday, October 1, 1863

Stormy.....didnt march today on account of rain.....went on picket....expect to start tomorrow for Knoxville

Friday 2

Pleasant.....started this morning about 7 Oclock.....went about 12 mls....went into camp near Mt Vernon

Saturday 3

Pleasant.....started today at 10 AM.....went about 5 miles.....went into camp at Big Springs.....went in a cave.....went through Mt Vernon

Sunday, October 4, 1863

Pleasant & cool.....marched about 12 miles.....started about 7 A. M......went into camp at Little Rockcastle River

Monday 5

Pleasant.....started this morning about 7 Oclock.....went 8 miles in 2 hours and 40 minutes

Tuesday 6

Pleasant.....nothing to do today.....in camp near London

Wednesday, October 7, 1863

Pleasan*t Stormy.....nothing to do today.....wrote to Father.....went to town*

Thursday 8

Pleasant .....nothing else to do.....had dress parade

Friday 9

Pleasant.....went on drill.....nothing else to do.....expect to march tomorrow

Saturday, October 10, 1863

Pleasant.....orders to move at 12 M.....went about 9 mls.....went through London.....went into camp at Laurel creek

Sunday 11

Pleasant.....started this morning at 7 Oclock.....went 20 mls.....went into camp near Barboursville

Monday 12

Pleasant.....started this morning at 7 Oclock.....went about 16 mls.....went into camp at Cumberland Ford

Tuesday, October 13, 1863

Stormy.....started this morning about 7 Oclock.....marched about 12 mls..... went into camp near Cumberland Gap

Wednesday 14

Cloudy & stormy.....started about 8 Oclock.....marched about 15 mls.....went into camp near Tazewell Tenn.....Then went through Cumberland Gap..... saw Parson Brownlow and family

Thursday 15

Pleasant....went to the town of Tazewell Tenn.....had a good time.....wrote to Francis

Friday, October 16, 1863

Stormy.....started this morning about 1 Oclock.....went about 12 miles..... crossed the Clinch River

Saturday 17

Cloudy.....started this morning.....went about 13 miles.....went through Maynardsville

Sunday 18

Stormy.....started this morning about 6 Oclock.....went about 17 miles..... went through (—)stown

Monday, October 19, 1863

Cloudy.....started this morning at 9 Oclock.....went about 14 miles.....went into camp near Knoxville

Tuesday 20

Pleasant.....went on drill.....orders to move tomorrow.....expect to go to Louden bridge about 28 miles from here

Wednesday 21

Stormy.....orders countermanded.....the 1ˢᵗ Brigade had a fight at Louden Bridge yesterday

Thursday, October 22, 1863

Pleasant.....warm.....went to town on a pass.....had a good time.....orders to move this afternoon

Friday 23

Stormy.....left camp last night about 8 Oclock.....slep at depot last night..... took cars for Louden 2 PM.....went through Concord

Saturday 24

Cloudy.....cool.....went into camp near Louden Bridge.....expected a fight..... Burnside drove the Rebs about 6 miles

Sunday, October 25, 1863

Pleasant.....cool.....not much to do today.....received a letter from Francis..... all quiet

Monday 26

Pleasant.....cool.....moved our camp about 100 yards behind a hill.....wagon train got to us today

Tuesday 27

Cloudy & stormy.....had reveille at 2 AM.....went down the river.....troops recrossing took up the Bridge

Wednesday, October 28, 1863

Cloudy.....went into camp last night near the river.....started this morning for Lenoire

Thursday 29

Pleasant.....went into camp yesterday at Lenoire station.....first division went into camp near us.....all quiet

Friday 30

Pleasant.....not much to do today.....first division got orders to build them log houses

Saturday, October 31, 1863

Pleasant.....not much to do today.....everything all quiet.....had to clean up camp today

Sunday, November 1

Pleasant.....nothing to do today.....received a letter from C J Gerry..... everything quiet

Monday 2

Pleasant & warm.....commenced camp duty today.....went on two drills..... everything quiet

Tuesday, November 3, 1863

Cloudy.....went on two drills.....wrote to Mary.....going to commence on our house tomorrow

Wednesday 4

Pleasant & warm.....commenced to work on our house.....received a letter from Father

Thursday 5

Stormy.....not much to do today....went on one drill.....wrote to Francis

Friday, November 6, 1863

Pleasant.....went on two drills.....worked on our house....everything all quiet.....no news

Saturday 7

Pleasant & cool.....washing day.....I am on guard.....Al has gone foraging..... received a letter from Father Lucretia & C J Gerry

Sunday 8

Pleasant.....went on inspection.....wrote to C J Gerry.....went on dress parade

Monday, November 9, 1863

Cold.....had no drill.....went on dress parade.....wrote to father.....Leut Hudson returned.....brought a bundle of letters from mother and Hattie

Tuesday 10

Cold.....went on compy drill.....built us a fireplace.....went on dress parade..... orders for reveille at 5 tomorrow morning

Wednesday 11

Cold.....went on picket over the Clinch River at 4 PM.....laid a pontoon bridge across.....no other duty to do

Thursday, November 12, 1863

Cold.....came off picket about 12 oclock.....went on dress parade.....had a goose stew for supper.....like to froze my but last night Lt Pope under arrest (Lieutenant Albert A. Pope, Boston, Massachusetts, commissioned Seconded Lieutenant , Thirty-fifth Regiment, Massachusetts Volunteers)

Friday 13

Pleasant & cool.....went on two drills.....Al on guard.....went on dress parade

Saturday 14

Stormy.....got up this morning at 2 Oclock.....expect the Rebs destroyed the pontoon Bridge.....first division started for Louden—.....lay in the sun all day

Sunday, November 15, 1863

Pleasant & cold.....revellie at 2 A.M......started for Louden.....1ˢᵗ Brigade had a skirmish with the rebs.....we supported them.....retreated back to Lenoire

Monday 16

Pleasant & cool.....started last night for Knoxville.....had to help the battery through the mud.....had a small fight with the rebs at Campbell station.....4 men wounded

Tuesday 17

Pleasant.....arrived at Knoxville.....went into camp near the city.....building defenses around the city

Wednesday, November 18, 1863

Pleasant.....fighting down on left.....went on skirmish.....didnt see any rebs..... expect them tomorrow

Thursday 19

Pleasant & cool.....on skirmish all night.....came off about 5 A.M.......Regt in the rifle pits.....rebs fired a few shot this morning.....came near hitting Burnside (surrounded by rebs)

Friday 20

Pleasant.....went in to the Rifle pits last night.....detailed as sharpshooters this morning.....went into a house near the Bridge.....rebs fired a shot into the house

Saturday, November 21, 1863

Stormy & cool.....not much to do today.....rebs fired a shell into the house last night.....had a pretty smart firing

Sunday 22

Pleasant & cool.....not much stirring today.....a little cannoning this evening.....living on quarter rations.....heavy firing heard down the river

Monday 23

Pleasant & cool.....a little skirmishing today.....rebs charged on our picket this evening and drove them in.....burned a lot of buildings

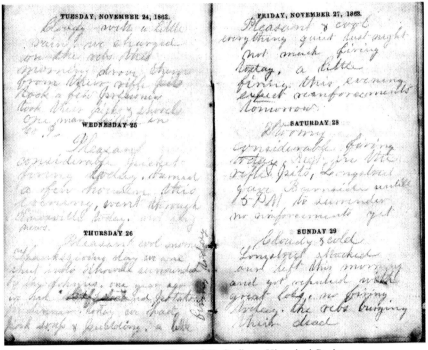

George F. Moore Diary 1863. Sudbury Historical Society

Tuesday, November 24, 1863

Cloudy with a little rain.....we charged on the rebs this morning.....drive them from the rifle pits.....took a few prisoners.....took their picks and shovels.....one man killed in Co J

Wednesday 25

Pleasant.....considerable picket firing today.....burned a few houses in the evening.....went through Knoxville today.....not any news

Thursday 26

Pleasant cool morning.....Thanksgiving day we are shut into Knoxville surrounded by the Johnnies.....one year ago we had beef steak and potatoes for dinner.....today we had pork soup and pudding.....a little firing today

Friday, November 27, 1863

Pleasant & cool.....everything quiet last night.....not much firing today.....a little firing this evening.....expect reinforcements tomorrow

Saturday 28

Stormy.....considerable firing today.....Regt in the rifle pits.....Longstreet gave Burnside until 5 PM to surrender.....no reinforcements yet

Sunday 29

Cloudy & cold.....Longstreet attacked our left this morning and got repelled with great lobs.....no firing today.....the rebs burying their dead

Monday, November 30, 1863

Pleasant & cold.....not much firing today.....froze last night.....Albert went on picket this morning.....had good news from Grant today

Tuesday, December 1

Pleasant & cold.....not much going on this morning.....had a little firing this evening.....had some more good news today

Wednesday 2

Pleasant & cool.....Considerable firing this morning.....thawed some today.....had some pretty heavy firing today

Thursday, December 3, 1863

Pleasant & cool.....thawed some today.....froze last night.....Considerable firing this evening.....nothing new

Friday 4

Pleasant & cold.....not much firing this morning.....thawed considerable today.....heavy firing this evening.....reinforcements coming

Saturday 5

Stormy.....the rebs have gone and left us.....took quite a lot of deserters..... we went out about 5 miles

Sunday, December 6, 1863

Pleasant & warm.....not much doing today.....signed the pay roll 3 ½ P.M...... got paid off.....Saw Gen Sherman and Burnside

Monday 7

Pleasant.....turned out at 6 A.M......started on a march about 7 ½.....went into camp at 3 P.M......went about 12 miles

Tuesday 8

Pleasant & cool.....turned out this morning at 5 Oclock.....started on a march about 11 A.M......went about 6 miles.....went into camp about 4 P.M.

Wednesday, December 9, 1863

Pleasant & cool.....started this morning about 7 ½ Oclock.....went about 14 miles.....went into camp near Rutledge at 2 P.M.

Thursday 10

Pleasant & warm......turned out this morning about 5 Oclock.....expected to march but didnt get started.....reported that we are going back to Knoxville

Friday 11

Pleasant & warm.....nothing to do today.....had a game of cards.....one year ago today was the Bombardment of Fredericksburg

Saturday, December 12

Cloudy & stormy.....turned out this morning about 5 ½ Oclock.....lay in camp all day.....had an inspection of shoes.....received a letter from John

Sunday 13

Stormy.....had an inspection.....went on guard last night.....came off at 11 Oclock.....expect to move in a day or two

Monday 14

Stormy morning.....Cold day.....rained last night.....had no tents with us..... turned out this morning at 5 Oclock.....orders to move at 7.....didnt move

Tuesday, December 15, 1863

Pleasant, cold last night.....Al & Spofford slept in a negros hut.....turned out this morning about 6 Oclock.....formed a line of battle about 11 A.M...... lay there all day

Wednesday 16

Pleasant & cool.....started on a march last night about 7 P.M......marched until about 12½.....started this morning.....went about 6 miles.....formed line of battle about 3 P.M.

Thursday 17

Stormy morning.....lay in line of battle all night.....Cavalry ahead of us..... our pickets were driven in.....we deployed as skirmishes.....fired a few shots at the Jonnies

Friday, December 18, 1863

Cloudy & cold.....on skirmish all night.....ground froze.....we advanced this morning about ¾ of a mile.....saw a few rebs.....relieved about 3 P.M.

Saturday 19

Pleasant & cold.....got paid off last night.....had a good nights rest.....pretty cold.....ground froze.....kept froze all day

Sunday 20

Pleasant & cold.....didnt thaw any today.....received a letter from Francis

Monday, December 21, 1863

Pleasant & cold.....in camp at poo(––)Valley.....received a letter from H G Sherman.....our knapsacks came up to us today.....it is reported that we are going out of the Department

Tuesday 22

Pleasant & cool.....nothing to do today.....I wrote to C J Gerry.....living on short rations.....havent drawn anything today.....shoeless and ragged

Wednesday 23

Pleasant & cool.....advanced our lines about 3 or four miles.....went back to camp.....nothing else to do

Thursday, December 24, 1863

Pleasant & cool.....not much to do.....drawed no rations today.....expect to move one of these days

Friday 25

Pleasant & cool.....nothing to do today.....went foraging.....got christmas dinner.....bought some chickens, molasses, potatos & (––).....got a dollar of B to make (–––).....Had a good time

Saturday 26

Stormy.....rained most all day.....looks like clearing off tonight.....expect to move Monday.....wrote to John.....had a chicken stew for dinner & supper

Sunday, December 27, 1863

Stormy.....rained most all day.....expect to move in a day or two.....went to the 21st(———).....bought a razor and brush

Monday 28

Cloudy.....stormed most all night.....went on picket last night.....no signs of moving today.....went foraging.....got some meal

Tuesday 29

Pleasant & cool.....on picket.....will be relieved tonight......Al went foraging..... got some more meal and some molasses

Wednesday, December 30, 1863

Cloudy & cool.....nothing to do today but clean up for muster tomorrow..... no movement yet

Thursday 31

Stormy day.....stormed all night last night.....mustered in for our pay.....owe us two months.....Sherman returned to the Regt.....gave me a shirt.....loaned him five dollars.....Harry Hale returned with him.....we are going to draw coffee, sugar, pork, and beans tomorrow for new year

George F. Moore

1864 Diary

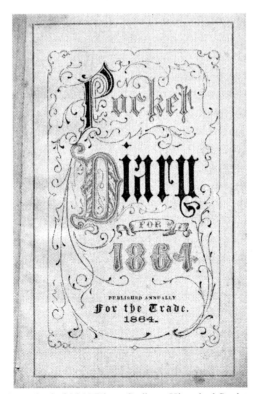

Inner leaf of 1864 Diary, Sudbury Historical Society

Friday, January 1, 1864

Pleasn & cold....Camped at Blanes Cross Road.....nothing to do.....living on half rations.....have not got much clothing.....dont know when we shall get any.....almost barefoot.....ground covered with snow

Saturday, January 2, 1864

Cloudy & Cold.....nothing to do today.....Corpl Spring detailed.....Spofford and Campbell went foraging.....got some pork corn molasses dried peaches 3c.....Gen Grant at Knoxville.....report that Longstreet has left East Tenn..... no clothing yet

Sunday, January 3, 1864

Cloudy & Cold.....nothing to do.....Hall & Bowen went foraging.....got some corn and corn cakes.....rained a little today.....no clothing yet

Monday, January 4, 1864

Stormy & cool.....nothing to do today.....rumor that we are going to Newport News.....wrote to Francis.....no clothing yet

Tuesday, January 5, 1864

Pleasant & cool.....nothing to do today.....no clothing yet.....the 21ˢᵗ Mass expected to start for home in a day or two.....what did not reenlist are coming into our Regt

Wednesday, January 6, 1864

Stormy.....nothing to do.....played cards with John Morse and Geo Spofford.....no clothing yet.....didnt get any mail.....awful dull

Thursday, January 7, 1864

Stormy.....nothing to do.....Corpl Marchant went on picket for me.....the ground is covered with snow.....no clothing yet.....the 21ˢᵗ Mass started for home today.....some of the boys came into our Regt.....the Regt took some prisoners with them

Friday, January 8, 1864

Pleasant & cold.....the ground covered with snow.....nothing to do.....wrote to Addie Tower.....no clothing.....almost barefoot.....gave us some rawhides to make a covering for our feet.....living on half rations yet

Saturday, January 9, 1864

Pleasant & cold.....had a cold night.....Corpl Sherman and I went foraging..... got some meal.....had a good supper at Mr Joffers.....hard traveling.....went about 7 miles

Sunday, January 10, 1864

Pleasant & cold.....nothing to do.....had an awful cold night.....troops going up the river.....rumored that Longstreet offored to surrender all but his officers.....no clothing yet.....snow on the ground

Monday, January 11, 1864

Pleasant & cold.....had the coldest night we have had this season.....nothing to do.....no clothing yet.....thawed a little this afternoon.....played cards with Al, Campbell and Spofford this evening (George A. Spofford, Company D of Wayland)

Tuesday, January 12, 1864

Pleasant & warm.....nothing to do.....Al and Campbell went foraging.....got some corn and pork.....no clothing yet.....wrote to Hattie

Wednesday, January 13, 1864

Cloudy.....went on picket.....warm day.....no clothing.....expect some every day

Thursday, January 14, 1864

Pleasant & warm.....ground thawed today.....came off picket about 10 AM.....got some shoes today.....expect more clothing in a day or two

Friday, January 15, 1864

Cloudy & warm.....nothing to do.....Al went on picket.....orders to move tomorrow.....everything quiet

Saturday, January 16, 1864

no entry

Sunday, January 17, 1864

no entry

Monday, February 15, 1864

Stormy & cool.....Received this Diary today.....started on a march about 10 AM.....went about 4 mls.....went into camp.....rained all day.....Al & W Bowen were left at our old camp.....both lame and couldnt walk

Tuesday, February 16, 1864

Pleasant & cool.....had a cold night.....slept with Rufus.....detailed for guard on the Ammunition train.....awful cold.....sent in a requisition for clothing

Wednesday, February 17, 1864

Cloudy & cold....snowed some today.....awful cold night last night.....slept in a corn barn near Gen Wilcox's headquarters.....not much to do today..... only to keep warm

Thursday, February 18, 1864

Cloudy & Cold.....snowed today.....cold night.....slept in the old corn barn last night.....went to camp.....had orders to move.....went about 1 ml..... headquarters in Knoxville.....Awful cold

Friday, February 19, 1864

Pleasant & cold.....pretty cold last night.....slept in an old barn with some straw in it.....not much to do today.....went through town.....got some bread..... weather more moderate today.....wrote to Father

Saturday, February 20, 1864

Pleasant & cool.....Cold last night.....slept in an old barn on some straw..... not much to do today.....went to the Regt.....got a letter from Clara.....drew rations for 9 days.....no news.....all quiet

Sunday, February 21, 1864

Pleasant & cool.....nothing to do.....went to camp.....got our rations.....had some beans and rice for dinner.....all quiet.....teams drawing wood into town

Monday, February 22, 1864

Pleasant & warm.....Washingtons birthday.....not much to do today.....went into town.....wrote to Clara.....Al got Ellen's and Edgars pictures.....Col Carruth arrived here tonight.....said the 9th Corps were going North soon

Tuesday, February 23, 1864

Pleasant & warm.....nothing to do.....Al and Corpl Sherman came over here today.....went to town.....got some bread......all quiet.....rumor that the Rebels are retaliating and that the first Division were going over the Mountain soon

Wednesday, February 24, 1864

Pleasant & warm.....Regt & Corps started for Strawberry plain.....light marching order.....had a thunder shower.....quite a heavy shower.....went to town.....got some bread.....saw Edgars & Ellen's pictures yesterday..... the Rebels have left here

Thursday, February 25, 1864

Pleasant – warm.....nothing to do.....went to town.....got some bread.....saw a lot of prisoners go aboard the cars bound for Chattanooga.....expect to start for the Plains tomorrow.....turned over the Ammunition.....wrote to Mary and M A Jones

Friday, February 26, 1864

Pleasant & cool.....started for Strawberry plains about 10 A.M......arrived there about 4 ½ P.M......orders to march tomorrow.....left our knapsacks at the Depot.....Col Carruth in command of the Brigade

Saturday, February 27, 1864

Pleasant & cool.....started on a march about 8 A.M......crossed the river in boats.....went about 1 mile.....went into camp.....lot of troops here.....expect a long march.....Al left behind with a lame foot.....Col Carruth in command of Brigade

Sunday, February 28, 1864

Pleasant & warm.....drew two days rations of meat.....started on a march at 10 ½ A.M......went about 14 mls.....went into camp at Mossy Creek.....went through the Village of Friends Station, New Market and Mossy Creek

Monday, February 29, 1864

Stormy.....started on a march about 7 A.M......went about 14 miles.....went into camp near Morristown at 1 ½ P.M......stormed all day.....went through the village of Panther Creek

Tuesday, March 1, 1864

Stormy.....lay in camp all day.....most of the men on picket.....camped near Morristown.....drew four days rations.....report that we start back towards Knoxville tomorrow

Wednesday, March 2, 1864

Pleasant & warm.....Started on a march about 6 A.M......went back to Mossy Creek.....arrived there about 1 P.M......went foraging.....got some biscuit Corn cake bread and a canteen of milk.....got back from foraging about 8 P.M......went 3 miles

Thursday, March 3, 1864

Pleasant & warm.....routed out last night about 11 Oclock.....packed up..... lay there about 1 hour.....had orders to turn in for the night.....lay in camp all day.....nothing to do.....everything quiet

Friday, March 4, 1864

Pleasant & warm.....nothing to do.....no news.....everything quiet.....cleaned up for inspection.....making out the muster rolls.....expect to be mustered for four months pay

Saturday, March 5, 1864

Pleasant & cool.....received a letter from Father and Addie Tower.....pickets were attacked by a few rebs.....went on picket about four oclock P.M......got a supper for some coffee.....everything quiet tonight

Sunday, March 6, 1864

Pleasant & warm.....came off picket about 10 A M.....no news.....nothing to do

Monday, March 7, 1864

Cloudy & warm.....everything quiet.....turned out last night.....lay about 1 hour.....orders to pitch tents.....moved camp today.....received letters from Francis & Albert.....tent with Rufus, Bill and Harry Hall

Tuesday, March 8, 1864

Pleasant & warm.....nothing to do today.....no news.....the 11 N.H.V. went out on a scout last night.....went about 10 miles didnt see any Johnnies..... came into camp today.....received a letter from Addie Tower.....wrote to Al

Wednesday, March 9, 1864

Pleasant & warm.....nothing to do today.....the 11th and 2^{ed} Maryland went on drill.....we commence to drill tomorrow.....Harry Hall is sick.....Rufus getting well

Thursday, March 10, 1864

Pleasant & warm.....rained last night.....went on two drills today.....drew rations for 5 days.....Hall is sick.....went on picket about 4 P.M......no news..... everything quiet

Friday, March 11, 1864

Pleasant & cool.....came off picket about 5 P.M......went out to find the Johnnies.....didnt see any.....orders to march tomorrow at 5 A.M.

Saturday, March 12, 1864

Pleasant & warm.....started on a march at 5 A.M......went about 14 miles.....left out load.....went out after the Johnnies.....went about 5 miles.....didnt see any..... went back and went about 1 mile to camp.....went about 25 miles in all

Sunday, March 13, 1864

Pleasant & cool.....had revelle at day light.....packed up.....lay by the fire til about 11 A.M......started for Morristown.....arrived there about 1 P.M......went into camp on our old camping ground.....got a mail.....got two letters for Al

Monday, March 14, 1864

Pleasant & cool.....lay in camp all day.....drew rations for five days.....got a mail.....our cavalry had a skirmish with the Johnnies yesterday.....today the 1st Division captured a few rebs.....no news

Tuesday, March 15, 1864

Cloudy & cold.....lay in camp today.....nothing to do.....went on Dress parade.....had a mail.....no news.....1st division got some more Johnnies today

Wednesday, March 16, 1864

Pleasant & cold.....laid out a camp today.....cleaned all up.....Al came to the company.....signed the pay rolls.....orders to move tomorrow at 6 A.M...... rumor that we are going North

Thursday, March 17, 1864

Pleasant & cold.....Started on a march about 6 A.M......went about 12 miles.....took dinner at 12M.....started again at 1 A.M......went to New Market.....marched about 18 miles.....went into camp.....orders to start at 6 ½ tomorrow morning

Friday, March 18, 1864

Pleasant & cold.....Started this morning at 6 ½ oclock.....went about 12 miles.....took dinner.....started again about 1 P.M......went within 6 miles of Knoxville.....went into camp.....orders to march at 6 ½ A.M.

Saturday, March 19, 1864

Pleasant & cold.....started this morning about 6 ½ Oclock.....went about 7 miles....went into camp near Knoxville.....got mustered for four months pay.....expect to be paid tomorrow.....received a letter from William J Forsyth

Sunday, March 20, 1864

Pleasant & cold.....lay in camp all day.....Gen Wilcox ordered the paymaster not to pay us here.....going to start over the mountains in a day or two..... sick go by way of Chattanooga & Nashville

Monday, March 21, 1864

Pleasant & cool.....started a 9 ½ A.M. for Kentucky.....went to Clinton..... went into camp about 6 P.M......marched about 19 miles.....Al went by way of Chattanooga.....received a book from Francis

Tuesday, March 22, 1864

Cloudy morning.....started about 8 A.M......Crossed the Clinch River.....went about 15 miles.....went into camp.....went through Clinton.....snowed most all day.....awful cold.....start again tomorrow at 6 A.M.

Wednesday, March 23, 1864

Pleasant & cold.....started about 6 ½ A.M......went about 6 miles to the mountains.....stopped and drew rations.....went through Jacksborough..... started again about 1 ½ P.M......went over the mountains.....went about 8 miles.....went into camp about 5 P.M.

Thursday, March 24, 1864

Stormy.....started this morning about 6 ½ oclock.....went about 10 miles..... took dinner.....started again about 1 P M.....went about 6 miles.....went into camp about 5 P.M......crossed a large mountain

Friday, March 25, 1864

*Stormy.....*snowed all day til about*.....started this morning about 6 1/2..... went about 10 miles.....took dinner.....started again about 1.....went about 5 miles.....crossed the line into Kentucky.....went into camp about 5 P.M.*

Saturday, March 26, 1864

Cloudy morning.....started this morning about 6 ½.....went about 12 mls..... took dinner.....started again about 3 P M....drew one days rations.....went into camp about 7 P M.....went about 6 mls.....pleasant night

Sunday, March 27, 1864

Pleasant & warm.....started this morning about 5 ½.....went about 6 mls..... stoped at Burnside point.....cleaned out the sulters.....took dinner.....started at 11 ½ A M.....went through Somerset.....went into camp about 1 mile from town.....went about 10 miles

Monday, March 28, 1864

Pleasant & cool.....stormed last night.....started this morning at 6 ½.....went about 10 mls.....took dinner.....started again at 1 PM.....went about 7 mls..... went into camp.....went through Cuba and Jonesboro

Tuesday, March 29, 1864

Stormy morning.....started this morning at 6 ½.....went about 10 miles..... took dinner.....started again about 1 PM.....went through Halls Gap.....went into camp.....marched about 13 miles today.....drew rations

Wednesday, March 30, 1864

Stormed all night.....started this morning at 6 ½.....went about 18 miles..... took dinner.....went through Stanford and Lancaster....went about......started again at 2 PM.....went about 4 miles.....went into camp

Thursday, March 31, 1864

Cloudy & stormy.....started this morning at 6 ½.....went about 12 mls.....went into camp at camp parks on our old camp ground.....one Brigade started for Covington

Friday, April 1, 1864

Stormy.....lay in camp until 2 P.M......broke camp.....went to Nicholasville..... went into the Depot to sleep over night

Saturday, April 2, 1864

Cloudy.....started on the cars this morning about 7 ½.....went to Lexington..... stopped about 2 hours.....started again 11.....went as far as Cynthiana..... stopped here about 5 hours.....started for Covington

Sunday, April 3, 1864

Pleasant.....arrived at Covington about 4 A.M......got a mail.....got a letter from John, Francis & Addie Tower.....crossed the river into Cincinnati..... took the cars for Columbus

Monday, April 4, 1864

Stormy.....arrived at Columbus about 6 ½ AM.....stopped about 2 hours..... started again for Pittsburg Penn......rode all day.....passed a number of towns

Tuesday, April 5, 1864

Cloudy.....Arrived at Pittsburg about 6 AM.....got some breakfast at the P Relief Association.....stopped about 3 hours.....went around the place..... started again for Harrisburg.....rode all day.....rained some this afternoon

Wednesday, April 6, 1864

Pleasant & cool.....rode last night through the mountains.....they were covered with snow.....arrived at Harrisburg about 6 A.M......got some breakfast.....started again about 9 for Baltimore.....crossed the river on the biggest bridge I ever was on.....arrived at Baltimore about 5 P.M.

Thursday, April 7, 1864

Pleasant & warm.....stopped in Baltimore last night.....staid in Eutaw street Barracks.....wrote to Father.....left Baltimore for Annapolis about 12 M arrived there about 3 ½ PM.....went into camp

Friday, April 8, 1864

Pleasant.....moved camp today about 1 mile.....saw quite a number of the boys that were left at Knoxville.....expect to draw A tents in a day or two..... drawing full rations.....going to get some clothing.....Al got 5 letters today

Saturday, April 9, 1864

Stormy.....Al and Rufus went to Convalescent camp.....Al & I got 13 letters today.....nothing to do.....expect our tents tomorrow.....Burnside rode through camp today.....I got letters from Father, Francis, Hattie, Dick Jones & C J Gerry.....wrote to C J Gerry

Sunday, April 10, 1864

Cloudy.....nothing to do today.....got a pair of draws.....wrote to W J Forsyth, Addie Tower and Hattie.....expect to be paid in a few days

Monday, April 11, 1864

Cloudy.....not much to do today.....expect the pay muster tomorrow.....wrote to W.J Forsyth & O J Smith & L J Brigham

Tuesday, April 12, 1864

Pleasant.....not much to do today.....got our tents pitched today.....got paid of 4 months pay.....went to town.....got some paper

Wednesday, April 13, 1864

Pleasant.....cleaned up camp today.....reviewed by Genls Grant and Burnside.....wrote to C J Gerry.....Mr Stickney was here yesterday (George A. Stickney Co. D of Waltham, MA)

Thursday, April 14, 1864

Pleasant.....nothing to do today.....Mr. Stickney started for home.....Al & I sent 30 dollars to Francis by him.....received a letter from father.....went to town to a circus.....had a good time

Friday, April 15, 1864

Pleasant.....nothing to do today.....played cards and read all day.....expect camp duty to commence tomorrow

Saturday, April 16, 1864

Cloudy & stormy.....nothing to do today.....wrote to Father.....expect camp duty to commence Monday

Sunday, April 17, 1864

Pleasant & cool.....had an inspection today.....nothing else to do.....wrote to Francis.....camp duty commences tomorrow

Monday, April 18, 1864

Pleasant & cool.....camp duty commenced today.....had two drills & dress parade.....received a letter from C J Gerry.....bought some pictures and sent mother

Tuesday, April 19, 1864

Pleasant & warm.....had two drills today and a dress parade.....Charles Campbells wife came out to see him today.....Lt Hudsons[1] father is here also.....nothing new

Wednesday, April 20, 1864

Pleasant & warm.....nothing new this morning.....Mr Draper came here today.....had an introduction to Mrs Campbell today.....the 57th Mass Regt came here today.....there was some Marlboro fellows in it.....got orders to draw shelter tents and be ready to move at any time

Thursday, April 21, 1864

Pleasant & warm.....nothing to do today.....Maj Watts arrived today..... he brought us a football.....turned in our A tents.....pitched our shelters..... wrote to C J Gerry

Friday, April 22, 1864

Pleasant & cool.....had two drills today.....nothing else to do today.....orders for reveille at 2 ½ Oclock tomorrow morning.....Rufus and Bill got their box today

Saturday, April 23, 1864

Pleasant & warm.....had reveille at 2 ½ A.M......lay in Camp until about 9.....started on a march.....went about ½ mile when father & Mr. Morse came to us.....we got a pass to go back & stop 24 hours.....father gave me his picture

Sunday, April 24, 1864

Pleasant & warm......stopped at the Hotel last night.....got my pass lengthened til tomorrow morning.....went to church today

Monday, April 25, 1864

Stormy.....left Annapolis for Washington this morning.....left Father at Annapolis Junct.....arrived at Washington about 9 A.M......saw George Smith and Mr. Johnson.....Regt came through about 2 P.M......joined them and marched to Fairfax Seminary

Tuesday, April 26, 1864

Pleasant & warm.....lay in camp all day.....nothing to do.....expect to march tomorrow.....wrote to C J G.....drew 3 days rations......no news.....quite a lot of citizens in camp today

Wednesday, April 27, 1864

Pleasant & cool.....started this morning about 10 A.M......went past Fairfax Seminary.....went to Fairfax court House.....went into camp.....one of the 57 Mass dropped dead today and 2 of the 56 Mass.....nothing new

Thursday, April 28, 1864

Pleasant & cold.....Started this morning about 8 Oclock.....the 35th was detailed to guard the teams.....went through Centerville and past Bull Run and Manassus Junction.....went into camp at Bristol Station.....marched about 17 miles

Friday, April 29, 1864

Cloudy & cold.....Started this morning about 8 ½.....went about 13 miles..... went into camp.....got a mail.....Received a letter from Addie Tower.....our corps is going to releive the 5th Corps.....no news.....went past Warrenton Junction

Saturday, April 30, 1864

Cloudy with some rain.....started this morning about 10 A.M......went about 6 miles.....went into camp at Bealton station.....nothing new.....we relieved the troops that were stationed here

Sunday, May 1, 1864

Cloudy & cold.....changed camp.....Al & I & Rufus pitched tent together..... nothing to do.....expect to go on picket tomorrow

Monday, May 2, 1864

Pleasant & cool.....went on picket about 8 A.M......saw Alfred & Ed Moulton today.....their Regt arrived here today and went into camp.....had a big shower.....tent blew down

Tuesday, May 3, 1864

Pleasant & warm.....came off picket about 9 A M......tent blew down last night.....got a little wet.....went to see Allie.....had a good time.....orders to move tomorrow

Wednesday, May 4, 1864

*Pleasant & cool.....turned out this morning at 5 A.M......cars run off the track.....broke up a lot of barrels of coffee and sugar.....started on a march about 6 A.M......went about 12 miles.....*went into camp about 2 ocl

Thursday, May 5, 1864

Pleasant & warm.....got into camp last night or this morning at 2 Oclock..... turned in and slept till 6.....started again about 7 A.M......went about 12 miles.....crossed the Rapidan River.....can hear the fighting.....went into camp about 7 P.M......company went on picket

Friday, May 6, 1864

Pleasant & hot.....crossed the river last night.....went into camp near it..... started this morning about 6 A.M......went about 3 miles.....stopped all day.....saw John.....stopped with him in the afternoon.....considerable fighting today

Saturday, May 7, 1864

Pleasant & awful warm.....John stopped with us till 11 Oclock last night then we had to pack up and leave.....went about ¼ mile.....stopped til morning.....waiting for our train to get along.....saw John today.....not much fighting on the right today.....went about 5 mls today.....went into camp

Sunday, May 8, 1864

Pleasant & warm.....marched about 3 miles.....stopped in the woods all day....got a mail.....got a letter from L J Brigham.....saw Gardner

Darling.....heard Ally was wounded.....we are still on the train.....have not seen any fighting yet.....went through Chancelorville (Gardner Darling, Sixteenth Regiment, Company H, wounded at the Battle of Fair Oaks, prisoner - traded. Ally refers to Alfred Moore who was wounded at Cold Harbor.)

Monday, May 9, 1864

Pleasant & warm.....started this morning.....went about ¼ mile.....went into the woods.....stopped all day......nothing to do.....saw a few prisoners..... considerable fighting today.....Al is detailed at Brigade Commissary..... Rufus is sick

Tuesday, May 10, 1864

Pleasant & warm.....lay in camp all day.....nothing to do.....Company on guard on the Ammunition train.....General Stevenson killed today.....Major Waly going home with his body.....still on the train.....pretty heavy firing today.....moved about 1 ½ mls today

Wednesday, May 11, 1864

Pleasant & warm.....lay with train all day.....Rufus pretty sick today..... considerable firing going on today and a large number of wounded went past our camp.....get a great many reports but cant tell what is true

Thursday, May 12, 1864

Stormy.....in camp most all day.....started on a march about 4 P.M......saw a lot of prisoners.....our forces captured Gen Johnson & Stewart and 5,000 prisoners last night

Friday, May 13, 1864

Stormy.....got stuck in the mud last night.....stopped all night.....started again this morning.....went about 3 miles.....went into camp within 3 miles of Fredericksburg.....my birthday.....no news of importance today

Saturday, May 14, 1864

Stormy.....lay in camp all day.....nothing to do only guard Ammunition train at night.....Bill got a detail today.....no news from the front.....Al went to the

*front today.....Tim Thompson and Sergt Davidson came to the company.....
saw Nelson Howe*

Sunday, May 15, 1864

*Stormy.....had orders to move at 6 A.M......hitched up the teams and lay in
camp all day.....awful bad roads.....teams all going to Fredericksburg.....no
news today.....saw John.....didnt hear from Alfred yet*

Monday, May 16, 1864

*Stormy.....started for Fredericksburg this morning.....arrived there about 12
M.....went into camp.....no news from any of the boys.....wrote to Mother.....
going to send it by Capt Lyons*

Tuesday, May 17, 1864

*Pleasant & warm.....no news today from any of the boys.....The Regt started
to join the Brigade today.....our company detached from the Regt.....we are
on the train yet.....saw Mr Fisher of Waltham today.....loaned Byrnes $1.00
today*

Wednesday, May 18, 1864

*Pleasant With shower.....nothing to do today.....the 35th in battle today.....got
some bread and pork that the troops threw away.....wrote to Addie Tower
and L. J. Brigham.....on guard tonight*

Thursday, May 19, 1864

*Pleasant & warm.....went to the front today for rations.....saw some of
the wounded of the 35th Mass.....not much news.....the rebs were near the
road when we came back.....had to run our horses to get past them.....They
attacked our supply team.....took a few horses*

Friday, May 20, 1864

*Pleasant & warm.....moved camp about ½ mile today.....saw a lot of Rebel
prisoners.....no news of importance.....got a mail.....received a letter from
Father, Dick Jones and C J Gerry.....drew some rations*

Saturday, May 21, 1864

Pleasant & warm.....orders to move at 4 AM.....packed up.....lay in camp til afternoon then started on a march for Bowling green.....went about 10 miles.....saw Ed Moulton

Sunday, May 22, 1864

Pleasant & warm.....traveled most all night last night.....went into camp today about 8 AM.....lay in camp til about 4 P.M......orders to move..... commenced a letter to father.....no news of importance today

Monday, May 23, 1864

Pleasant & warm started last night about 9 PM.....traveled all night and til about 10 today.....went through Bowling Green and went into camp at Milford station.....considerable fighting today

Tuesday, May 24, 1864

Pleasant & warm.....lay in camp all last night and today.....considerable firing today.....no news.....orders to move at 6 P.M......had a big shower with rain and hail.....wrote to father

Wednesday, May 25, 1864

Pleasant & warm.....started last night about 11 O'Clock.....went about 2 mls.....went into camp.....no news of importance.....our forces crossed the North Anna River.....had a shower this afternoon

Thursday, May 26, 1864

Stormy morning.....lay in camp all night last night.....no news today..... everything quiet.....Reinforcements going to the front.....orders to move tomorrow

Friday, May 27, 1864

Pleasant & warm.....stormed all last night.....started on march about 10 A.M......went about 16 miles.....went into camp.....no news of importance today.....saw some of our wounded yesterday

Saturday, May 28, 1864

Pleasant & warm.....started this morning about 7 oclock.....went about 12 miles.....went into camp near Dunkirk.....went through Newtown.....got some mail today....have not had any rations for two days.....no news of importance today.....saw a few prisoners

Sunday, May 29, 1864

Pleasant & warm.....started this morning about 8 Oclock.....went about 15 mls.....went into camp about 6 P.M......crossed two rivers.....went through Eliot and Dunkirk.....no news today

Monday, May 30, 1864

Pleasant & warm.....started this morning about 8 oclock.....went about ½ mile.....lay beside the road for other teams to pass all day.....nothing to do..... no news.....considerable firing today

Tuesday, May 31, 1864

Pleasant & warm.....went about 3 miles today.....went into camp near the river.....no news of importance.....heavy firing.....saw some prisoners.....got a letter from C J Gerry.....wrote to her

Wednesday, June 1, 1864

Pleasant & warm.....lay in camp till about 4 P.M......got orders to move..... went about 3 mls.....went into camp.....stopped all night.....heavy firing at the front today.....report that our army occupy Nicholasville

Thursday, June 2, 1864

Pleasant morning.....stormy afternoon.....lay in camp all last night.....got orders to take our Ammunition to the front about 1 P.M......went about 1 ½ mls on the wrong road.....turned around went about 5 mls the other way..... turned around went back about 3 mls.....went into camp

Friday, June 3, 1864

Pleasant & warm.....started this morning went about 4 miles.....went into camp.....saw John.....been with him all day.....had a good time.....rebs made a charge last *tonight and got repulsed.....went through Hanover or old Church Village*

Saturday, June 4, 1864

Cloudy & stormy.....lay in camp all day today.....no news of importance..... considerable firing....rebs made a charge on the 2ed Corps last night and got repulsed with great loss.....been with John most all day

Sunday, June 5, 1864

Pleasant & warm.....nothing to do today.....everything quiet.....rebs made a charge on the 2ed & 6th this evening and got repulsed with great loss. Been with John most all day

Monday, June 6, 1864

Pleasant & warm.....lay in camp all day.....no news.....some Artly firing today.....went over to the 13th mass.....saw all the boys.....everything quiet this evening

Tuesday, June 7, 1864

Pleasant & warm.....nothing to do today.....went to see Al.....saw John and all the rest of the Sudbury boys.....had a good time.....everything quiet today.....no news

Wednesday, June 8, 1864

Pleasant & warm.....nothing to do today.....Al came over to see me.....we went over to the 13th mass....saw all the boys.....had a good time.....wrote to Francis.....no news.....considerable firing tonight

Thursday, June 9, 1864

Pleasant & warm.....nothing to do today.....went over to the 18th mass..... saw all the boys.....saw Al.....heard from Henry Smith.....Curtis Smith is taken prisoner

Friday, June 10, 1864

Pleasant & warm.....moved camp into the woods this morning.....the Ammunition ordered to the landing.....started about 1 P.M. for that place..... arrived there about 7 P.M......went into camp

Saturday, June 11, 1864

Pleasant & warm.....went to the landing today.....got some things at the Sutlers.....detailed to go to the front this afternoon with ammunition..... received a letter from Francis today

Sunday, June 12, 1864

Pleasant & warm.....went about 6 miles last night.....camped for the night..... started this morning.....went to headquarters.....left my load at the 27 mich.....loaded with ammunition and rations.....went back to landing..... saw Albert

Monday, June 13, 1864

Pleasant & warm.....started this morning.....went about 18 miles.....went into camp.....went through Berryville.....got some Cherries.....the first of the season.....Army on a move.....saw the Regt.....got a mail

Tuesday, June 14, 1864

Pleasant & warm.....turned out this morning about 2 Oclock.....had the teethache all night.....started on a march about 7 A.M......went about 6 miles.....went into camp.....saw Albert

Wednesday, June 15, 1864

Pleasant & warm.....stopped in camp all last night.....no news today of importance.....lay in camp all day.....orders to move tonight at 6 Oclock

Thursday, June 16, 1864

Pleasant & warm.....started last night about 9 P.M......went about 3 miles..... stoped 1½ hours.....started again.....went to the James River.....crossed the Chickahominy Heard some firing today.....report that our forces have captured Petersburg

Friday, June 17, 1864

Pleasant & warm.....started last night.....crossed the James River.....went about 1 mile.....stopped til morning.....started again.....went about 5 mls..... went into camp for the night.....heavy firing today towards Petersburg..... crossed the James at Wilcox's landing

Saturday, June 18, 1864

Pleasant & warm.....started about 7 A.M......went about 8 mls.....went into Rank for the night.....saw John.....considerable firing today.....our men advancing slowly in to Petersburg.....went into the rebs (———)works

Sunday, June 19, 1864

Pleasant & warm.....no news of importance today.....went to the Regt.....saw all the boys.....saw John and Al.....got some candles and (———) of Al.....saw Eli.....read some letters that Al & John received from home

Monday, June 20, 1864

Pleasant & warm.....nothing new today.....considerable firing.....drew rations.....staid in camp all day

Tuesday, June 21, 1864

Pleasant & warm.....no news of importance today.....went to see John and Albert.....considerable firing today

Wednesday, June 22, 1864

Pleasant & warm.....nothing to do today.....not much news.....rebs charged on our lines today.....got repulsed.....saw Al & John.....wrote to Dick James.....got some dollars of Albert

Thursday, June 23, 1864

Pleasant & warm.....no news of importance today.....considerable firing..... lay in camp all day.....all the able bodied men ordered into the ranks..... expect to join the Regt in a few days

Friday, June 24, 1864

Pleasant & warm.....nothing to do today.....heavy firing today.....drew rations.....ordered to the Regt tomorrow.....no news of importance

Saturday, June 25, 1864

Pleasant & warm.....moved our camp yesterday.....Uncle Smith & myself had a wall tent.....stopped in it overnight.....ordered to the Regt this morning.....

went to work this afternoon chopping.....got a letter from Rufus.....no news of importance

Sunday, June 26, 1864

Pleasant & warm.....nothing of importance to do today.....got a letter and picture from Clara.....saw Al and John.....worked last night.....considerable firing while we were at work.....bullets flew around us

Monday, June 27, 1864

Pleasant & warm.....worked all day today.....no news of importance.....wrote to Rufus, John Morse and George Spofford.....went to City Point today..... Al got a letter from father today

Tuesday, June 28, 1864

Pleasant & warm.....lay in camp all day.....got to go to work on a fort tonight.....wrote to Clara Gerry.....no news of importance

Wednesday, June 29, 1864

Pleasant & warm.....worked all night.....considerable firing last night.....Co D commanded the fort under considerable heavy fire.....Al got a letter from Alfred.....got to go to work tonight again

Thursday, June 30, 1864

Pleasant & warm.....lay in camp all day.....worked all last night.....Co D worked in open field under a heavy fire again.....no news of importance..... mustered today for four months pay.....saw Bill and Eli

Friday, July 1, 1864

Pleasant & warm.....lay in camp all day.....worked all night.....considerable heavy firing last night of Artillery.....did not amount to much.....got a letter from Father.....Al go one from Mother

Saturday, July 2, 1864

Pleasant & warm.....lay in camp all day.....worked all last night under a considerable heavy fire.....report that the 19th Corps has arrived here from Banks Department.....expect to have some hard fighting in a few days

Sunday, July 3, 1864

Pleasant & warm.....lay in camp all day.....nothing to do.....worked all night.....wrote to Francis today.....no news of importance today.....expect there will be some heavy firing in the morning

Monday, July 4, 1864

Pleasant & warm.....nothing to do today.....worked all night.....nothing unusual today.....borrowed 8 dollars of Eli yesterday

Tuesday, July 5, 1864

Pleasant & warm.....nothing to do today.....no news of importance..... worked all night.....a fellow in Co D got killed.....2 in Co C got wounded yesterday

Wednesday, July 6, 1864

Pleasant & warm.....no news of importance.....the usual firing kept up..... did not work last night.....received a letter from father.....saw Spencer & W. Jones

Thursday, July 7, 1864

Pleasant & warm.....did not work today.....no news of importance.....received a letter from mother.....wrote to Father.....Al got a letter from Francis and W H Bent

Friday, July 8, 1864

Pleasant & warm.....went to work today making implements and getting ready to fortify.....no news of importance today.....saw John.....Al got a letter from Mary and A Clark.....I got a book from Francis

Saturday, July 9, 1864

Pleasant & warm.....no news of importance today.....everything quiet.....saw John and Al.....gave Al my letters to send home by John

Sunday, July 10, 1864

Pleasant & warm.....no news today.....Packed up everything this morning..... orders to move at 7 ½ A.M......left our knapsacks and went out to work in

the woods.....worked all day.....came back to camp tonight.....got a letter from Rufus

Monday, July 11, 1864

Pleasant & warm.....went to work again today in the woods making gabions.....no news of importance today.....saw John and L. Haynes.....Had a small shower this evening (Leander A. Haynes, Thirteenth Regiment, company H)

Tuesday, July 12, 1864

Pleasant & warm.....no news of importance today.....got a letter from L P Brigham.....saw John and L Haynes this morning.....they went to City Point today.....the 16th Mass left here today for Home

Wednesday, July 13, 1864

Pleasant & warm....went to work today......no news of importance except that Rebel Raid into Maryland.....commenced a letter to mother today..... worked all day.....no mail today

Thursday, July 14, 1864

Pleasant & warm.....worked all day.....wrote to mother.....no news of importance.....movement of troops......2ed Corps gone into camp

Friday, July 15, 1864

Pleasant & warm.....worked all day today.....troops filling up the old entrenchments.....no news of importance.....only from Mary and Al sent me a Coiled Heart

Saturday, July 16, 1864

Pleasant & warm.....worked all day today.....no news except from Maryland.....expect there will be a move made here within a few days..... we keep upon firing day and night

Sunday, July 17, 1864

Pleasant & warm.....nothing to do today except to clean up camp.....wrote a letter to Francis.....went over and took dinner with Albert.....no news of importance except from Maryland

Monday, July 18, 1864

Pleasant & warm.....went to work today again at usual.....worked all day..... expected an attack from Gen. Longstreet last night.....considerable firing..... everything quiet today.....no news of importance

Tuesday, July 19, 1864

Stormy.....went to work today.....rained so hard that we had to quit.....got all wet through.....wrote to L. Brigham and R H Hurlbut.....Everything quiet..... no news of importance

Wednesday, July 20, 1864

Cloudy morning.....Pleasant afternoon.....went to work today at the usual time.....worked all day.....no news of importance.....everything quiet..... report that Sherman has got Atlanta with 15000 prisoners

Thursday, July 21, 1864

Pleasant & warm.....went to work today at the usual time.....worked all day.....no news of importance except from Sherman.....President has called for 200,000 more men.....received a letter from W J Forsyth.....everything quiet.....saw Al and Eli today

Friday, July 22, 1864

Pleasant & warm.....went to work at the usual time this morning.....no news of importance.....considerable firing today.....received a letter from W J Forsyth

Saturday, July 23, 1864

Pleasant & warm.....no news of importance about this part.....good news from Sherman.....not much from today.....worked today as usual.....received a letter from Francis

Sunday, July 24, 1864

Pleasant & cool.....did not work today.....went over and took dinner with Al.....wrote to Francis, Hattie and W.J. Forsyth.....no news of importance only from Georgia.....everything quiet here.....got a letter from Hattie

Monday, July 25, 1864

Pleasant & cool.....went to work at the usual time this morning.....rained all night.....worked all day.....no news except from Georgia.....everything quiet here.....received a letter from Mary

Tuesday, July 26, 1864

Pleasant & warm.....went to work at the usual time today.....worked all day.....no news of importance except from Georgia.....everything quiet here

Wednesday, July 27, 1864

Pleasant & warm.....went to work at the usual time this morning.....worked all day.....wrote to Mary.....no news of importance.....heavy firing on our right this morning

Thursday, July 28, 1864

Pleasant & cool.....nothing to do today.....wrote to Alfred.....no news of importance.....got to go to work at the front tonight.....everything quiet except a little picket firing

Friday, July 29, 1864

Pleasant & warm.....nothing to do today.....worked last night til 2 ½ this morning.....Al got a letter from John today.....no news.....expect to go to the front again tonight

Saturday, July 30, 1864

Pleasant & hot.....turned out this morning about 2 A.M.....joined the division.....went to the front.....blew up the Reb fort.....division made a charge.....took two lines of troops but had to abandon them.....fell back to our old positions.....lost heavy

Sunday, July 31, 1864

Pleasant & Hot.....not much to do today.....Grant sent in a flag of truce today to bury his dead and the Johnnies wouldnt let him.....everything quiet today except the picket firing.....saw Al

Monday, August 1, 1864

Pleasant & warm.....the Rebs gave Burnside the privilege of burying his killed.....they would not accept of a flag of truce from Grant.....my Regt buried all the dead in our division

Tuesday, August 2, 1864

Pleasant & warm.....nothing to do today.....had an inspection last night..... received a letter from Clara, Allie and Clara Powers.....no news..... everything quiet except the usual firing.....wrote to Clara

Wednesday, August 3, 1864

Pleasant & warm.....no news of importance today.....wrote to Clara Powers.....nothing to do.....everything quiet.....expected an attack on our line today

Thursday, August 4, 1864

Pleasant & warm.....nothing to do today.....no news of importance.....fast day.....wrote to Alfred.....everything quiet.....saw Al.....got some sugar.....Al got a letter from Francis

Friday, August 5, 1864

Pleasant & warm.....nothing to do today.....drew some clothing.....no news..... got a letter from Father and Dick Jones.....the Rebs blew up our fort today or attempted to but didnt amount to anything

Saturday, August 6, 1864

Pleasant & warm.....nothing to do today.....a detail is going out to work tonight.....does not include me.....it was only a false skirmish line the rebs blew up yesterday.....wrote to Father today.....got a letter from Alfred today.....no news of importance

Sunday, August 7, 1864

Pleasant & warm.....nothing to do today.....pretty heavy Cannoneding today.....dont know what the results was.....went over to see Al and Eli today.....saw Bill Bowen.....everything quiet.....tonight get to go to the front to work

Monday, August 8, 1864

Pleasant & warm.....nothing to do today.....received a letter from Hattie..... carried a letter to Al from John and a paper and book to Eli & Al.....nothing unusual happened today.....got to go to work again tonight

Tuesday, August 9, 1864

Pleasant & warm.....nothing to do today.....wrote to Hattie.....Explosion in the Ordinance Dept at City Point.....great loss of life.....no news of importance.....saw Al today.....he got a letter from Father

Wednesday, August 10, 1864

Pleasant & warm.....nothing to do today.....wrote to Dick Jones.....no news of importance.....expect the Paymaster in a few days.....everything quiet since the Battle.....Saw Al & Eli.....got a box for Eli

Thursday, August 11, 1864

Pleasant & warm.....nothing to do today.....wrote to Alfred.....no news of importance.....everything quiet.....got to go to work tonight

Friday, August 12, 1864

Pleasant & warm.....nothing of importance.....got paid off four months pay.....had quite a (––) today.....nothing to do tonight.....got some supper

Saturday, August 13, 1864

Pleasant & warm.....nothing to do today.....heavy firing in the night.....dont know what was up.....wrote to John today.....no news of importance..... expect to go to work tonight.....went out last night about 12 O'clock

Sunday, August 14, 1864

Pleasant & warm.....nothing to do today.....received a letter from Mother..... no news of importance.....report that Gen Butler had a victory yesterday..... had a little rain tonight.....expect to go to work again tonight

Monday, August 15, 1864

Pleasant & warm.....went to work last night.....worked til about 12 Oclock..... got orders to march.....went about 8 miles.....relieved part of the 5th Corps doing picket duty on the left of the army

Tuesday, August 16, 1864

Pleasant & warm.....not much to do today.....moved camp.....received a letter from Addie Tower and one from Francis.....not very well today..... orders to have our arms where we can take them at a moments notice

Wednesday, August 17, 1864

Sick.....unable to do duty.....nothing new today

Thursday, August 18, 1864

Sick.....got a letter from Alfred & Rufus

Friday, August 19, 1864

Sick.....sent down to stop with Al til I get well.....got letters from Father and Mary

Saturday, August 20, 1864

Rained today.....we moved the cattle up near the front today.....they put my knapsack on one of the cattle.....everything quiet

Sunday, August 21, 1864

Sick.....stopping with Albert.....got a letter from John and Hattie.....Regt was in a fight today

Monday, August 22, 1864

Went to the Hospital today

Tuesday, August 23, 1864

Pleasant.....in division Hospital

*There are no further daily notations in the diary.

[1] Charles Hudson of Lexington was a member of Congress for four terms, an ordained Universalist minister since 1819, served on the State Board of Education, a naval officer in the Port of Boston, selectman in Lexington, MA, wrote a comprehensive history of the town of Lexington, MA. The town of Hudson MA was named after him in 1866 when Feltonville, which had been part of the town of Marlborough, petitioned the state to become a separate town. Charles Hudson gave the town $500.00 for a library if they would name the town after him.

Sarah Elizabeth Jones

Diary 1867

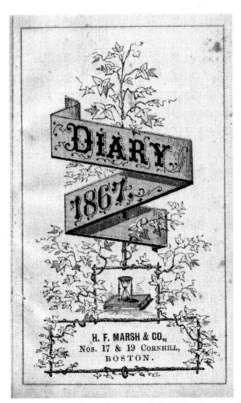

Sarah Elizabeth Jones 1867 Diary, the Year of Her Marriage to George Moore.
Sudbury Historical Society

Many names appear often in the diary, and to aid the reader a little in understanding the identities of some: Allie is Alfred Moore, Al is Albert Moore, Charlie is George's younger brother and Hattie could be his sister or Harriet Garrison who married Alfred Moore, Abby is Abby Jones, Sarah's oldest sister and Lucella or Leu is another older sister, Johnnie Morse is John Morse who was in the Thirty-fifth, Kate Tower is the girl who marries Rufus Hurlbut. Sarah Jones was a schoolteacher in Sudbury in 1867 when she wrote this diary.

Tuesday, January 1

Not very pleasant. Went to school in the forenoon. School did not keep in the afternoon as we were getting ready for our tea which we held in the evening. Had a pleasant time. George gave me a pair of skates for a New Years present.

Wednesday 2

Pleasant day. Staid at home in the forenoon as Leu had gone to Boston. Went to school in the afternoon. Intended to have gone down to the singing school but had such a cold I could not sing. George came down

Thursday 3

Pleasant day. Uncle E, Aunt Abbie and Fannie came up to our house. Staid at home in the forenoon to wash. Went to school in the afternoon. Went up to hear the band play in the evening. It was their last meeting.

Friday, January 4, 1867

Beautiful day. Went to school all day. Emma Browne was in school in the afternoon. Went to the Musical Union in the evening but could not sing I had such a cold.

Saturday 5

Pleasant day. Staid at home nearly all day. Went up to the store and in to see Mrs. Taylor a few minutes. George came down and we went down to the Library.

Sunday 6

Snowed part of the day. Went to Church all day, but few present as was so unpleasant. Reverend Mr. Dickinson preached text AM 2 Chron 4:18 PM 2 Coron 5:13,14. George came down in the evening.

Monday, January 7, 1867

Pleasant day. Father carried me to school in the morning. Very good sleighing. Did not go home at noon. George came down in the evening and we did examples.

Tuesday 8

Pleasant day. Went to school all day. Went to the prayer meeting in the evening in the vestry. The Methodist met with us. We are to have meetings every night this week.

Wednesday 9

Pleasant day. Went to school all day. George came in school in the afternoon. George, Leu, Nell & I were up to Miss Hunts in the evening. Had a nice time

Thursday, January 10, 1867

Pleasant day. Went to school all day. Lu went to Weston this afternoon and I had the work to do after school. Ironed in the evening. George came down.

Friday 11

Pleasant day. Went to school all day. Mr. Thompson was in school. Mary Moore and Em Brigham stopped for me to go down to the singing school so I went. George was sick. Enjoyed the evening very much.

Saturday 12

Pleasant day. Staid home all day. Wanted to go down to the Library but the horse was not at home. George came down in the evening.

Sunday, January 13, 1867

Pleasant day. Went to Church all day. Reverend Mr. Dickinson preached. Text Sabbath School Concert in the afternoon. Mrs. Colby played the organ in the morning. Went up to the Methodist Church in the evening.

Monday 14

Pleasant day. Staid at home in the forenoon. George & Charley came up to the school house at noon. In the evening went out coasting with the boys & girls, then went down to George's and sang. Had a splendid time.

Tuesday 15

Pleasant day. Went to school all day. Mrs. Hunt, Mrs. Howe and Miss Leland were in school. Ellen Haynes came over to our house in the evening. George came down.

Wednesday, January 16, 1867

Pleasant day. Went to school all day. Lucille and I talked of going to the Library but it was most too cold and Hattie stopped and told Leu they wanted her at the shop tomorrow.

Thursday 17

Very hard snow storm. Went to school all day. Father came after me at night and it was very hard work to travel. The snow blows and drifts terribly. Shall have some sleighing.

Friday 18

Unpleasant day. No school today and no hat shop for Leu. The wind has blown the snow round so that it is very much drifted. Very little passing as the snow is very deep.

Saturday, January 19, 1867

Pleasant day. Staid at home all day. People have been breaking out the roads nearly all day. George came down in the evening.

Sunday 20

Pleasant day. Went to Church all day. Reverend Mr. Dickinson preached. Text ..Meeting was held in the vestry so there was not a great many. George came down.

Monday 21

Snowed part of the day. There was no school. Leucilla and I did the washing. The roads are not much better for breaking out as they are covered up again.

Tuesday, January 22, 1867

Pleasant day. I'm not going to school any more as Leucilla goes to the shop. Went today. George came down in the evening.

Wednesday 23

Pleasant day. Staid at home all day. Aunt Caroline called. Went up to Mrs. Taylor's a few minutes. Rode up on Mr. Moore's sled as he was carrying the boys home. George came home with me.

Thursday 24

Splendid Day. Staid at home all day . Towards night went up to Mrs. Hunt's and up to the school house. The scholars were snow balling after school at a great rate.

Friday, January 25, 1867

Pleasant day. Staid at home all day. Went up to the Musical Union in the evening. Had a splendid time singing. Are getting ready for a concert.

Saturday 26

Not very pleasant. Staid at home all day. George came and spent the afternoon and evening. Went over to Mrs. Heards and after the milk. He brought the organ down tonight.

Sunday 27

Pleasant day. Went to Church all day. Reverend Mr. Dickinson preached. Text There was no meeting in the evening so we sang and played.

Monday, January 28, 1867

Pleasant day. Staid at home all day. Leu cut me a jacket today so I helped Mother. Went up to the school house a few minutes and up to Mrs. Hunt's in the eve.

Tuesday 29

Pleasant day. The folks went down to the village today so I was alone. George stopped on his way home. Went to the Unitarian fair in the evening.

Wednesday 30

Pleasant day. Staid at home all day. Helen Shaw came here at night and staid all night. George stopped a few minutes as he was going home from Boston.

Thursday, January 31, 1867

Pleasant day. Staid at home all day. Helen staid at our house in the forenoon. George came down a few minutes and then went up to the band meeting.

Friday, February 1, 1867

Pleasant day. Went up to the store in the morning. Went up to the Musical Union in the evening. Sang the piece that I am going to sing at the concert.

Saturday 2

Pleasant in the morning. Staid at home in the forenoon. Walked down to the Library in the afternoon with Hattie. George came down in the evening. Rains hard tonight.

Sunday, February 3, 1867

Pleasant day. Went to Church in the morning. Staid at home in the afternoon as I was not well. Went to a lecture in the eve by Mr. John Parker, a colored man.

Monday 4

Pleasant day. Sick all day. Did not get up until ten o'clock and then lay on the lounge the rest of the day. Hope I shall be better tomorrow.

Tuesday 5

Pleasant day. Staid at home all day. Lay down a part of the day. Braided some and played some. Am tired of being sick. George came down in the evening.

Wednesday, February 6, 1867

Pleasant day. Staid at home all day. Felt rather better until towards night my head began to ache worse than it has any time. Went to bed early.

Thursday 7

Debate should President Johnson be impeached. Pleasant day. Staid at home all day. My head has not ached quite so much today. Went up to the Temperance Meeting in the evening. Stopped at Mrs. Hunt's to sing. George Called for me.

Friday 8

Pleasant overhead but not underfoot. Terribly muddy. Went up to the Hall in the afternoon to rehearse. Went to the Concert in the evening. Quite a large attendance. Commenced to rain a little.

Saturday, February 9, 1867

Unpleasant day. Very dark , damp and misty. Staid at home all day. The snow has gone off so much the people have begun to go in wagons. George came down in the evening. Poured hard nearly all night.

Sunday 10

Pleasant day. Very windy. Staid at home in the forenoon. Went to Church in the afternoon. Reverend Mr. Dickinson preached Text for J 28:28. Staid at home in the evening.

Monday 11

Pleasant day. Staid at home all day. Father went to Cambridge today as jury man. Went up to hear the band play. Lizzie Towle was up from Waltham.

Tuesday, February 12, 1867

Pleasant day. Went over Mrs. Curtis Moore's a little while in the afternoon. George came down in the evening.

Wednesday 13

Pleasant day. Staid at home all day. Went to the Methodist Band of Hope & Sabbath School Exhibition in the Hall. Liked very much although I did not feel very well.

Thursday 14

Pleasant Day. Staid at home all day. Aunt Abby spent the afternoon at our house. Went to the exhibition which was continued from last eve. Al Moore was up. Had a gay time.

Friday, February 15, 1867

Pleasant day. Staid at home all day. Lizzie Moore called. Went to the Musical Union. John and Al Moore said they were coming home with me but when they got to the corner they ran home and let George come, polite fellows.

Saturday 16

Rainy day. Staid at home all day. Father came home from Cambridge tonight. George could not bring the organ down it was so rainy but he came himself so I was satisfied.

Sunday 17

Pleasant day. Went to Church all day. Text A.M. Mark 5:86. P.M. Reverend Mr. Jordan preached Text Went up to the Methodist meeting.

Monday, February 18, 1867

Pleasant day. Staid at home all day. Did not feel very well today so did not try to work much. George came down in the evening.

Tuesday 19

Pleasant day. Staid at home all day. The Doctor called today and said I had the Erethema Tuberosa. There is a few little spots broken out on my leg. George came down.

Wednesday 20

Pleasant day. Staid at home all day. Have not felt any better today. Father went down to the Library. George came down in the evening.

Thursday, February 21, 1867

Snowy day. Staid at home all day. It has been trying to snow all day. Will not be a very good night for the Temperance Meeting. George came down.

Friday 22

Pleasant day. Staid at home all day. Mary Heard came in a few minutes in the afternoon and played the organ. George came in. Wanted to go to the sing very much but could not.

Saturday 23

Pleasant day. Staid at home all day. Mr. Thompson and Mr. Balcom were at our house to dinner as the schools were examined. George came down in the eve.

Sunday, February 24, 1867

Pleasant day. Staid at home all day. There is a little snow on the ground but it has melted very fast today. George came down.

Monday 25

Pleasant day. Staid at home in the forenoon. Have felt a little better to do so I went down to Julia Jones and carried my braid. George and Nell came down.

Tuesday 26

Pleasant day. George came down in the afternoon and we went up to Lizzie's a few minutes. Went into Miss Taylor's. Expected Levy & Allie down in the evening but they did not come. George came down.

Wednesday, February 27, 1867

Pleasant day. Aunt Susan, Uncle Gardner, Aunt Pamela & Uncle Farwell & Hattie spent the afternoon at our house. Miss. Taylor & Nell came down in the evening. George & Mr. Hunt came down after the cousins and we had a sing.

Thursday 28

Pleasant day. Went down to Ellen Clarks and up to Miss Taylor's in the forenoon. Ellen Clark & Anna Haynes spent the afternoon at our house. George and I went up to Miss. Taylor's in the evening.

Friday, March 1

Rainy day. Staid at home all day. George came down in the afternoon. Did not expect there would be any sing but G. came down about half past 7 and said Mr. Smith had come so he carried us up.

Saturday, March 2, 1867

Pleasant day. Staid at home all day. Miss Taylor called a few minutes in the morning to bid us goodbye. Lizzie Hurlburt called. George came down in the evening

Sunday 3

Pleasant day. Went to Church all day. Reverend Mr. Stone an agent for the Freedmen preached Text A.M. Luke 11:2. P.M. Went to the Methodist meeting in the evening.

Monday 4

Snowy day. Uncle Adams folks spent the day at our house while he went to Town meeting. George came down in the evening.

Tuesday, March 5, 1867

Pleasant day. We all went visiting today. Went to Aunt Pamela's in the forenoon and Aunt Susan's in the afternoon. Staid at home in the evening and braided.

Wednesday 6

Pleasant day. Staid at home all day. Have been braiding all day. George came down in the evening and did my hair up on hair pins for me before he went home.

Thursday 7

Snowy day. Staid at home all day. Some of the Musical Union were going to Waltham tonight to sing at a fair but we had to stay at home.

Friday, March 8, 1867

Splendid day. Staid at home in the forenoon. Leu & I went over to Saxonville with Father. Mary Heard called. Went to the Musical Union in the evening

Saturday 9

Pleasant day. Staid at home all day. Lulie came down in the forenoon. Went after the milk. Braided 11 yards today. George came down in the evening.

Sunday 10

Snowed nearly all day. Went to Church all day. Text Acts 12:13-15. Prayer meeting in the afternoon at Mr. Dickinson's. Attended a funeral. Commenced to storm hard after meeting. Staid at home in the evening.

Monday, March 11, 1867

Not very pleasant. Staid at home all day and braided. Am very tired of such unsettled weather, wish we could have more than one pleasant day. George came down.

Tuesday 12

Snowed nearly all day. Aunt Caroline came down in the morning and wanted me to come up there so I went up and staid all day. George came down in the evening. Braided 12 yards.

Wednesday 13

Pleasant day. Went up to the store in Mrs. Hunt's and down to Nell's a few minutes. She was having her hair curled. George came down and we thought of going up to the Hall to a show but did not

Thursday, March 14, 1867

Pleasant day. Staid at home all day. Went down to Waltham to a Concert at which the Musical Union sang. Liz and Allie went with us. It was very cold coming home. Had a grand supper (after we got home).

Friday 15

Pleasant day. Staid at home all day. Ellen Haynes came over. Mary Heard called. Went up to the Musical Union in the evening. Splendid evening but rather cold.

Saturday 16

Pleasant day. Staid at home all day. Aunt Susan Haynes spent the afternoon at our house. George came down in the evening. Commenced to snow.

Sunday, March 17, 1867

Snowed hard nearly all day. Did not go to Church as the snow was so deep. There were very few persons went. Staid at home in the evening.

Monday 18

Pleasant day. Staid at home in the forenoon. Went over to Mrs. Dickenson's in the afternoon. Mary & Alice played quite well. Went out and snowballed George when he went home. He came down in the evening.

Tuesday 19

Pleasant day. Staid at home all day. George came down in the evening and went up to the store with me. It was a perfectly splendid evening.

Wednesday, March 20, 1867

Pleasant day. Staid at home all day. Father asked me to go to Weston but I wanted to make my braid up so I did not go. Aunt Maria came home with Father and staid at our house over night

Thursday 21

Pleasant day. Went over to Mrs. Moore's in the afternoon but saw Emma Browne go to the house so had to go home. George came down in the evening. Hope it will be pleasant tomorrow.

Friday 22

Not very pleasant. Very windy. Aunt Maria came down in the forenoon. Went up to the hall in the evening. Went to the festival and Concert in behalf of the Freedmen in the evening. Had a splendid time.

Saturday, March 23, 1867

Pleasant day. Staid at home all day. Jerusha Haynes came down in the afternoon. Went over to Clara Powers and up to the store. George came down in the evening.

Sunday 24

Pleasant day. Went to Church all day. Reverend Mr. Dickenson preached 1st Text A.M. John 2:20 A.M. & P.M.. Went up to the Methodist meeting in the evening. Mr. Jordan's last night here.

Monday 25

Rainy day. Rained nearly all day. Staid at home and braided. Leucella went down to the shop. Cleared off at night.

Tuesday, March 26, 1867

Pleasant day. Staid at home in the forenoon. Went over to Miss Nancy Jane Moore's in the afternoon. Played on the organ. George came down in the evening.

Wednesday 27

Pleasant day. Staid at home all day. Went down to the Library and brought Lu home. Went up to the office and down to Nell's and she came home with me and spent the evening.

Thursday 28

Pleasant day. Went up to Mrs. Jonas Hunt's and spent the afternoon. George came down and we went up to the Methodist Band of Hope.

Friday, March 29, 1867

Pleasant day. Staid at home all day. Went after the milk. Went to the Musical Union in the evening. Not many spectators. Had a nice sing.

Saturday 30

Pleasant day but very windy. Staid at home all day. Lucy and Nancy Bogle called, also Nell. Went after the milk. George came down in the evening. It is growing warmer today.

Sunday 31

Very pleasant. Went to Church all day. Reverend Mr. Hill of Saxonville preached Text A.M., P.M. John 3:30. Staid at home in the evening as there was no meeting of the Methodists.

Monday, April 1, 1867

Rainy day. Staid at home all day. Aunt Susan came up in the afternoon and staid while Uncle Gardner went to town meeting. George came down in the evening.

Tuesday 2

Pleasant day. Staid at home all day. Went up to the office and down to Nell's. Went up to Lizzie's and Nell was there and we staid all the evening. The organ was there and we sang.

Wednesday 3

Pleasant day. Staid at home all day. Mrs. Dexter Jones came up in the evening. George came down and helped me about my Arithmetic.

Thursday, April 4, 1867

Pleasant day. Went to Church all day. Alfie was there in the forenoon & sang. George came home with me and I went down to his house after meeting. Allie and Leuy came down, rode horseback a little. Temperance meeting in the evening. Question : does reading works of fiction do more evil than good?

Friday 5

Rainy day. Lulie spent the day at our house. Had two callers to go to the Poorhouse. Cleared off a bit at night. Went up to sing in the evening.

Saturday 6

Pleasant day. Carrie's baby born today. Staid at home in the forenoon. Went down to the Library, the store and the Cal-shop. Came home with Clara Powers & George. George came down in the evening.

Sunday, April 7, 1867

Pleasant but very windy. Went to Church in the forenoon. Reverend Mr. Dickinson preached Text John 17:11. Staid at home in the afternoon. Meeting in the vestry.

Monday 8

Pleasant day. Staid at home all day. Father has gone to Weston today and is not coming home nights. Went up to the office. George came down.

Tuesday 9

Pleasant day. Staid at home all day. Mother went down to the village in the afternoon. Went up to the office. Went to walk with George. He came down.

Wednesday, April 10, 1867

Pleasant day. Staid at home all day. Aunt Susan, Aunt Pamela, Lucy and Nancy Bogle spent the afternoon at our house. Went up to the office.

Thursday 11

Pleasant day. Staid at home all day. Nell came down a few minutes at night then I went up to the office with her. George came home with me.

Friday 12

Pleasant day. Florence, Mary & Carrie Smith spent the day at our house. Went down to Nell's to have my hair curled to go to the Concert which the I.M.A. held at Saxonville.

Saturday, April 13, 1867

Pleasant day. Went up to Charles Thompson's office to be examined but he said I need not be but might have the school. Went down to the village up to the office and into Emma Brown's. George came down. (Mr. Thompson was the school headmaster).

Sunday 14

Pleasant day. Went to Church all day. Reverend Mr. Dickenson preached text (——) S. School Concert in the afternoon. After meeting, father carried Miss. Kimball and I up to Assabet. To N Puffin where we are to board.

Monday 15-

Pleasant day. Commenced school today. We have a very nice school room. Have about 58 scholars, nearly all Irish. Went to walk after school.

Tuesday, April 16, 1867

Rained some today. Went to school all day. Has been rather uncomfortable in the schoolroom as we had no fire. Went down to the store and called at Mr. McGorts.

Wednesday 17

Rainy day. Went to school as usual. Mr. Thompson, Mr. Harriman and Mr. Vose were in school. Went down to the store. Had a letter from G.

Thursday 18

Pleasant day. Have a very bad cold so that I could hardly speak. George came up and I went to the concert in the hall by the I.M.U.. I could not sing. George went home with me and rode home with Rufus.

Friday, April 19, 1867

Pleasant day. Could not talk out loud today so that I had to dismiss school at noon and not keep any more. George came up after me at night. Had a nice ride home.

Saturday 20

Pleasant day. Hannah Parmenter who is going to teach at our school was at our house today. Went down to the Library and at night went and carried Miss Parmenter home. George came down.

Sunday 21

Pleasant day. Went to Church all day. Reverend Mr. Dickenson preached text J 2:19. Could not sing today as my cold still troubles me. George carried me up to Assabet.

Monday, April 22, 1867

Not very pleasant. Went to school all day. Addie and I went out to walk tonight and got caught in a thunder shower. It rained quite hard before we got home. Very hard shower.

Tuesday 23

Pleasant day. Went to school all day. In the afternoon, Mrs. Puffer and I hitched a team and went to S. Acton. I got me a new dress and we called on Mrs. Puffer's niece. Had a nice ride.

Wednesday 24

Not very pleasant. Went to school all day. Went down to the store and called at Mrs. Maxwell's to see Kate Bowen and at Mr. Fitzpatrick's. Had a letter from George tonight.

Thursday, April 25, 1867

Pleasant day. Went to school all day. Mrs. Puffer went to Boston today. After she was gone her Mother and her sister came to see her. At night Addie and I went to walk. Called at Mrs. Phineas Puffer's , Mr. Morrison, Mr. McCormack and Miss Sherwood's. Had an introduction to Morris O'Donnel.

Friday 26

Pleasant day. Went to school all day. Mrs. Puffer came home a little after noon. She brought Addie and I a bouquet of trailing Arbutus. George came up after me. Went to the Concert in the Hall in the evening.

Saturday 27

Pleasant in the forenoon. Rained some in the afternoon. Staid at home all day. Worked in the garden some. Went up to the office at night. George came down in the evening. Cleared off very pleasant.

Sunday, April 28, 1867

Pleasant. Went to Church all day. The Baptist minister of Northboro preached A.M. 14:7 P.M. Josh (———).George Carried me up to Assabet. Did not get up quite early enough to go to meeting.

Monday 29

Not very pleasant. Went to school all day. After school took all my scholars and went to walk up on Summer Hill, a very high hill not far from Mrs. Puffers. Addie went with us. Went to a Temperance Lecture in the evening.

Tuesday 30

Pleasant day. Went to school all day. Went to walk after school with Addie and her scholars. Went into the woods and got some evergreens and had a pleasant time though we were very tired.

Wednesday, May 1, 1867

Not very pleasant. Went to school all day. Went down to the office after Lu and we intended to go to meeting in the evening but it began to rain very hard so we staid at home.

Thursday 2

Pleasant day. Went to school all day. Went down to see Mrs. Stone. Had a pleasant visit. Mrs. Puffer's niece and Miss Whittenmore called at Mrs. Puffer's. Sang with them a little while.

Friday 3

Pleasant day. Went to school all day. In the afternoon went to the door and was very much surprised to see Father and Lu. They came in school and then brought me home. George came down.

Saturday, May 4, 1867

Pleasant day. Staid at home all day. Nell called for me to go to the Library but I had so much sewing I could not go. Went up to the office and over to Mr. Towers. George came down.

Sunday 5

Pleasant day. Went to church all day. Reverend Mr. Dickinson preached Text A.M. Phil P.M. 2 Chron 33:12,13. George brought me up to Assabet. The folks had gone away so we could not get in. Addie went down to Fanny Haynes and John brought her home and went to meeting with us but George could not stay.

Monday 6

Pleasant day. Went to school all day. They were very noisy today. Went to the office and to see Kate. Called at Mrs. Starks & Mrs. Carter's, Kity Simonds & Graham's.

Tuesday 7

Pleasant day. Went to school all day. Had a little trouble today but nothing very serious.

Wednesday 8

Rainy day. Went to school all day. Has rained very hard all day. Had an invitation to the Sewing Circle but did not go. Stopped raining at night so we went to the office and then to the prayer meeting.

Thursday 9

Rainy day. Went to school all day. Went down to the office at night and then went to walk. Kate called to see us. Cleared off quite pleasant at night.

Friday, May 10, 1867

Pleasant day. Went to school all day. George and Nell came up for the afternoon. They staid a time and then we came home. Went down to the choir meeting at the village. George came in awhile.

Saturday 11

Pleasant day. Went to walk down in the meadow in the forenoon. Went to walk with George on the hill. Went up to the office and over to the Towers. George came down.

Sunday 12

Pleasant day. Went to Church all day. Reverend Mr. Coleman of Acton preached. Text A.M. 18:17 P.M. Ruth 1:16. George carried me up to Assabet. Did not go to meeting as it was too late.

Monday, May 13, 1867

Pleasant day. Went to school all day. Had the pleasure of receiving two more scholars today. Went down to the office. Called at Mrs. Proudmoy. Going home got caught in the rain.

Tuesday 14

Rainy day. Went to school all day. It has rained hard nearly all day so we could not go out at night. Staid at home and braided and read. Braided 3 yards today.

Wednesday 15

Pleasant day. Went to school all day. Addie and I called at Mrs. Lupples, Mrs. Sullivans's. Went to meeting. Came home with Mrs. Puffer. Introduced to Mrs. Ed Smith.

Thursday, May 16, 1867

Pleasant day. Went to school all day. After school went to walk with Addie, Maggie Morrison, Annie Sherman, Celia Rafferty and Carrie Puffer. Went to the choir meeting with Mrs. Puffer in the evening.

Friday 17

Not very pleasant. Went to school all day. Commenced to rain a little at night. Called at Mrs. Hutchers. George came up after me. Had a very hard shower.

Saturday 18

Not very pleasant. Tried to work in the garden but every time we went out it began to rain. Called at Mrs. Dickenson's. Went down to the Library after supper with George. Splendid eve.

Sunday, May 19, 1867

Pleasant day. Went to Church in the forenoon. Reverend Mr. Dickenson preached Text (——) Went up to the Reverend Mr. Chapman's in the afternoon. Text Matt 19:20,21. George carried me home. Went to meeting up there.

Monday 20

Rainy day. Went to school all day. Went down to Kate's to get some ribbon for my hat, but concluded to get a new one instead. Am glad I have got through one more day.

Tuesday 21

Not very pleasant . Went to school all day. Some expected Mr. Thompson in but he did not come. Went down to the office with Cilia Rafferty & May Morrison.

Wednesday, May 22, 1867

Rain today. Went to school all day. It was very cold in the school room as we could have no fire. Got pretty wet going to school. Got a letter from George.

Thursday 23

Not very pleasant. Went to school all day. The choir met at Mr. Puffer's. Staid to help them sing a little. Had a splendid time tho no ladies came but Kate.

Friday 24

Pleasant day. Went to school all day. Kate came in in the after noon. Went down to Kate's at night. Kate and Mother came up after me. George came down.

Saturday, May 25, 1867

Pleasant day. Went up to see Carrie and her baby and down to Nell's. In the afternoon went down to Aunt Susan's. George came down to the Library to come home with me.

Sunday 26

Rainy day. Went to Church all day. Reverend Mr. Dickinson preached A.M. & P.M. Luke 18:28,29,30. Henry Gould was up and came in a few minutes. George carried me up and went to meeting with me.

Monday 27

Splendid day. Went to school all day. School was very noisy today as is usual on Monday. Went fishing with Bheney and some of the girls. Rufus, Lizzie, Meg Granville & Kate came to see me and we went down to Kate's.

Tuesday, May 28, 1867

Splendid day. Went to school all day. As we were to have Election day I thought I would walk home. Got rather tired but not as much as I expected. George was at the house.

Wednesday 29

Pleasant day. George came down after dinner and helped me work in the garden. Then we went fishing and staid til nearly dark. Went up to the office. George came down.

Thursday 30

Not very pleasant. George carried me back this morning and we took Al and went to ride. Went down to Mr. Reily's & to the choir meeting in the evening.

Friday, May 31, 1867

Pleasant day. Went to school all day. George came up after me. We went down to the Apothocary's shop and Addie went with us. Went to sing a few minutes in the Unitarian Church.

Saturday, June 1, 1867

Pleasant day. In the afternoon attended the funeral of Sarah Fairbanks. After that George, Abbie, Leu & I went to ride down to Hurd's pond. Stopped at Aunt Sarah Hunts and got some (——) Got a splendid lot of flowers.

Sunday 2

Pleasant day. Went to Church all day. Text Reverend Communion in the afternoon. George carried me up at night. Did not go to meeting.

Monday June 3, 1867

Rained part of the day. Went to school all day. The scholars behave as usual on Monday morning. Had three new ones. Went down to Kate's and to the store. Got some trimming for my hat.

Tuesday 4

Pleasant day. Went to school all day. One of the Irish women came in at me today for whipping her boy and I sent her out. She called me in at night and apologized. Went down to the store.

Wednesday 5

Pleasant day. Went up to Mrs. Puffer's and Mr. Arthur's. Went to school all day. Anna Haynes came in the forenoon. Went down to Kate's and to the office. Walked up the railroad. Had a letter from G.

Thursday, June 6, 1867

Pleasant day. Very hot. Went to school in the forenoon. In the afternoon Addie and I walked down to visit Fannie Haynes school. Staid at Fannie's to (———) and she brought us home.

Friday 7

Pleasant day. The committee came in school in the forenoon. It was so warm in the forenoon seemed as if I couldn't stand up. Had a hard shower at night. George came after me. Addie came home with me.

Saturday 8

Not very pleasant. Addie and I went up to the store and over to Mrs. Towers. Went down to the Library. Ellen Clark called. George came down and we went up to the store.

Sunday, June 9, 1867

Pleasant day. Went to Church all day. Reverend Mr. Turner of Waverly preached Text A.M. Mark 11:13 Judges 6:28. After meeting went down to George's. The boys and girls were all at home. Went to the Methodist meeting and then George brought us home.

Monday 10

Pleasant day. Went to school all day. After school called at Mrs. Hunt's. After tea Addie and I called at Mrs. Snow's. Then went down to town. Had very pleasant calls.

Tuesday 11

Pleasant day. Went to school all day. After tea Addie & Mrs. Puffer and I called at Mrs. Smith's. Addie & I went to walk when we got home from there.

Wednesday, June 12, 1867

Pleasant day. Went to school all day. After tea Addie and I went to the Office and then walked a little ways. Had a letter from George.

Thursday 13

Pleasant day. Went to school all day. Had a beautiful shower after school. After that Addie and I went out calling. Went down to Kate's. After we had gone to bed Kate and Rosa came & serenaded us.

Friday 14

Pleasant day. Went to school all day. Lucilla and Abbie came up after me and came in school. Went down after Father when I got home. George came down.

Saturday 15, 1867

Pleasant day. Staid at home all day. Went down to the Library at night with George and down to the store. Sewed after I got home until nearly 11 o'clock.

Sunday 16

Pleasant day. Went to Church all day. Reverend Mr. Dickinson preached Text A.M. Psalms. Did not go up tonight as it commenced to rain after meeting and rained until it was too late.

Monday 17

Not very pleasant. Got up very early and Father brought me up. The folks had not got up. Mr. Puffer's son was at home. Went to school all day. Rained at night.

Tuesday, June 18, 1867

Rainy day. Went to school all day. Len went off this morning. Addie made him a bouquet to carry. Staid at home after school and sewed as it was rainy.

Wednesday 19

Very pleasant. Went to school all day. After school called at Mrs. Supplers and at Mrs. Whitneys with Al and Mrs Puffer and Mrs Grea's with Kate. Had a letter from George.

Thursday 20

Pleasant day. Went to school all day. Otis Puffer and his wife were at our house spending the afternoon. Called at Mrs. Floods after supper.

Friday, June 21, 1867

Pleasant day. Went to school all day. Am very glad that another week is finished out, that school is almost done. George came up with me and we went to the Rehearsal in the Church.

Saturday 22

Pleasant day. Clara Powers and Maryanna called in the morning. Went down to the Library, over to Mrs. Dickinson's and up to the office. George brought me down a box of strawberries.

Sunday 23

Pleasant day. Went to Church all day. Reverend Mr. Dickinson preached. Went to the Methodist meeting as I was not going back.

Monday, June 24,1867

Pleasant day. Lucella carried Father and I up to Assabet this morning. Father took the cars to go to Cambridge. Went down to the store and got some cloth for a jacket. Went to the dressmakers to get it cut. Mrs. Ed Smith was there. Rode home with her and stayed awhile.

Tuesday 25

Not very pleasant. Went to school all day. Worked on my jacket after school as I wanted to get it done for examination. Finished my letter to George.

Wednesday 26

Pleasant day. Went to school all day. Went over to the school house and cleaned a little. Went down to the store to get my letter. A young gentleman from Vermont spent the night at our house.

Thursday, June 27, 1867

Rainy day. Went to school all day. Addie went with Mrs. Harriman to Libbie Granwell's Ex. Had the school house cleaned in the afternoon. Had to sit up late and work after school.

Friday 28

Pleasant day. My school was examined in the forenoon and Al's in the afternoon. Got through as well as I expected. Lu and George came up. The scholars made me a pocket of anise Lintype album.

Saturday 29

Pleasant day. Went to Fannie Haynes examination in the forenoon. Staid at home in the afternoon. Went up to the office and sat on the Hall steps with the girls.

Sunday, June 30, 1867

Pleasant day. Went to Church all day. Reverend Mr. Dickinson preached Text A.M. Came out of meeting in the afternoon as I had a very bad headache. Went to the Methodist meeting.

Monday July 1

Pleasant day. Staid at home all day. Spent the forenoon in washing. George and I went up to Assabet at night. Went to see Addie and she and I went to Mrs. Harriman's. Went to the store and called at Mrs. Cheneys.

Tuesday 2

Pleasant day. Staid at home all day. It has been very hot today and hard work ironing. Went up to the store and down to Olive Rice's with Nell, George & Mrs. Smith.

Wednesday, July 3, 1867

Pleasant day. Leu and I went to Boston with Father today. He went to Cambridge and we went round alone nearly all day. Bought four dresses and numerous little things. Came home and went to washing. George came down.

Thursday 4

Pleasant day. Staid at home in the forenoon. After dinner went down to Georges. The boys were all at home. John brought up a girl with him. I liked her very much. Went to Framingham to the Hotel for supper. Just before we got home it rained as hard as it could pour. John tied his horse at the gate and it got frightened and ran away and broke the carriage some. But on the whole I had a very nice time and got home safe through the mud.

Friday 5

Rainy day. Staid at home all day and sewed. George stopped when he went home. No choir meeting as it was not pleasant.

Saturday, July 6, 1867

Pleasant day. Sewed in the afternoon. Carrie and her baby came up today. She came down to our house and I went home with her to see the baby. Went up to the office. George came down.

September 16, the wedding day of George and Sarah, was also Sarah's eighteenth birthday.

Sunday 7

Pleasant day. Went to Church all day. Reverend Mr. Curtis who is preaching at Wayland preached A.M.. Got ready to go to meeting at night but the bell did not ring.

Monday 8

Pleasant day. Helped wash in the forenoon. Staid at home in the afternoon. Leu went down to the village and then went up to town with me.

Tuesday, July 9, 1867

Pleasant day. Staid at home all day. Leu went berrying after Father got home. Leu and I went down to the store. Saw the great balloon Hyperion. Went up to the store. (The Hyperion was a British airship developed by Colonel Musgrove Montgomery in 1867).

Wednesday 10

Pleasant day. Staid at home all day. After supper Leu and I went to ride down to Aunt Susan's. Stopped at the Library as we came home.

Thursday 11

Pleasant day. Leu and I went berrying in the afternoon and got quite a lot. Went up to the office and George came home with me. Nell and Mear came down a few minutes.

Friday, July 12, 1867

Pleasant day.(———) the day. Abbie and I intended to have gone to ride but it poured hard at noon so staid at home. Went up to the office and went to walk with George. Very warm tonight.

Saturday 13

Pleasant day. Helped Mother in the forenoon. In the afternoon carried Abbie to ride. Stopped at Aunt Susan's as we came home. Aunt Maria and Uncle Gary called at night.

Sunday 14

Pleasant day. Went up to Church all day. Reverend Mr. Ward preached Text A.M. Num 23:0 P.M. James 4:13,14,15. Went up to the Methodist meeting at night. Splendid evening.

Monday, July 15, 1867

Pleasant day. Staid at home all day. Went down to Alfie Jones at night to get some cherries with George, Mae Smith, Leu Brigham and Lucille. Had a nice time . Came home in the moonlight.

Tuesday 16

Pleasant day. Went down with Father and took the horse back and Addie and I went to ride. Went up to the office at night and went to walk with George.

Wednesday 17

Pleasant day. Went to ride in the afternoon with Abbie and Mother. Nell came down a few minutes and I went a little way with him and met George and went down to his house with them.

Thursday, July 18, 1867

Pleasant day. Leu and I went berrying in the morning but we did not stay long as it began to rain. Went into Mrs. Goodnows to see the baby and into Mrs. Kids.

Friday 19

Pleasant day. Staid at home all day. Whitman Rice's house burnt up. Went to the choir meeting. Letter from Addie Connor. Commenced to rain.

Saturday 20

Rainy day. Rained hard nearly all day and I was unable to get out. George came down at night. Went after the milk for me.

Sunday, July 21, 1867

Very rainy day. Went to Church all day. Reverend Mr. Chapman preached in the forenoon Text: Dan 6 A.M. Staid at home in the evening. Some signs of clearing up.

Monday 22

Pleasant day. Did not help wash much today but sewed instead. Leu and I went berrying in the afternoon. Went up to the office.

Tuesday 23

Pleasant day. Staid at home all day. George stopped a few minutes in the forenoon as he went home from work. Went up to the office and went home with George.

Wednesday, July 24, 1867

Pleasant day. Carried Addie down to Aunt Pamela's in the morning and came home at noon. Went down again in the afternoon and staid until night. Very hot day.

Thursday 25

Pleasant day. Staid at home all day. Signs of shower in the afternoon. Men all hurrying to get their hay in. Went to the Band of Hope in the evening.

Friday 26

Rainy part of the day. Staid at home all day. Went up to the office and after the milk. Went to the choir meeting in the evening. Had a nice time.

Saturday, July 27, 1867

Pleasant day. Staid at home and sewed nearly all day. Lizzie Hurlburt called, Johnnie Morse went past in the afternoon and I gave him a bouquet. Went to (———).at night.

Sunday 28

Pleasant day. Went to Church all day. Text Rom. Mr. Reverend and Mrs. Darling were at church and Mrs. Smith came in the afternoon. Sick with the headache after meeting, sing closed down.

Monday 29

Pleasant day. Staid at home all day but did not work any as I was sick. Abbie Smith and Kate Tower called. Had to go after the milk as Leucretia was gone. George came down.

Tuesday, July 30, 1867

Pleasant day. Went to Aunt Susan's with Abbie in the forenoon. Went down back of the house in the afternoon to get some berries for tea. Went up to the office. George came down.

Wednesday 31

Pleasant day. Staid at home all day. Aunt Mary, Ellen, Frank and the children called in the afternoon. Went up to the office and into Emily Willis'.

Thursday, August 1, 1867

Not very pleasant. Rained some in the forenoon. Went berrying in the afternoon with Edna Gulleson and Freddie Dickinson. Cleared off a bit before night. George came down.

Friday, August 2, 1867

Rainy day. Staid at home all day. Lucella and P (——) spent the day in overhauling old boxes and books. Continued to rain very hard and bids fair for another rainy day.

Saturday 3

Rainy day. Rained hard all day. Helped Mother in the forenoon. My teeth troubled me very much. George came down in the evening.

Sunday 4

Pleasant day. Went to Church all day. Reverend Mr. Shorry preached in the forenoon. Text Corinthians in the afternoon. Did not go to meeting at night as I had a toothache. George came down after meeting.

Monday, August 5, 1867

Pleasant day. Staid at home all day. After supper went up to Lizzie Garrison's and staid awhile. Stopped at Clara Powers. Went to the office and George came down.

Tuesday 6

Pleasant day. Staid at home in the forenoon. Leu and I went berrying in the afternoon. Went up to the office and then down to George's. Leu and Em Brigham were there and we sang all evening.

Wednesday 7

Pleasant day. George and I went down in the stage. Met Hattie in Boston and went shopping. Got me a dress. Had a nice time though I got very tired.

Thursday, August 8, 1867

Pleasant day. Staid at home in the forenoon. Went down to Mrs. Benjamin Richardson's and spent the afternoon with Emma Dakin, S. Goodnow, Maggie Jones & Lu . Had a nice time.

Friday 9

Pleasant day. Went berrying in the forenoon. Went up to Lizzie G's at night. Went to the sing at the meeting house but Marsh did not come so we did not sing much.

Saturday 10

Pleasant part of the day. Staid at home all day. Had a very hard shower in the afternoon. Went up to the office. Hattie and Al Moore came up. George came down.

Sunday, August 11, 1867

Pleasant day. Went to Church all day. Reverend Mr. Dickinson preached Text A.M. Rev 21: P.M. Mark 10:17. Went down to the S T Concert with Lizzie. George could not come out today as he had the toothache.

Monday 12

Pleasant day. Helped wash in the forenoon. Lizzie Garrison came down at night. Went up the office and then down to see Hattie Moore. Splendid evening.

Tuesday 13

Pleasant day. Went berrying in the forenoon. Splendid moonlight evening. Played croquet with a lot of the boys & girls.

Wednesday, August 14, 1867

Showery day. Staid at home all day. Intended to have gone to Waltham but the rain prevented it. Went up to the office. George came down.

Thursday 15

Terrible rainy day. Staid at home all day. Sat up in the attic and braided and read. Has rained hard enough today to last a year.

Friday 16

Rainy day. Staid at home all day. Did not go up to the office and anywhere. George came down. The moon shines tonight and it may be pleasant tomorrow.

Saturday, August 17, 1867

Very changeable today. Has rained part of the time and been pleasant a part. Went berrying a while in the afternoon and lost my breast pin. George came down.

Sunday 18

Pleasant day. Went to church all day. Reverend Mr. Dickinson preached. Went up to the Methodist meeting tonight. Has been the hottest day we have had for some time.

Monday 19

Pleasant day. Helped wash in the forenoon. Went berrying in the afternoon. Went up to the office. George came down. Georgie Goodnow, Kate Tower & Rufus called.

Tuesday, August 20, 1867

Pleasant day. Lucilla carried me down to Waltham to see Carrie. She went shopping with me and then came home. Carrie and I went out in the afternoon and evening.

Wednesday 21

Pleasant day. Staid at home all day. Went up to Mrs. Wilson's to get my dress. Carrie went to the depot with me. Found Emma Brown in the cars so had her for company.

Thursday 22

Not very pleasant. Staid at home all day. Nell came down in the forenoon. George and Charlie came down. Went to the Band of Hope. Very interesting meeting. Rained hard coming home.

Friday, August 23, 1867

Rainy day. Rained nearly all day. Went up to the store in the forenoon and staid at home the rest of the day and sewed on my dress.

Saturday 24

Pleasant day. Helped Mother as Lue is over to Mrs. Dickinson's at work. Went down to the Library. George came down but did not stay long. He has a very sore finger and it pained him so he could not stay.

Sunday 25

Pleasant day. Went to Church all day. Reverend Mr. Dickinson preached. Mr. Henry Cutler presided over the organ in the forenoon. George did not go as his hand pained him.

Monday, August 26, 1867

Pleasant day. Helped wash in the forenoon but did not feel very well. George stopped a few minutes. Went home with him at night and staid awhile.

Tuesday 27

Pleasant day. Staid at home all day. George came down awhile in the afternoon. Went up to the office and stopped at Mrs. John Goodnow's. George came down.

Wednesday 28

Pleasant day. Got up in the morning intending to do the work all alone but instead of that I went to bed and spent the forenoon. George came down in the afternoon.

Thursday, August 29, 1867

Rainy day. Staid at home all day and sewed. Lue and I have both been at work on my dress all day. Went after the milk at night. George came down.

Friday 30

Pleasant day. Went up to the Store in the morning and up to Lizzie's. Grandmother came down in the forenoon. Nell came down. Aunt C made me a present of a butter dish. Went with George to look at the rooms over the store.

Saturday 31

Pleasant day. Sewed nearly all day. Went up to Lizzie's in the afternoon. Nell came down a few minutes. Went up to the office and up to Lue's with George and then we came home.

Sunday, September 1, 1867

Not very pleasant. Went to Church all day. Reverend Mr. Curtis of Wayland preached Text Acts, PM James. Went up to the Methodist meeting in the evening. Saw Libbie Gamode.

Monday 2

Pleasant day. Staid at home in the forenoon. In the afternoon went to ride with Abbie. Carried Mrs. Dickinson and Alice. George came down.

Tuesday 3

Pleasant day. Staid at home in the forenoon. Went down to Aunt Susan's with Abbie and up to Mrs. John Brown's. George came down in the evening.

Wednesday, September 4, 1867

Pleasant today. Went to Boston today with George and Hattie. Father carried us to Saxonville and came after us. Went out to Brookline. Saw Al and Charley. Got very tired.

Thursday 5

Not very pleasant. Staid at home all day. In the evening went to the Temperance meeting in the Hall. Arrangements were made for the Convention to be held next week. Sat with Libbie G.

Friday 6

Pleasant day. Staid at home all day and sewed. Went up to the office. Nell came home with me and I went a little way back up with her. George has gone to Boston.

Saturday, September 7, 1867

Pleasant day. Staid at home all day and sewed. George came down in the forenoon and afternoon. Went down to his house after supper.

Sunday 8

Pleasant day. Went to Church all day. Reverend Mr. Dickinson preached. Went down to the Sabbath School Concert in the evening. Pleasant.

Monday 9

Pleasant day. Helped wash in the forenoon. Had a very large washing. George and I went up to Fannie Haynes with Addie Kimbal. Had a pleasant time.

Tuesday, September 10, 1867

Pleasant day. Did not iron much today as the clothes did not get dry. Went up to the store at night. Staid at home in the evening.

Wednesday 11

Pleasant day. Staid at home all day. Carrie came down in the afternoon with the baby. Went up to the office. George and I went down to the Library.

Thursday 12

Pleasant day. Staid at home in the forenoon. Went down to the store with Mother and Abbie. In the evening went up to the Hall to rehearse for the Convention.

Friday, September 13, 1867

Pleasant day. Attended the Temperance Convention in the Hall. Aunt Maria and Albert were up. Staid at the Hall all day. Had a very interesting meeting. Went up to the office.

Saturday 14

Pleasant day. George came down a few minutes in the forenoon. In the afternoon went up to our house to work. Nell and Hattie came up. George came down.

Sunday 15

Pleasant day. Went to Church all day. Reverend Mr. Dickinson preached. Went to the Methodist meeting in the evening. The boys came up today to attend the grand wedding tomorrow.

George Frederick Moore and Sarah Elizabeth Jones were married by Reverend Erastus Dickenson on the evening of Monday, September 16, 1867.

Monday, September 16, 1867

Pleasant day. Went up to the house and cooked all the forenoon. Al and Charley were up with Nell and Hattie came down at night and helped me dress. Feel very happy tonight in my new home and hope I always shall.

Tuesday 17

Pleasant day. Had to get up this morning and get breakfast for myself instead of having Mother get it for me. Went home a few minutes in the morning. Went home with George.

September 16, the wedding day of George and Sarah, was also Sarah's eighteenth birthday.

Wednesday 18

Pleasant day. Staid at home all day. Mrs. Curtis Moore ,Grandmother, George's Mother called. Went home a few minutes. George and I went down to the Library.

Thursday, September 19, 1867

Pleasant day. Staid at home all day. George went grapeing. Emma Brown and Louisa called. Nell came up. Went to the Band of Hope in the evening. Quite good.

Friday 20

Pleasant today. Went over to S. Acton with Abbie to carry Grandmother. Saw Addie Kimbal, Aunt Caroline & Carrie. Mrs. Hunt, Clara Powers and Nell called. Went home.

Saturday 21

Pleasant day. Staid at home all day. Abbie came up in the forenoon. Lue came a few minutes in the afternoon. Em & Leu Brigham called. Went home with George after milk.

Sunday, September 22, 1867

Pleasant day. Went to Church all day. Text 2Cor 2:12. Went to the Methodist in the afternoon. Text Rev 3:11. The people did the usual amount of staring on such an occasion.

Monday 23

Pleasant day. Went home and did my washing in the forenoon. Went down after Father at noon. Went down to Nellie. Nell, Lizzie, Hattie, Leu B., Alfie and Rufus called.

Tuesday 24

Beautiful day. Staid at home all day. Baked bread and washed floors in the forenoon. Miss my husband very much. Aunt Jane called gave me a V. Bully.

Wednesday, September 25, 1867

Pleasant day. Baked all forenoon and ironed in the afternoon. Leu came up and staid awhile. Went home with her and staid til George came home. Went down to his Mother's and staid awhile.

Thursday 26

Pleasant day. Discussion on Women's Rights H. Rogers & S. Moore. The funeral of Mr. Balltes took place today. Did not go as I did not feel well. Mrs. Burbeck and Mrs. Willis called also L & H Hurlburt in the evening. Attended Temperance Meeting.

Friday 27

Pleasant day. Went up to Aunt Caroline's with my folks and spent the afternoon. Went home with George in the evening and had a sing. Saw Dick.

Saturday, September 28, 1867

Pleasant day. Baked in the forenoon. Went down to Mother's in the afternoon and she came home with me a few minutes. Went down to the Library with Leu. Mea Nell came home with George.

Sunday 29

Pleasant day. Went home a minute in the morning. Nell came up and did my hair. Went to Church all day. Text AM.

Monday 30

Rainy day. Staid at home alone all day. Not feeling very well. Sat in the rocking chair and read most of the time. Have felt pretty lonesome today.

Tuesday, October 1, 1867

Pleasant day. Went home in the morning and helped wash. Staid at home to dinner. Went over to the store and into Mrs. Hunt's a few minutes. Very tired tonight.

Wednesday 2

Pleasant day. Staid at home in the forenoon. Leu came up and did my work for me as I was sick. Went home and spent the afternoon. Aunt Caroline and Carrie were there. Kate and Rufus called.

Thursday 3

Pleasant day. Staid at home all day. Mrs. Hunt came in a few minutes. Mrs. John Goodnow called. Hattie came up in the afternoon to help me fix my dress. Carrie called and Edna Gilbertson & Alice.

Friday, October 4, 1867

Not very pleasant. Went over to Concord to the Cattle Show with George, Lue & Mip Maxwell. There were hundreds of people there but it was so cold that we could not enjoy it so well.

Saturday 5

Rainy day. Staid at home alone all day. Baked in the forenoon. Went into Mrs. Hunt's a minute and into the store. Finished a letter to Miss Taylor. Storm hard.

Sunday 6

Pleasant day. Staid at home in the forenoon. Went to Church in the afternoon. Communion. Went to the meeting in the evening.

Monday October 7, 1867

Pleasant day. Went home in the forenoon and washed. Came home did up my work and mixed some bread. Went to a Tem Lecture by Reverend Mr. Nason. Received congratulations of Dea. Richardson and wife.

Tuesday 8

Pleasant day. Staid at home in the forenoon. Went down to see Nell in the afternoon. In the evening G. went to a meeting in the Hall so I went down home.

Wednesday 9

Pleasant day. Nell came up a few minutes. Went home a few minutes. Went to Mrs. Dickinson's baby's funeral. Went home with George.

Thursday, October 10, 1867

Pleasant day. Went down to Mother's and made some sweet pickle. Went to Mrs. Haynes funeral in the afternoon. Went home with George. Em & Leu came in.

Friday 11

Rainy day. Did my baking today instead of tomorrow. Mrs. Hunt came in, in forenoon went over there and heard Mrs. Colby play. Had a letter from Mary M..

Saturday 12

Rainy day. Helped Mrs. Hunt clean up the attic. Nell came up in the afternoon. Libbie Gramwell came up and spent the evening. John staid a few minutes when he came after Leu.

Sunday, October 13, 1867

Pleasant day. Went to Church all day. Text AM 2 Cor 15:31, PM Rev 21:2-3. Went over to Mother's at noon. Services were held at the Unitarian Church in the evening. Text Cor 16:1.

Monday 14

Pleasant day. Went home in the forenoon and washed. Went down to Nell's and down home in the afternoon. Staid alone awhile in the eve.

Tuesday 15

Pleasant day. Went up to Assabet with Father, Lizzie Hurlburt & Miss Maxwell to visit the schools. Had a little thunder shower but did not get wet.

Wednesday, October 16, 1867

Pleasant day. Mother and Abbie came up to see me. Nell, Mea and Leu Brigham called. Went down to Em Brigham's to sing. Had toothache. Splendid eve.

Thursday 17

Pleasant day. Went home a few minutes. Aunt Susan and Aunt Pamela called also Fannie Haynes and Addie Kimball. Went up to see Leu in the eve.

Friday 18

Pleasant day. Baked in the forenoon. In the afternoon went to ride with Abbie & Mother. Went down to the store. Allie & Lucy came up in the evening.

Saturday, October 19, 1867

Pleasant day. Worked round until noon and then went over to Mrs. Hunts and took dinner. Nell came up in the afternoon. Went up to Lucy's. Emma Garfield called

Sunday 20

Pleasant day. Went to Church all day. AM Reverend Mr. Phillips of Groton Junction preached. Text Gal 6:14 PM. Reverend Mr. Chapman 1Cor 9:25. Went to a Temperance Lecture by Reverend Mr. Anthony of Marlboro.

Monday 21

Not very pleasant. Went down and washed in the morning. Aunt Sarah Guild came, was very glad to see her. George and I staid to supper and carried Aunt S. down to the village.

Tuesday, October 22, 1867

Rainy day. Went over to Mrs. Hunt's. Aunt Susan, Aunt Pamela & Aunt Sarah called also Mrs. Brigham, Anna Richardson and Mother Moore called.

Wednesday 23

Pleasant day. Went down to Aunt Pamela's and staid to dinner with the folks. After dinner Leu and I carried Aunt Sarah over to Saxonville. Went to the Band of Hope.

Thursday 24

Pleasant day. Went over and sewed for Mrs. Hunt a little. Went to a Temperance Lecture in the Hall by Mr. Parker of Natick. Very good.

Friday, October 25, 1867

Pleasant day. Went home and carried my work in the afternoon. Nell Shaw called and went over to S. Acton with Leu and I after Father. Staid down to Nell's in the eve.

Saturday 26

Pleasant day. Staid at home in the forenoon. Mabel Hunt came in. Went over to Mrs. Hunt's awhile. Leu Brigham called in the evening also Nell Shaw, Clara Powers. Mary Moore called.

Sunday 27

Pleasant day. Went to Church all day. Reverend Mr. Dowse of (———) Text AM Ex 10:22-23 PM Went to a Lecture by Reverend Mr. Chapman, but did not hear much of it as I was too sleepy.

Monday, October 28, 1867

Pleasant day. Went down home and washed in the forenoon. Leu came up in the afternoon. Aunt Olive called in the evening also Ma and Nell. Went to the office.

Tuesday 29

Rainy day. Went over to Mrs. Hunt's in the forenoon and down to Nell's in the afternoon. Rained very hard as I came home and rained pouringly all the evening.

Wednesday 30

Rainy day. Staid at home all day for a wonder. Mrs. Hunt came over in the afternoon. Aunt Susan Haynes called. Does not rain much tonight.

Thursday, October 31, 1867

Pleasant day. Leu came up in the forenoon a few minutes. Rachel Ann and Jerusha Haynes called in the evening. Went over to the office and down after the milk.

Friday, November 1

Pleasant day. Went down to Mother's a few minutes in the morning. Mrs. Chapman called in the morning. Leu and Mother came up. Went to Assabet after Ad but she was sick.

Saturday 2

Pleasant day. Ironed, baked and cleaned up. Mrs.Wotton called, also Abbie Smith. Went over to Mrs. Hunts a little while. Nell came up a few minutes.

Sunday, November 3, 1867

Pleasant day. Did not go to Church in the morning. Went to the Sabbath School and to Church in the afternoon. Text (----) Went to a Lecture by Reverend Mr. Gould of Saxonville.

Monday 4

Pleasant day. Went home in the forenoon to wash. Leucella came up a few minutes in the afternoon. Went over to the office.

Tuesday 5

Pleasant day. Staid at home all day. Spoke with Henry & Herbert Gerry. Mary and Nell came up and spent the afternoon and staid awhile in the eve. Went to the office.

Wednesday, November 6, 1867

Pleasant day. Went to Boston with Father and Mother. Went as far as Waltham with the horse. At night met Alfie at the depot and she rode home with us. Got pretty tired.

Thursday 7

Pleasant day. Went to the examination of Lizzie Hurlburt's school. Went down to Mothers to dinner. Went into Mrs. Maxwell's school. Attended the first of the course of Lectures by Mr. J. O. Pick.

Friday 8

Dull and Cloudy. Staid at home all day. My face is swelled and my teeth very sore. Mabel Hunt came in the afternoon. Staid at home in the evening.

Saturday, November 9, 1867

Pleasant day. Staid at home all day. Did not go out until evening when I went over to Mrs. Hunt's while George went away.

Sunday 10

Pleasant part of the day. Did not go to Church as my face was swollen. Read and slept and passed a rather tiresome day.

Monday 11

Pleasant day. Went home to wash in the morning. Nell and Mary came up. George went to Boston today. Went over to the office.

Tuesday, November 12, 1867

Not very pleasant. Went down to Ness's in the afternoon to have my hair done. Went to the Unitarian Fair in the evening. Had quite a good time. A little snow fell in the evening.

Wednesday 13

Pleasant day. Nell and Mary came in a few minutes. Em Brigham came and gored my dress. Went into Mrs. Hunt's to practice for the Band of Hope.

Thursday 14

Pleasant day. Staid at home all day. Mother came up in the forenoon and Leu a few minutes in the afternoon. Attended the Temperance meeting.

Friday, November 15, 1867

Pleasant day. Staid at home all day. Nell and Leu came up a few minutes. Went over to the office and to the second lecture by Reverend Mr. Peck.

Saturday 16

Not very pleasant. Did housework nearly all day. Went over to Mrs. Hunt's twice and down to Mother's. Spoke to Frank Gerry. Went over to the office. Abbie Smith and Libbie came up awhile.

Sunday 17

Pleasant but pretty cold. Went to Church all day. Reverend Mr. Hall of Saxonville preached Text AM 122 Psalms. Went down to Mother Moore's and up to Lizzie's to see her and Alice.

Monday, November 18, 1867

Pleasant day. Went to Boston today with George and Nell. Nearly froze coming home. Went up to the Unitarian fair and went down to Mr. D's and stood up with Kate and Rufus and them back to the fair.

Tuesday 19

Pleasant day. Went down and washed in the forenoon. Went over to Mrs. Hunt's and saw Mrs. Charles Gerry. Some of the band of Hope met here to practice in the eve.

Wednesday 20

Pleasant day. Went down to Mother's a few minutes. Went over to Mrs. George Goodnow's. Went to the Band of Hope in the eve. Pretty full meeting.

Thursday, November 21, 1867

Pleasant day. Cleaned house nearly all day. Went to the Service by Reverend Mr. Butler but was so tired and sleepy could not hear much of it. Kate and Rufus came in a minute.

Friday 22

Pleasant day. Staid at home all day. Ironed in the forenoon. Nell came up awhile in the afternoon. Went into Mrs. Hunt's to see Polly Rice.

Saturday 23

Pleasant day. Made my meat pies. Leu came up and helped me. Cleaned my buttery in the afternoon. Got very tired.

Sunday, November 24, 1867

Not very pleasant. Went to Church in the forenoon. Reverend Mr. Richardson of Lincoln preached (——) Text.John 6:35. No meeting in the AM. Staid at home in the eve.

Monday 25

Pleasant day. Went down home and washed. Came home and cleaned house all afternoon. Went home and carried Abbie some supper. Am very tired.

Tuesday 26

Pleasant day. Cleaned house all day. Took the windows out of the kitchen. George helped me wash them. Went into Mrs. Hunt's.

Wednesday, November 27, 1867

Pleasant day. Cleaned house all day. Had got on my hands and knees scrubbing the floor and in walked John and Abbie. Was glad to see them but was sorry to look so.

Thursday 28

Rainy day. Went down to Mother's and staid to dinner then Father carried us down to George's Mother's where we spent the rest of the day. They were all at home and we had a grand time.

Friday 29

Unpleasant day. David Gerry called. Al Rice and wife came in the evening. Al came in the morning and H (——)and (——) in the afternoon. Went up to Hallie's with Geo, K.Herl & Mary. Al & Mary came and staid to tea. Alice came too.

Saturday, November 30, 1867

Pleasant day. Al called Hallie. Mae and Nell called. Went down to Mother's and staid while George went to the village. Saw Miss Rogers, our teacher. Very cold out. Allie called and staid while Geo went home.

Sunday, December 1

Pleasant day. Did not go to meeting in the morning. Went to the S. School. Intended to have gone in the afternoon but did not. Went to the Methodist in the eve.

Monday 2

Pleasant day. Washed at home for the first time and George hung up the clothes for me. Went down home a few minutes.

Tuesday, December 3, 1867

Pleasant day. Baked in the forenoon. Went down home in the afternoon. Mrs. Dickinson was there. Attended the Lecture by Reverend J. McKown. Hattie called.

Wednesday 4

Pleasant day. Went down to Mother's and staid all day to sew. Leu sewed for me. Went up to the store. George came down after me and we staid awhile.

Thursday 5

Pleasant day. Staid at home in the forenoon. Went down to have Hattie cut my dress in the afternoon. Aunt Susan Haynes and Mrs. Chapman called.

Friday, December 6, 1867

Not very pleasant. Staid at home in the forenoon. Went down and called on Kate and Rufus in the afternoon. Went to the singing school but few present as it stormed.

Saturday 7

Pleasant day. Staid at home all day. George had to do the work as I was sick. He went down to the Library. Mother came up a few minutes.

Sunday 8

Pleasant day. Staid at home all day with the sick headache. Abbie Smith came in a minute. George went to church in the afternoon. Leu came up.

Monday, December 9, 1867

Pleasant but very cold. Staid at home all day. I could not wash as I was not able. Leu came up in the afternoon. Father came in a few minutes in the eve.

Tuesday 10

It snowed in the morning but cleared off pleasant at noon. Went over to Mrs. Hunt's a few minutes. Nell and Mary called, also Father. Went to the singing school in the eve.

Wednesday 11

Pleasant day. Baked some in the forenoon. George went chopping. Went down home and sewed. Staid at home in the evening. George went to sleep.

Thursday, December 12, 1867

Cloudy and very cold. Staid at home in the forenoon. George has gone chopping. Went down home in the afternoon. Staid at home in the evening.

Friday 13

Pleasant day. Staid at home all day. Allie came home today, came in to see us. Got ready to go to the Temperance meeting, but George heard that there was none.

Saturday 14

Not very pleasant. Went down home in the forenoon and in the afternoon to sew. Sewed a little in the eve to get my dress done for Sunday.

Sunday, December 15, 1867

Not very pleasant. Went to Church all day. Reverend Mr. (——) of Assabet preached. Text- John 1:17. He made some interesting remarks in the S. School. Staid at home in the eve.

Monday 16

Pleasant day. Went down to George's home in the afternoon. Went over to Mrs. Chapman's with George to rehearse for the Band of Hope. Went down home a minute.

Tuesday 17

Pleasant day. Washed in the forenoon. Leu came up a few minutes also Kate and Rufus. Went to the Singing School in the evening. Used "The Temple Choir" tonight.

Wednesday, December 18, 1867

Pleasant day. Went down to Waltham with George. Saw Lizzie Towle. Most froze coming home. Got thawed out and went to the lecture by Reverend Mr. Upham on D(———).

Thursday 19

Very pleasant but cold. Went down home and spent the afternoon. Went to the Band of Hope in the Hall. Sang a song. Enjoyed the meeting very much.

Friday 20

Snowed some. Went down home and carried my work. George did not go chopping as it snowed. Staid at home in the evening and read.

Saturday, December 21, 1867

Beautiful day. Went over to Mrs. Hunt's a few minutes. Went down home and staid while George went away and Mother made us stay to supper. Some of the girls came in.

Sunday 22

Stormy day. Went to Church all day. Reverend Mr. (——) of Boston preached Text AM–Josh 28:11 PM-Mark 17:12. Did not go out in the eve as it was stormy.

Monday 23

Pleasant day. Went home a minute in the morning. Leu came up in the afternoon. Staid at home in the morning for a change.

Tuesday, December 24, 1867

Pleasant day. Washed in the forenoon. Mother came up a few minutes in the afternoon. Went to the singing school in the evening. Had a gay time.

Wednesday 25

Not very pleasant. Went down to Father Moore's and spent the day. The boys did not come up. Tried to go up to Assabet but did not make out. Leu came up.

Thursday 26

Pleasant day. Staid at home in the forenoon. Called at Mrs. John Goodnow's and went down home. Attended the Lecture by Mr. Mallebien of Boston.

Friday, December 27, 1867

Pleasant day. Staid at home all day. Leu came up in the afternoon. Lizzie called. George Harrington carried us and Mr. Chapman's folks down to the Temperance meeting.

Saturday 28

Very pleasant. Went up to Lizzie's. Went over to Saxonville with Leu and Lizzie. Staid down home to supper and staid awhile in the evening.

Sunday 29

Pleasant day. Went to Church all day. Text AM-Luke 9:20-PM-2Cor 4-9. Went to the Methodist meeting in the evening.

Monday, December 30, 1867

Pleasant day. Staid at home all day. Nell came for me to go skating but I thought I would not go. Went after the milk. Mr. Dickinson & his wife called also Mary, Nell & Liz in AM.

Tuesday 31

Pleasant day. Washed in the forenoon. Mrs. Goodnow called in the afternoon. Aunt Becky and Mrs. Jones called. Went to the singing school in the evening.

May my next diary contain as many pleasant events as this.
Sarah E. Jones Moore

In cash account-January
1 Bottle of Cologne .26, ¾ yard of ribbon .6, 4 yards cotton cloth $1.00, Hoop Skirt $2.25, handkerchief .25, Boot Lacing .4, 75 yards of Braid at 3 cents per yard $2.25, 8 yards Punel at 20 cents per yard,

June 8
5 yards of Cotton Cloth at 25 cents per yard $1.25, Pair of hose .25, 2 yards of Mearsailles $1.80, cutting Jacket .25, trimming .16, Cards .50, 8 yards Muslin at 25 cents per yard $2.00, Parasol $1.25, Pair of Shoes $1.50, 2 yards of Velvet .20, 21 yards of Cotton Cloth at 21 cents per yard $4.41, 6 Spools of thread at 7 cts .42, 34 yards of Cotton Cloth $6.95, 6 ½ yards Bleached Cotton at 21 cts per yd $1.37, 4 ½ Cotton Cloth at 24 cts per yd $1.08, 15 yards of Silk at $2.00 per yard $30.00, Corsets $2.50, Hoop Skirt $1.25, Collar and Cuffs $1.00, Handkerchief $1.00, Mending glasses .50, 3 Yards Cambric at 13 cts per yard .36, 1 Yard Silicia .25, 1 doz Buttons .50, 2 ½ yards Lace at 30 cts .75, Sewing Silk .22, Twist .6, Alpacia Braid 5 yards at 5 cts per yard .25, 7/8 yard Belt Ribbon .70, 5 yards Cotton Cloth at 19 cts per yard .95, 7 yards Calico at 12 ½ per yard .87 ½, 3 yards at 18 .54, 1 pound of Cotton Batting .30, ½ yard Calico .9, 4 yards Cloth at 21 cts .84, Spool of thread .7, Sack $14.00, Gloves $2.00, Breast Pin $1.00, Velvet .45, Buttons .33, Table Cloths $2.26, 6 Yards Crash at 18 cts per yard $1.08, Match Safe .10, Stove Polish .10, Loon Spoon .15, Tin Dish .25

Cash account October
Table Cover $1.33, Bed Spread $3.25, 7 ½ yards paper at 7cts .51, 1 Yard Crash .48, 7 ½ yards Cord at 2 ½ .17, 2 yards Ticking .84, 2 ¼ yards Cloth

at 25 .56, 2 yards Print at 12 ½ .25, Crockery Ware .92, ½ Day Plates .44, ¼ Day Plates .11, 1 Bowl .25, ½ lb Teas .25, Soap Dish .42, 2 yards Crash at 25 .50, 2 Doilies .36, Hair Brush .35, 1 ½ yds Ribbon at 15 .20Cash Account November

Serpentine Braid .06, Bell Pins .02, 1 doz Hair Pins .05, Crockery & Furniture $30.00, Ribbon .20, Collar 5, Thread .14,

The Moore Family After the War

At the end of the Civil War, John, Albert, George, and Alfred, returned home to Sudbury. After four years of war the family was together again.

Uriah Moore was fifty-seven years old in 1861 when his sons went off to war. He died in 1871, ten years later. Little is known of Uriah after the war. In 1871 he was buried in Wadsworth Cemetery in Sudbury, Massachusetts next to his son, Francis.

Uriah Moore 1806-1871. Sudbury Historical Society

Mary Hayward Dakin Moore Courtesy of Marion Hurlbut Eaton Collection

Following the death of her husband in 1871, **Mary Hayward Dakin Moore** resided in Sudbury, Boston, and Maine with her children. Her obituary of 1896 describes her life as follows:

> Mrs. Mary Hayward Moore died at the residence of her son, James Edgar Moore, Brookline, Massachusetts on Tuesday, Oct. 13, 1896. The end of a long and worthy life came peacefully and almost painlessly after a brief illness from pneumonia. Mrs. Moore was born June 18, 1811, at South Sudbury, Massachusetts, and was a daughter of Abel Dakin and Mary Hayward Dakin. Her husband, Uriah Moore, a descendent of the Howe family, famous in connection with the old "Wayside Inn," and who was a Captain in the State Militia, died about 30 years ago, leaving her his widow. She was the mother of 10 children, Francis U. Moore, deceased, Albert H. Moore of Boston, Massachusetts, Mary Drew of Natick, Massachusetts, John H. Moore of Everett, Massachusetts, George F. Moore of Kennebunk, Maine, Alfred M. Moore of Malden, Massachusetts, Mrs. Bangs S. Baker (Harriet) of Roxbury, Massachusetts, Charles H. Moore of Providence, Rhode Island, Mrs. Arthur A. Cook (Ellen) of Everett, Massachusetts, and James E. Moore of Brookline, Massachusetts. Six sons, three daughters, eleven grandchildren and three great-grandchildren survive her. All but one of her sons and daughters were at her side at the time of her death. Physically, Mrs. Moore was of slender form and of light weight, yet all her long life of 85 years, she has enjoyed good health and strength, and her stalwart and healthful children bear good testimony to the stock from which they came. Only one severe illness prior to her last and one serious accidental fall interrupted her long continued strong and healthful life. To the last days she retained the full use of both hearing and sight, reading newspaper print without the aid of glasses of any kind. Of a buoyant, cheerful, sunny temperament, the world for her was always a bright and happy one. Retiring, quiet and gentle in disposition and demeanor, her presence was always a delight and a benediction. Patient, persevering, industrious, her hands always sought helpful work of some kind wherever she

was-even against the protest of her children, with whom, visiting from time to time in turn, she spent the latter years of her life-always a welcome member in any and all of the homes of her children. She deeply and wisely loved children and had the pleasure of seeing a large family of boys and girls grow up under her care to honorable successful manhood and womanhood. She cultivated in her children ties of family affection and a sense of the beauty of family unity, which has always conspicuously appeared in the large almost unbroken family reunions at Thanksgiving, where this mother, with her descendants of three generations to the number of twenty-three, and with wives and husbands making over thirty, annually greeted each other in heartiest love and sympathy. In the house, wherever she happened to be, she was as young in feeling as the youngest and was always glad to share in the sports and good time of the most youthful members of the family. The summer of 1895 saw her at Kennebunk, Maine going with the boys and girls, her children and grandchildren, on a hay rack ride to see the River Carnival, in the fullest enjoyment of all the fun, even though then she was eighty-four years of age. She gave the services of four of her sons for three years each in the late Civil War, which was always a source of much satisfaction to her. Four days before her death she passed the sixty-fourth anniversary of her wedding day. One of the last requests was that her body might be borne to its last resting place by her six sons. Her life was throughout consistent, practical, influential, Christian, honoring the church membership of The Congregational Church of South Sudbury, Massachusetts. The casual visitor in her presence could not help being attracted to her by her sweet, gentle and intellectual nature. No member of this large family could be more sincerely missed and mourned than she.

Mary Moore is buried with her husband Uriah and their son Francis in Wadsworth Cemetery.

Mary Moore and family. Photograph courtesy of the Marion Hurlbut Eaton Collection

Francis Uriah Moore was 31 years old when he died in 1865 at Dansville, New York at "Our Home on the Hillside." He was buried in New York when weather conditions prevented transporting his body back to Sudbury. Later, at some unknown time, Francis's body was moved from New York and returned to Sudbury, where according to town cemetery records, he is buried in the Moore family lot in Wadsworth Cemetery.

Albert Henry Moore was mustered out on June 9, 1865, at Alexandria, Virginia. Following the war, Albert moved about the country. According to his pension form he lived in Brookline, Boston, and Gloucester, Massachusetts from 1866 through 1872. He lived in San Francisco and Santa Barbara, California in 1874 and 1875 and then moved back to Boston, where, on July 26, 1883, he married Thankful Emily Crosby Nickerson. Thankful, the daughter of Joshua Crosby and Thankful Baker of Orleans, Massachusetts, had three children, Henry, Alville, and Grace, from her first marriage to Henry Nickerson. In 1899 Thankful died of breast cancer leaving Albert a widower. She was buried in the Crosby family lot in Orleans with her parents and her first husband. Following her death, Albert resided in Boston with his step daughter Grace who, according to the 1900 federal census, was a "Practitioner of Christ." Albert returned to California, and resided there through 1912. His occupation was always listed as "upholsterer" in city directories and census records. An advertisement in the 1884 Boston Directory lists his company as *Interior Decorators* on Washington Street. In 1917, in poor health, Albert entered Togus Veterans Hospital in Maine. Togus (an Indian name for mineral waters) was a National Home for Disabled Volunteer Soldiers which opened after the Civil War in 1866. Known as the Eastern Branch, now the Togus Veterans Medical Center, the Home offered a place for disabled veterans to live if they could not care for themselves or if their pensions did not provide them enough financial support. The facility still exists today and retains its peaceful, rural landscape that the Board of Managers felt was integral to the well-being of the veterans.[1] Albert died two years later on March 26, 1919, of arteriosclerosis. His body was returned to Sudbury, in care of his brother James Edgar, to be buried in the family lot in Wadsworth Cemetery next to his parents and his brother Francis.

ALBERT H. MOORE & CO.

Interior Decorators.

DRAPERIES,

Upholstery & Window Shades.

Sofas, Easy Chairs, Lounges, Divans, and Fine
Furniture of Every Description to Order.

No. 548 WASHINGTON ST.

(Opp. Adams House),

BOSTON, MASS.

Advertisement in the City Directory, Boston, 1884.

Mary Elizabeth Moore married Romanzo Eastman Drew, son of Nehemiah and Mary (Jennsion) Drew of Natick, Massachusetts on May 1, 1870. They were married by clergyman Philander Thurston in Sudbury and they had one son who died at birth in 1872. Romanzo died in Natick in 1878 but no information has been located about Mary.

John Hayward Moore served for three years in the Thirteenth Regiment Massachusetts Volunteers and mustered out on August 1, 1864, at Boston, Massachusetts. He returned home to Sudbury for a short while. According to his 1904 pension application he had returned to the war in 1864 as a member of the Christian Commission, transporting wounded soldiers, until the war ended. In 1865, the town of Sudbury paid John and the men of the Thirteenth Regiment for their military service. John was paid $240. (See Appendix I) John's pension record showed that his initials were marked in india ink on his arm.

Census records show that following the war John resided in Sudbury, Brookline, Malden, Waltham, and Everett, Massachusetts listing his occupation as cabinet maker, carpenter, builder, and architect. It is recorded on his pension application that he "helped to build the Soldiers Home in Hampton, Virginia." John is listed in the book, *Building the City of Home and Industry-the Architectural and Historical Development of Everett, Massachusetts,* by Elizabeth Duffee Hengen, as one of the important builders in Everett in the late nineteenth century. He is included on a list with other important architects of the day.

> Most of these men began their careers as carpenters and builders and expanded into real estate, insurance and architecture as their businesses prospered. They advertised profusely in newspapers, local directories and trade journals, offering land, houses and tenements to the public. (Hengen)

JOHN H. MOORE,

Architect and Builder.

Plans and Estimates furnished and Contracts executed with despatch at reasonable rates.

RESIDENCE, 57 LIBERTY ST., EVERETT.

City Directory, Everett. Shute Memorial Library, Everett, Massachusetts

On January 13, 1875, John married Albertine Simpson of Sudbury at the First Parish Church in Malden, Massachusetts. Albertine was the daughter of Horatio G. and Charlotte Caroline (Lewis) Simpson of Roxbury, Massachusetts. That same year their only child, a daughter, Ella, was born. On November 13, 1906, John died of pneumonia, just two days after his wife, Albertine, died of pneumonia.

Albertine Simpson Moore – courtesy of Jill Cook

Obituary of John Hayward Moore from the Everett newspaper in 1906 follows:

> John H. Moore, an old resident of this city, died Tuesday evening, of pneumonia, following very closely that of his wife who died of the same disease on Sunday. They lived at 57 Liberty Street. Mr. Moore was one of the old residents of this city, having come here when it was sparsely settled, and, as a carpenter built a large portion of the houses in the section around Liberty Street. At one time he owned a large amount of property in the central part of the city. He was born in Sudbury sixty-six years ago and was one of a family of nine, six boys and three girls. Until this spring the family circle remained unbroken, but at that time the death of a brother occurred. Mr. Moore is the second of the family to pass away. At the outbreak of the Civil War, Mr. Moore enlisted in the Thirteenth Massachusetts Regiment and for three years fought for his country, participating in all the battles with his regiment. He was a member of the James A Perkins Post 156, GAR. He is survived by a daughter, four brothers and three sisters. Mrs. Albertine Moore was 52 years old. She was born in Roxbury, Massachusetts. (the writer of this obituary was unaware of Francis Uriah Moore who died in 1865)

John and Albertine are buried in Mount Wollaston Cemetery in Quincy, Massachusetts alongside his youngest brother, James Edgar, and Edgar's wife Annie Delight Souther.

George Frederick Moore was discharged at the rank of Corporal on June 9, 1865, at Alexandria, Virginia. After returning to Sudbury, he and his brother Albert found they were required to make a request of the town for the military payment the town promised them when they enlisted. The paperwork the town needed had been lost. They were the only men from the group that left together in August of 1862 who had to ask the town for their money. Their request is recorded in the Sudbury Archives. On October 25, 1865, an article at Town Meeting was submitted requesting the town to pay both Albert and George Moore $100, including interest for the notes given them at their enlistment. They again requested payment in November. The selectman's report on the town debt for 1865 and accepted April 2, 1866, showed money paid as interest on the Town debt by the selectmen. Listed among the thirty persons were Albert H. Moore with a note of $20.38 and George F. Moore with a note of $20.15. These records show that the men received only the interest on the money owed them. The last notation on file regarding Albert and George's request for their money states that it was decided to leave the decision of payment in the hands of the selectmen. A record of the men's final payment was not located.

George was married to Sarah Elizabeth Jones by the Reverend Erastus Dickinson on September 16, 1867, (Sarah's birthday) at the First Parish Church of Sudbury. Sarah, a Sudbury school teacher, was the daughter of Samuel and Lucy (Smith) Jones of Sudbury. George and Sarah resided in Sudbury and had three children, Alice Elizabeth, Samuel Albert, and Albert Jones. Samuel died at 17 days from cholera. While living in Sudbury, George worked as a carpenter. He built the West School House for the town in 1872 and was paid $1,600. The family moved to Malden, Massachusetts for a short time where George was listed as an architect in the Malden City Directory of 1874-1875. In 1876 the

Albert Jones Moore 1873-1948.
George and Sarah Moore's son.
Sudbury Historical Society

family moved to Kennebunk, Maine where he worked at the Rogers Fiber Company and the Mousam Manufacturing Company. During his years in Maine, between 1876 and 1894, George was awarded at least seven US patents for improvements in boot and shoe making. (Appendix A) One of his patents, dated 1877, was held jointly with Rufus H. Hurlbut, his cousin. George was also the director and leader of Moore's Military Marching Band which performed at many functions and parades in the Northeast.

In 1905, when George was sixty-three, he pension was six dollars a month, in 1907 it increased to twelve dollars, in 1912, twenty-four and in 1917, thirty dollars. When George died he was receiving sixty-five dollars a month and Sarah had to apply for a widow's pension.

When George retired, he and Sarah returned to South Sudbury where they made their home on King Phillip Road until his death on January 26, 1929. Following her husband's death, Sarah resided with her son Albert in Andover, Massachusetts until her death in 1940. George and Sarah are buried in the Moore family lot in Wadsworth Cemetery.

GAR in Parade at corner of Concord Road and the Boston Post Road, Sudbury, Massachusetts. The Richardson Collection, Sudbury Historical Society.

George's obituary from the Kennebunk, Maine newspaper reads as follows:

> George F. Moore, Civil War veteran and highly esteemed citizen of Kennebunk thirty and more years ago, died at his home in South Sudbury, Mass., January 25, aged 86 years, eight months and 12 days. Funeral services

were held on the following Monday and he was buried in Wadsworth Cemetery in that town with full military honors conducted by the Legion and Sons of Veterans of South Sudbury. He was the last but one of the 1861-65 veterans residing in Sudbury where he was born May 13, 1842, the son of Uriah and Mary (Dakin) Moore. In 1876 he moved to Kennebunk, at the time the late Homer Rogers and Stephen Moore took over the old Leatheroid company, from which developed the present Rogers Fiber company and affiliated companies. Mr. Moore had charge of the Counter department. He invented and improved counter-making machinery, some of which is still in use. He was very much interested in music and organized Moore's Military band, one of the finest bands in this section with a state-wide reputation, which made trips to Boston, Montreal and other cities to furnish music for large parades. He personally financed and conducted the band for several years, building up his organization by employing men at the factory who were musicians. Only two of the original band still resides in Kennebunk, Charles H. Cole and Oscar Mitchell. Mr. Moore was also interested in sports of all kinds, and at one time financed the local baseball club, and in company with the late Caleb Gurney carried on the local skating rink which was located on Brown Street. He was a member of the Kennebunk Congregational Church, Myrtle Lodge, Knights of Pythias, and Webster Post, Grand Army of the Republic, being a past commander of the later society. On retiring from business in 1912, Mr. Moore moved to South Sudbury, continuing his residence there until his death. During his residence in Kennebunk he was an outstanding, public-spirited citizen who left a deep impression upon the community and the mention of his name has always recalled pleasant memories to residents of former generations. As a direct descendant of the Howe family of Wayside Inn fame, he was much interested in the restoration of the Wayside Inn and on several occasions was the personal guest of Henry Ford. Besides his wife, he leaves two children, Albert J. Moore, president of the J.F. Bingham Manufacturing Company of Lawrence, Massachusetts, and Mrs. Arthur Taylor of Melrose, Massachusetts, a grandson, Arthur Plummer of Auburn, Maine, three great grandchildren, and two sisters, Mrs. Hattie Baker of Orleans, Massachusetts, and Mrs. Ellen Cook of Quincy, Massachusetts.

The Wayside Inn, ca.1915 by Clifton Church.
Courtesy of the Wayside Inn Archives, Sudbury, MA.

Obituary from the *Maynard News* on February 1, 1929:

George F. Moore, the last surviving veteran of the Civil War who enlisted from this town died at his home on King Phillip Road, Friday evening, in his 87th year. There is left one member of the veterans association here, William Bills who enlisted from Waltham.

Mr. Moore was born May 13, 1842, the son of Mr. Uriah and Mary (Dakin) Moore. He was mustered into the Thirty-fifth Regiment Massachusetts Volunteers, August 16, 1862, at the age of 20 years. During his service he was made a corporal. He served for a term of three years when he was mustered out June 9, 1865.

After his return from the war he became a contractor and builder. He built several dwelling houses and one school house. One house that he built was on the plot of land between what is now owned by Frank Gerry and Mr. Harry Wetherbee. That was destroyed by fire.

He married Sarah Elizabeth Jones September 16, 1867. Later on he entered the employ of S. B. Rogers & Co. as a machinist. After a few years he moved to Kennebunk,

Maine, where he was employed in the Mousam Company and was an inventor of several machines.

Mr. Moore possessed great musical talent. While living in Kennebunk he was the leader of the best Brass Band in the state of Maine.

In 1909 he returned to his native town. He bought several acres of land and built himself a comfortable home in the field opposite what is now the Foss block. He worked about at carpentering. Later he sold his place to a Mr. Riggs and rented a small bungalow of Mr. Joseph Keene.

Mr. Moore was a smart, pleasant man, looking much younger than he really was.

He was taken sick with what appeared to be a bad cold but it later developed into bronchial pneumonia.

Funeral services were held from the Memorial Congregational Church, Monday afternoon. Reverend Elbridge Whiting officiated. The American Legion was present in a large body. Six members acted as pall-bearers. Mrs. Harvey Fairbank presided at the organ before and after the service. The casket was draped with a flag and flower tributes were beautiful and numerous. The Legion with its colors and firing squad escorted the cortege to the cemetery where the Legion conducted the military services. Interment was in Mt. Wadsworth cemetery. Mr. Moore is survived by his wife, a daughter, Mrs. Arthur Taylor of Melrose, a son, Bert Moore of Andover, one grandson of Lewiston, Maine and three great grandchildren, also of Lewiston.

Obituary from the *Concord Enterprise*, Wednesday, January 30, 1929:

LAST SUDBURY VETERAN DIES
George F. Moore passes away in 87th Year

Sudbury, George F. Moore, the last surviving veteran of the Civil War who enlisted from this town died Saturday in his 87th year. There is left one member of the Veteran's Association here, William Bill who enlisted from Waltham.

Mr. Moore was born May 13, 1842 the son of Mr. Uriah and Mary Dakin Moore. He enlisted in the Thirty-fifth Mass Volunteers on August 16, 1862, and was mustered out a corporal in June 1865. He married Sarah Elizabeth Jones in 1867. The couple lived in Kennebunk, Me for many years where Mr. Moore held a responsible position with S. B. Rogers and Co. of that place. He was leader of the brass band in that town and was also known as a musician of ability throughout the state being proficient on several instruments.

The couple returned to Sudbury when Mr. Moore retired from business a few years ago where they have made their home since that time. Besides his widow, he is survived by a son, Albert, a daughter, Alice, and two sisters, Mrs. Arthur Cook and Mrs. George Baker, all living near Boston.

Sudbury-The funeral of George F. Moore, one of the two surviving Civil War veterans residing in Sudbury, took place at his home in South Sudbury, yesterday afternoon. Reverend Elbridge Whiting officiated at the services, and Mrs. Harvey Fairbanks played the organ selections during the service. Sudbury Legion Post members under Commander A. F. Bonazzoli attended the funeral and took part in the exercises at Mount Wadsworth Cemetery.

Words read at the service in memory of Mr. George F. Moore, a Veteran of the Civil War

Soldier, rest ! thy warfare o're
Sleep the sleep that knows no breaking:
Dream of battled fields no more,
Days of danger, nights of waking.

As man may, he fought his fight,
Proved his truth by his endeavor:
Let him sleep in solemn night,
Sleep forever and forever.

Fold him in his country's stars,
Roll the drum and fire the volley!
What to him are all the wars?
What but death- bemocking folly?

Leave him to God's watching eye;
Trust him to the hand that made him,
Mortal love weeps idly by;
God alone has power to aid him.

Soldier rest! Thy warfare o'er,
Dream of fighting fields no more;
Sleep the sleep that knows not breaking,
Morn of toil, nor nights of waking.

Reverend Elbridge C. Whiting
Officiating clergyman

George had been receiving a government pension of sixty-five dollars a month when he died in 1929. Sarah's widow's pension was only forty dollars a month and when she suffered a stroke in 1940 and needed a great deal of care, with the help of her son, Albert, she petitioned the government to increase her pension. This was a lengthy process, requiring her to send notarized statements by local citizens, stating that she was indeed the wife of former Civil War veteran, George F. Moore. After many months, the government turned down her request because she and George had not been married until after the war.

George and Sarah's daughter, Alice Elizabeth, married Charles Mone Plummer of Maine on February 5, 1887, and they had one son, Arthur Plummer. Alice later married Arthur Taylor of England on October 23, 1903, and they lived in Melrose, Massachusetts before moving to Florida. Alice died in 1948 and both she and her husband, Arthur Taylor, who died in 1947, were buried in the Moore family lot in Sudbury. George and Sarah's son, Albert, married Agnes Woodward of Vermont, and they lived in Andover, Massachusetts, where Albert was a successful businessman. Albert died in 1948 and was buried in the Woodward family lot in Morrisville, Vermont. Agnes died in 1960, and was buried in Vermont with Albert.

Alfred Marshall Moore, was a private in the Fifty-ninth Regiment Company I. On May 6, 1864, only ten days after his regiment left Massachusetts he was wounded at the Battle of the Wilderness at the North Anna River. He was brought to the U.S. General Hospital Ward E, Satterlee Hospital in Philadelphia, Pennsylvania, on May 28, 1864, "with contusion of left chest and wounded wrist." His pension record stated "wounded by accident." Satterlee Hospital was one of the largest and best Union hospitals and treated over 12,000 soldiers during the war. It was torn down after the war. In January of 1865, Alfred was transferred into the Fifty-first Regiment, Second Battalion U.S. Veterans Reserve Corp (VRC) by Special Order #4. The VRC was informally known as the Invalid Corps. The Invalid Corps of the Civil War period was created to make suitable use in a military or semi-military capacity of soldiers who had been rendered unfit for active field service on account of wounds or disease contracted in line of duty, but who were still fit for garrison or other light duty, and were, in the opinion of their commanding officers, meritorious and deserving. The soldiers serving in the Second Battalion were made up of men whose disabilities were serious, who had perhaps lost limbs or suffered some other grave injury. These soldiers were commonly employed as cooks, orderlies, nurses, or guards in public buildings.[23] On September 19, 1865, Alfred was discharged from the Fifty-first Regiment from Satterlee Hospital and returned home to Sudbury.

On May 24, 1868, Alfred married Harriet Elizabeth Garrison, daughter of Hiram and Harriet Kent Garrison, of Framingham, Massachusetts. They were married by Reverend Erastus Dickinson at The First Parish Church of Sudbury. Alfred and Harriet were residents of Brookline, Massachusetts and Lockport, New York before they settled in Malden, Massachusetts with their three children, Elsie, Alfred, and Chester. Alfred's occupations between the years 1870 and 1920 were recorded in the census as carpenter, rubber shop worker, and shoe shank manufacturer. A Lockport, New York City Directory of 1891 lists his occupation as "inventor". US patents by Alfred M. Moore between the years 1889 and 1890 reveal his work in the shoe business, with three patents for "Boot Trees" and one for "Cutter Heads" used in shoe manufacturing. He also held a patent for "Gear Cases" in bicycle building. In 1896 Alfred, his brother George,

Alfred Marshall Moore wearing his GAR medal. Courtesy of Nancy Jahnig

and son Chester started a business making shoe shanks for the shoe industry. George later left the business, and it grew to become *The Moore Company* under Alfred and Chester. Alfred invented and patented a welt shank for welt shoes, and in 1925 *The Moore Company* became incorporated under the name of the *Moore Shank Company* with Alfred continuing to work at the plant until his death in 1926 at the age of 82. His son Chester continued the business until 1946. Alfred died June 9, 1926, and was buried in Forestdale Cemetery in Malden, Massachusetts with his wife, Harriet Garrison Moore, who died in 1923.

Harriet Amanda Moore married Bangs Smith Baker, a mariner, the son of Benoni and Lydia (Smith) Baker of Orleans, Massachusetts in 1870. Bangs, a veteran of the Civil War, was a member of the Thirty-third Regiment Massachusetts Infantry Volunteers Company I. He enlisted on July 28, 1862, and received a disability discharge on March 21, 1863. They had one daughter, Ethel Hayward Baker, and lived in Brookline, Boston, Sudbury, and Orleans, Massachusetts where Bangs listed his occupation as "mason" and she as "keeping house". Bangs entered Togus Veterans Medical Center in Maine in July 1914 and died there in October 1914 at 70 years. He is buried in the Togus National Cemetery. Harriet continued to live in Orleans where she died in 1947 at the age of 97. She is buried in the Orleans Cemetery.

Charles Herman Moore married Harriet Josephine Prosser, daughter of Willard and Susan (Maxson) Prosser of Rhode Island, on February 7, 1871. Around 1874-1875 they lived in Malden, Massachusetts, where Charles and Charles O. Prosser ran *Moore and Prosser Grocer*. Charles and Harriet moved to Rhode Island where Charles Hayward Moore was born in 1879. Harriet died in 1893, and Charles later married a woman named Jennie. Their son, Herman Uriah Moore, was born in January 1901, but died four months later. Charles Herman died at the age of 58 on June 9, 1928, and his son Charles Hayward Moore died one day later at the age of 27. All three are buried in the North Burial Ground in Providence, Rhode Island.

Ellen Maria Moore married Arthur A. Cook, a grocer, the son of Benjamin and Elizabeth (Slocumb) Cook of Lincoln, Massachusetts, on October 22, 1873. They were married in Sudbury by Reverend P. Thurston. In 1874, they lived in Boston, where Arthur is recorded at the New England Historical Genealogical Society (NEHSG) as a fish dealer. Their son, Edgar, was born March 11, 1874. The 1880 census lists the family as residents of the town of Kennebunk, Maine and lists Arthur's occupation as "leather-board factory worker". They returned to Massachusetts, first to Malden, and later to Brookline. In 1920, they lived in Brookline in the home of Ellen's widowed brother, James Edgar Moore. After Arthur's death in 1925, Ellen lived her last years with her daughter, Meltha, a secretary, in Quincy, Massachusetts. Ellen died in 1931 and was buried with her husband in Mount Auburn Cemetery, Cambridge, Massachusetts.

James Edgar Moore married Annie Delight Souther, on August 17, 1873. She was the daughter of Frances Souther of Quincy, and the late Francis Souther, a Civil War veteran. The NEHGS records this as her second marriage. In 1900 James and Annie lived in Brookline, Massachusetts where he listed his occupation as "provisions dealer". James Edgar's mother, Mary H. Moore, was living with her son, in Brookline at the time of her death in 1896. Jame's wife, Annie died on November 26, 1903 at

42 years of age, and was buried in the Souther family lot in Wollaston
Cemetery, Quincy, Massachusetts. James Edgar died in 1926, and was
buried with his wife Annie.

Cousins of the Moore siblings who were in the Civil War

Rufus Henry Hurlbut was born in Sudbury on July 16, 1842, the son of
Thomas Prentiss Hurlbut and Mary Ann Moore, sister of Uriah Moore. He
fought alongside his cousins, George F. and Albert H. Moore in Company D
of the Thirty-fifth Regiment. He was promoted to sergeant on May 8, 1865,
and was discharged June 9, 1865, at Alexandria, Virginia. He returned to
Sudbury, and on November 18, 1867, married Catherine Tower, daughter
of Jonas Tower and Almira Perry Tower of Sudbury. The ceremony was
performed by Reverend Erastus Dickinson. George and Sara Moore stood
up as witnesses for their marriage. Rufus and Catherine had four children,
Arthur, Marian, Grace, and Anza.

Rufus and Catherine Tower Hurlbut with children, Arthur Scollay,
Anza Prentiss, Grace Perry, and Marion Belle at home.
Courtesy of the Marion Hurlbut Eaton Collection

Rufus' obituary states the following:

> He took part in the battles of South Mountain under McClellan; Antietam, Fredericksburg, the siege of Vicksburg, under Grant; the siege of Knoxville, under Burnside; the Wilderness campaign, and the siege of Petersburg and "The Mine." He had many employees working under him in the Hurlbut-Rogers Machine Company in South Sudbury, which manufactured his own invention, a cutting-off lathe. This was considered the best lathe of its kind, and his machines were sold in nearly every industrial country in the world. During the World War he found it impossible to supply the demand from the munitions factories of the allies and many of his machines in France and Belgium were shipped into Germany. The factory was under his control for nearly forty years, finally being sold to Mac-Briar of Hudson in 1915, who moved much of the equipment to New Hampshire. A fire in 1923 destroyed the factory completely. Mr. Hurlbut was a representative of this district in the state legislature as a comparatively young man. For several years he was town moderator and deacon in the Memorial Congregational Church, and took part in civic affairs. He delivered an address at the dedication of the monument erected in honor of Revolutionary patriots on June 17, 1896. Rufus died September 9, 1920 and is buried in Wadsworth Cemetery in Sudbury.

Rufus's descendents continue to live in the home that Rufus built in Sudbury.

Rufus Hurlbut and John Morse, former members of Co. D, Thirty-fifth Regiment
years later in Sudbury. Photograph Courtesy of the Marion Hurlbut Eaton
Collection.

Henry A. Smith, born in Sudbury sometime around 1839, was the son of
Joseph Smith and Olive Moore. Henry married Elizabeth Nancy Tibbett's,
the daughter of James Tibbett's and Mary Webster on January 1, 1857. On
April 16, 1861, Henry enlisted as a Private in Company C, Third Infantry
Regiment Massachusetts Volunteers. He later enlisted in Company F,
Sixth Infantry Regiment Massachusetts Volunteers and on September 5,
1862, was promoted to full sergeant. He mustered out June of 1863, and

reenlisted on February 4, 1864, into Company E, Fifty-ninth Infantry Regiment Massachusetts Volunteers alongside his brother Curtis and his cousin Alfred Moore. He was promoted to brevet captain on March 25, 1865. This is the same day that George wrote his letter from Virginia stating that Lieutenant Henry Smith was wounded. In June 1865 Henry transferred into Company G of the Fifty-seventh Regiment Massachusetts Infantry Volunteers and on July 30, 1865, he mustered out of the service at Washington, D.C. Henry and Elizabeth and their six children made their home in Chelsea, Massachusetts. Elizabeth died in 1894 and in 1896 Henry married Emma Cole. In 1903 he married again, this time to Annie Furbush. Henry died in Hopkinton, Massachusetts at the age 67 and is buried in the Woodlawn Cemetery in Everett, Massachusetts.

Spencer Smith, son of Olive Moore and Joseph Smith of Sudbury, was born in 1841. On July 16, 1861, at the age of 21, he enlisted in the Thirteenth Regiment, Company F, as a member of a group from the Wadsworth Rifle Guards in Sudbury. He enlisted as a corporal, and was promoted to a full corporal on July 15, 1864. Spencer mustered out on August 1, 1864, in Boston, Massachusetts and returned to Sudbury. On April 14, 1866, Spencer and Susan Young, the daughter of Alfred and Maria Young of Waltham, were married by the Rev Erastus Dickinson of Sudbury and made their home in Waltham, Massachusetts where Spencer worked in a bleachery. Spencer died in 1878.

Curtis Smith, son of Olive (Moore) and Joseph Smith, was born in Sudbury December 22, 1842. On April 1, 1864, at the age of 21, Curtis enlisted as a private in the Fifty-ninth Regiment Company C, listing "farmer" as his occupation. Curtis was captured just two months later at Cold Harbor on June 2, 1864. He was taken prisoner and sent to Andersonville Prison in Georgia. Although Uriah's letter of December 4, 1864, describes Curtis as being a prisoner in Richmond Prison, Adjunct General Records, Regiment Records, Curtis's military records as well as the records at Andersonville Prison indicate that he indeed was a prisoner at Andersonville, and died there on October 24, 1864. Curtis was buried on the grounds of the prison. Historic documents from Andersonville record his grave as number 0 which means that he was reported to have died there but there was no identified grave. Curtis Smith may be one of the 460 unknowns buried under a stone marked "Unknown." There are 65 names of soldiers on record as dying on October 24, 1864. These men lie in graves 11375-11440. Of these graves only 11417 is marked as Unknown. It may be Curtis. It may not. (Kevin Frye, Andersonville Historian)

Camp Sumter, commonly called Andersonville, was
one of the largest military prisons established by the
Confederacy during the Civil War. In existence for 14
months, over 45,000 Union soldiers were confined at the
prison. Of these, almost 13,000 died from disease, poor
sanitation, malnutrition, overcrowding, and exposure to
the elements. The largest number held in the twenty-six
and a half acre stockade at any one time was more than
32,000 during August of 1864. Today the beauty of the
prison site belies the suffering that once took place inside
the stockade. The Andersonville National Cemetery
began as the final resting place for those who perished
while being held as POWs at Camp Sumter. Today it is
a National Cemetery, connecting the past to the present
by continuing to serve as an honored burial place for
modern-day veterans.[4]

The town of Sudbury continued to honor their Civil War veterans
long after the war ended. A group of G A R (Grand Army of the Republic)
veterans gathered in front of the Town House in Sudbury, Massachusetts
in 1891.

Sudbury, Massachusetts G. A. R Veterans in front of Town Hall. 1891.
Photograph from the Bradshaw-Rogers Collection, Sudbury Historical Society

1. Timothy L. Smith, *Togus Down in Maine, the First National Veterans Home* (Charleston, S.C.: Arcadia Publishing).

2. *Massachusetts Soldiers, Sailors, and Marines in the Civil War*: Norwood, Mass. 1933, vol. VII, 122-123.

3. http://en.wikipedia.org/wiki/Veteran_Reserve_Corps

4. http://www.nps.gov/ande/index.htm

Appendix A

Patents of George F. Moore

George F. Moore held over seven patents, that we know of, all related to shoe and boot manufacturing. Some patents were held in his name alone, some with the Mousam Manufacturing Company, and one with his cousin, Rufus Hurlbut. The cover page of three patents and the drawings on one follow. None of the descriptive text is included.

Mousam Manufacturing Company, Kennebunk, Maine, Courtesy of The Brick Store
Museum, 64.3.57, Kennebunk, Maine

Mousam Manufacturing Company, taken from the factory pasture. Kennebunk,
Maine, Courtesy of The Brick Store Museum, Kennebunk, Maine.

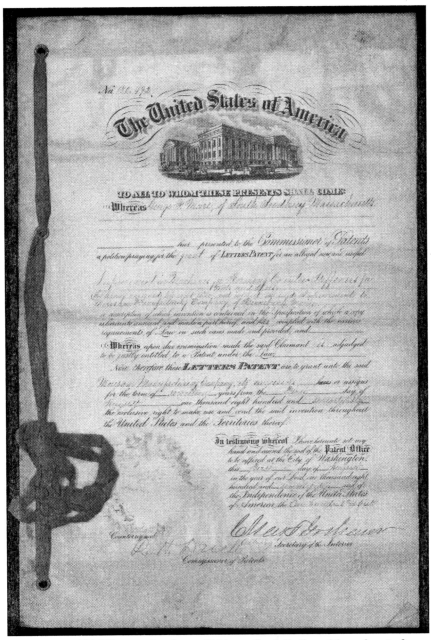

Patent No. 180.492 granted to George F. Moore, South Sudbury, Massachusetts for Improvements in Machines for Forming Counter Stiffeners for Boots and Shoes, August 1, 1876, Mousam Manufacturing Company, Kennebunk, Maine, Sudbury Historical Society, Photograph by Chuck Zimmer

Patent No.299.996, granted to George F. Moore of Kennebunk, Maine for Machines
for Shaping Heel Stiffeners, June 10, 1884, Mousam Manufacturing Company,
Kennebunk Maine, Sudbury Historical Society, Photograph by Chuck Zimmer

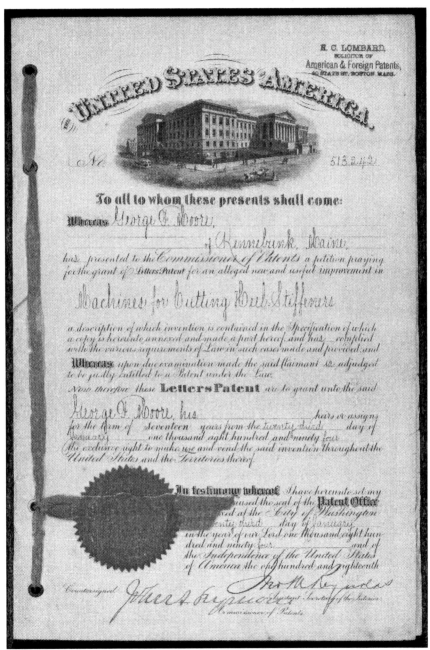

Patent No. 513.242, Granted to George F. Moore of Kennebunk, Maine, Machines for cutting Heel Stiffeners, January 23, 1894. Sudbury Historical Society, Photograph by Chuck Zimmer

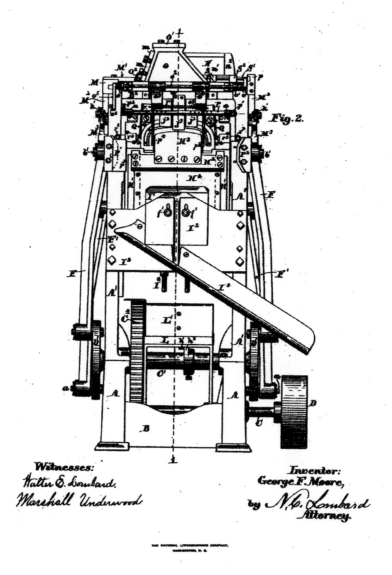

G. F. MOORE.

MACHINE FOR CUTTING HEEL STIFFENERS.

No. 513,242. Patented Jan. 23, 1894.

Fig.2.

Witnesses:
Walter E. Lombard.
Marshall Underwood

Inventor:
George F. Moore,
by N. C. Lombard
Attorney.

Patent drawing No. 01 of Patent 513.242. Sudbury Historical Society

(No Model.)

5 Sheets—Sheet 1.

G. F. MOORE.
MACHINE FOR CUTTING HEEL STIFFENERS.

No. 513,242.

Patented Jan. 23, 1894.

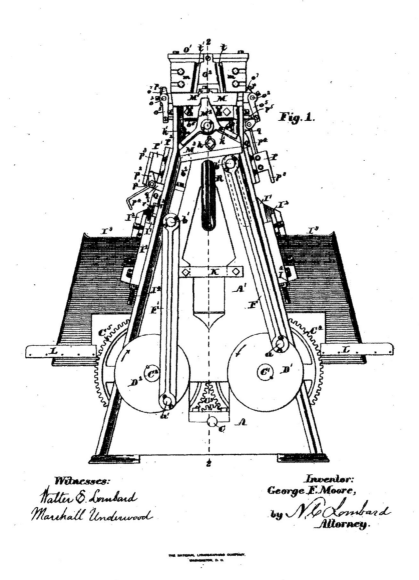

Fig.1.

Witnesses:
Walter E. Lombard
Marshall Underwood

Inventor:
George F. Moore,
by N. C. Lombard
Attorney.

Patent drawing No. 02 of Patent Number 513.242. Sudbury Historical Society

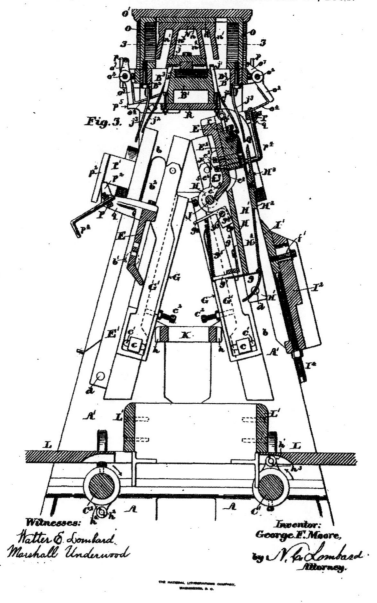

G. F. MOORE.

MACHINE FOR CUTTING HEEL STIFFENERS.

No. 513,242.   Patented Jan. 23, 1894.

Fig. 3.

Patent drawing No. 03 of Patent Number 513.242. Sudbury Historical Society

(No Model.)

5 Sheets—Sheet 4.

G. F. MOORE.
MACHINE FOR CUTTING HEEL STIFFENERS.

No. 513,242.

Patented Jan. 23, 1894.

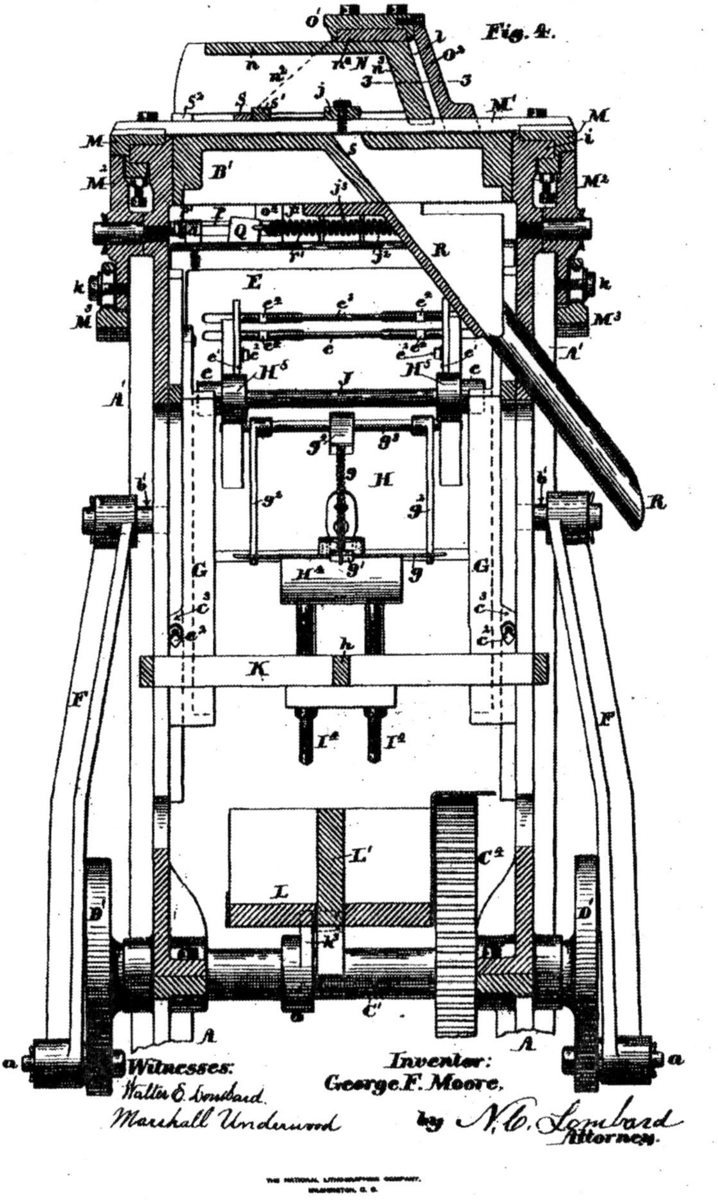

Fig. 4.

Witnesses:
Walter E. Lombard.
Marshall Underwood.

Inventor:
George F. Moore.

by N. C. Lombard.
Attorney.

THE NATIONAL LITHOGRAPHING COMPANY,
WASHINGTON, D. C.

Patent drawing No. 04 of Patent number 513.242. Sudbury Historical Society

Appendix B

Moore Genealogy

Ancestors of George F. Moore

Moore Family	Howe Family	Nixon Family
	John Howe 1620-1680 m.1640 Mary Martha Jones 1618-1672	
John Moore 1611-1674 m.1638? Elizabeth Rice 1619-1690	Samuel Howe 1642-1713 m.1663 Martha Bent 1642-1680	
Benjamin Moore 1648-1729 m.1686 Dorothy Wright 1662-1717	David Howe 1674-1759 m.1701 Hepzibah Death 1680-1769	Christopher Nixon 1703-1748 m.1726 Mary Seaver 1706-1748

Hezekieh Moore
1696-1794
m.1728
Mary Haynes
1709-?

Ezekiel Howe
1720-1796
m.1744
Bathsheba
Stone
1721-1772

John Nixon
1727-1815
m.1754
Thankful Berry
1735-1776
m.1778
Hannah Gleason
1744-1831

Uriah Moore
1752-1799
m.1776
Olive Howe
1758-1850

Olive Howe
1758-1850

John Nixon Jr
1757-?
m. 1779
Elizabeth Haynes
1757-?

Curtis Moore
1778-1855
m. 1776
Polly Nixon
1784-1853

Polly Nixon
1784-1853

The Children of
Curtis Moore 1778-1855
Polly Nixon 1784-1853
married 1805

Children		Spouse
Uriah	m.1832	Mary Hayward Dakin
1806-1871		1811-1896
Olive	m.1827	Joseph Smith
1807-1896		1806-?
Elizabeth Betsy		
1808-1856		
Mary		
1811-1813		
Curtis		
1812-1813		
Mary Ann	m1841	Thomas Prentiss Hurlbut
1814-1901		1820-1882
Nancy		
1816-1822		
Lucretia	m.1842	Rufus Brigham
1818-1887		1818-1896
Jane		
1820-1822		
Nancy Jane		
1824-1900		
Curtis	m.1861	Mary Elizabeth Brown
Benjamin		1841-1893
1828-1900		

The Children of
Uriah Moore 1806-1861
Mary H. Dakin 1811-1896
married 1832

Children		Spouse	Children
Francis Uriah 1833-1865			
Albert Henry 1835-1919	m.1883	Thankful Emily Crosby Nickerson 1848-1899	
Mary Elizabeth 1838-1914	m.1870	Romanzo Eastman Drew 1844-1878	Infant 1872-1872
John Hayward 1840-1906	m.1875	Albertine Simpson 1853-1906	Ella Hayward 1875-1967
George Frederick 1842-1929	m.1867	Sarah Elizabeth Jones 1849-1940	Alice Elizabeth, 1868-1948 Samuel Albert, 1871-1871 Albert Jones,1873-1948
Alfred Marshall 1844-1926	m.1868	Harriet Elizabeth Garrison 1849-1923	Elsie Lizzie 1869-1952 Alfred Goddard,1874-1956 Chester Marshall 1876-1965
Harriet Amanda 1846-1943	m.1869	Bangs Smith Baker 1843-1914	Ethel Hayward 1870-1966

Charles Herman 1848-1906	m.1871 m.1900	Harriet Josephine Prosser 1843-1893 Jennie Nelson 1863-	Charles Hayward Jr. 1879-1906 Herman Uriah 1901-1901
Ellen Maria 1850-1931	m.1873	Arthur Cook 1850-1925	Edgar Arthur 1874-1963 Bessie, Meltha 1883- 1890
James Edgar 1852-1926	m.1893	Annie Delight Souther 1860-1903	

The Children of
Joseph Smith 1806-?
Olive Moore 1807-1896
married 1828

Children		Spouse	Children
Emily 1827-1842			
Anderson 1829-?	m.	Eunice Marianna Capen 1833-1907	
Andrew 1829-?			
Mary 1831-1850	m.1850	Edmund Alphonse Capen 1825-1890	Edmund Alphonse Capen Jr. 1850-?
Sara 1833-?			
Lucretia 1838-1885	m.1854	Edmund Alphonse Capen 1825-1890	Emma 1856 Ernest-1858 Mary L-1860
Henry A 1839-1906	m.1857	Elizabeth N. Tibbets 1838-1894	Alvah-1861 Inez-1863
	m. 1896	Emma Cole 1854- ?	Florence-1868 Lillian-1871
	m.1903	Annie Furbush 1858-?	George-1874 Marion-1876
Spencer 1841-1878	m.1866	Susan Young 1847-?	
Curtis 1842-1864			
Emily 1845-1864			
Halina 1848-			

Mary Olive
1850-?

The Children of
Thomas Hurlbut 1820-1882
Mary Ann Moore 1814-1901
married 1841

Children		Spouse	Children
Rufus Henry	*m.1867*	*Catherine*	*Arthur S.1868-1901*
1842-1920		*Tower*	*Marian Belle, 1870-1961*
		1845-	*Grace Perry, 1876-?*
			Anza P. 1878-?
Elizabeth	*m.1888*	*Dexter Jones*	
1844-?		*1820-1893*	
Helen Mary			
1849-1893			

Appendix C

Sudbury Civil War Monument Dedication

Civil War Monument,
Sudbury, Massachusetts.
Photograph by m. e. hoover

Sudbury Civil War Monument

Gift of Samuel B. Rogers*

Tribute to the Loyal Sons of
Sudbury 1861-1865

Dedicated May 31, 1897

Inscription on the back is:
To those who died while serving their country

Names on the monument of Sudbury soldiers who died in the Civil War:

Horace Sanderson, John Forsyth, Edwin S. Parmenter, John P. Hudson, George T. Dickey, Thomas Corcoran, Thomas Smith, Curtis Smith, Abel Dakin, Hartson D. Sinclair, Cyrus E. Barker

On the afternoon of May 31, 1897 an elaborate program of prayer, music and orations by visiting honored guests with over a hundred school children strewing flowers at the base of the monument took place. Homer Rogers presented the monument which was received by Rufus Hurlbut.

Selected quotes from the address of Jonas S. Hunt follow.

Mr. Hunt said the following regarding the Moore, Smith and Hurlbut families:

Four volunteers from Sudbury, of one family; three from another, and one from a third; eight who were all brothers and cousins, all of whom were great great-grand-sons of General John Nixon, who was conspicuous for his bravery at the famous battle of Bunker Hill. These same eight were also lineal descendents of Colonel Ezekiel Howe, also of revolutionary fame. There was one family in town when the War begun in which there were seven sons; four of them enlisted, one was drafted and exempted, and it is said that the other two boys would have enlisted if they had been old enough.

Selected quotes from the oration of the Honorable John L. Bates:

But the contest of the century that we commemorate today, the contest of 1861 to 1865, differed from that in 1675 in that it was not for the protection of home and life. Nor was it, like the contest of 1775, a contest for political rights for a voice in the government. No. They were even higher motives than these that actuated the boys in blue. Theirs was a contest, primarily, to be sure, for the perpetuity of the Union, but behind that and above it was the irrepressible conflict for humanity, for fraternity, a conflict to make the Declaration of Independence a truth and not a lie in this country, a conflict to extend freedom and the right to the pursuit of life and happiness to every human soul whether the great Maker had set it in ebony or in ivory.

Sudbury failed not the colonists in their hour of need in 1676, nor did she fail the patriots in 1775. What was her course in 1861? She was true to her history and the character of the fathers was shown in the acts of the children. When the first echoes of the shots fired at Sumter came reverberating through the North, the stars and stripes went down on Sumter, but "they went up in every city and town North of Mason & Dixon's line;" unfurled they were from the loftiest trees of the forest, the highest spires of the city. Every one wore the colors. Sudbury without waiting for the formality of a legally called town meeting, gathered in her hall, discussed the situation with patriotic zeal, and took such action as it was possible for her to take, to make herself ready for the Government.

Her soldiers were in more than a dozen of the regiments of the Massachusetts Infantry. They were in several of the regiments of Cavalry and also in the Artillery. They acted a gallant part in many of the most serious and momentous conflicts of the great struggle.

It was not Sudbury's lot to furnish commanders, but to furnish men. To the generals of the war we would accord naught but honor, but sometimes we are inclined to overlook the man who served in the ranks, but who served his country, it may be, with yet the greater self-sacrifice, because he had not the allurements of fame to beckon him on.

In 1881, at four o'clock on a summer's morning, alone, in the darkness, I hastened across the bridge over the Potomac, up the heights beyond until I reached the Arlington National Cemetery. The king of day was just rising from the mists beyond the city, and tipping buildings of the noble capital of the nation with its golden spray. Far below me, the placid Potomac was rippling with smiles as it received the kisses of the morning sunbeams. The city was arousing itself from slumber and throwing off the veil of night. On the noble trees, whose boughs interlocked above me, the grey squirrels jumped from branch to branch, here and there pausing with saucy look to glance at the early intruder. On my left was a magnificent mansion with its stately columns, the former home of the great confederate chieftain, Lee. But my thoughts tarried not with the rising sun, not the waking city, not the playful squirrel, nor the ancient mansion, for at my right was a plain granite monument, and this was the inscription it bore: "Beneath this stone lie the remains of 2111 unknown Union Soldiers gathered from the battlefield." I raised my hat, for my feet pressed sacred soil. Visions of war were all about me. I saw you veterans, in the long and dreary wait on the banks of the Potomac impatient to meet the southerner's bayonet. I saw you in your reverses at Bull Run and Chancellorsville, reverses that but stimulated you to such victories as those at Antietam and Gettysburg. I saw the little Monitor, as in the cause of God she went forth and hurled the shot that felled the Goliath Merrimac. I saw you on the heights of Vicksburg wrestling the stubborn city from Rebellion's grasp, thereby cutting in twain the great Confederacy. I followed you in your triumphal march with the great Sherman from Atlanta to the sea. I saw your patient endurance of suffering and agony, as life ebbed out in Libby prison and Andersonville. I saw you facing death in a thousand skirmishes. I exulted in your victories on numberless battlefields. And as I looked ever and anon there came up to me your battle songs of freedom, as defense after defense gave way, while, under the mightiest chieftain of the age "Unconditional Surrender Grant," you marched through the Wilderness and hemmed in the capital of the confederate states. I saw you enter the streets, saw Lee's troops in flight, and Davis with pallid cheek leaving the doomed city; I saw Richmond on fire and the stars and stripes floating from the capital of the confederacy. I saw you in hot pursuit of the fleeing forces. I saw you at Appomattox where the white flag went up over the rebel hosts and the veterans in blue shared their rations with the veterans in gray. Throughout the north I heard the bells pealing; the cannon roaring as they joined in one triumphant anthem of victory from sea to sea. I saw the nation stagger when she was dealt that last foulest blow of treason that robbed her of her leader. Then I heard the sound as of the rushing of many waters, or the roaring of the pine forest in the gale. More distant and louder it became, and then I distinguished the tramp, tramp, tramp of a great host beneath which the earth was trembling. The long bridge below was covered with men, and each man wore a dusty coat of blue. The city, yonder, was decked in holiday attire. Banners streamed from every pinnacle. The rulers of the nation were there; the statesmen who had guided the ship of state through the storm of four years of civil war were there; the uncrowned sovereigns of America, the people, lined the streets on every hand, while the flag of my country, undimmed by the loss of a single star, waved from a thousand staffs. It was the day of the grand review of the greatest army that ever shook a continent or wielded the battle axe of God. Huzzas rent the air. Again and again, the triumphant sounds broke out afresh, as the remnant of a great regiment, or the crutch of a veteran, or the empty sleeve of a hero, or a tattered by victorious battle flag came into view. All along the line men bared their heads, the women waved their handkerchiefs. Tramp, tramp, tramp, three hundred thousand veterans, flag defenders, emancipators, heros are passing in review. The review is ended. I see the vast army lay down their arms and again become absorbed in the pursuits of civil life.

All of the above was taken from a pamphlet printed by the town of Sudbury on the proceedings at the dedication of the Civil War memorial statue by The Enterprise Printing Co. in 1897.

*Samuel B. Rogers, born 1813, was a successful local businessman engaged in the transportation of western hogs from Ohio to Brighton Massachusetts. After his retirement he started S. B. Rogers a manufacturer of leather-boards with two nephews and was at one time the owner of the Pratts Mills. He engaged in homebuilding and was President of Hurlbut-Rogers Machine Company, manufacturers of "cutting off lathes".

Appendix D

Civil War Soldiers from Sudbury, Massachusetts

The following is the most complete list to date of persons who enlisted into the service of the United States from the town of Sudbury, Massachusetts for the Civil War. These men were both residents and non-residents of the town, with their enlistment location of Sudbury, Massachusetts.

Last name	First name	Age	Rank	Regiment	Company	Occupation
Arnold	Robert	24	Private	33	C	farmer
Bacon	Asa B.	41	Private	45	F	
Bailey	William B.	25	Private	35	D	shoe maker
Baker	Marcus T.	21	Private	38	I	farmer
Barker	Cyrus E	23	Full Sgt.	13	H	powder maker
Barr	William	35	Private	26	E	weaver
Battles	Henry S.	24	Private	13	F	farmer
Black	Alexander		Private	4 HA*		
Blake	Edward	33	Private	13	H	butcher
Blake	Silas H.	38	Private	47	G	farmer
Boines	Patrick	32	Private	26	B	farmer
Bowen	William F.	20	Private	35	F	farmer
Brown	Francis F.	28	Asst. Surgeon	48	F	physician

Brown	Francis H.	19	Private	13	F	farmer
Brown	Lyman W.	18	Full Landsman	13	H	farmer
Brown	Samuel G.	27	Corp.	6	E	farmer
Buckley	Cornelius	38	Private	19	A	laborer
Butterfield	George	20	Full Corp.	1 Cav.	L	farmer
Butterfield	James	22	Private	45	F	farmer
Casey	John F.	19	Private	2 Cav.	I	shoe maker
Cheney	George W.	24	Private	12	C	clerk
Clear	Joseph	19	Private	4 HA	I	laborer
Conant	Albert	22	Private	13	H	farmer
Coombs	William F.	37	Private	1 HA	C	teamster
Corcoran	Thomas	21	Private	2 HA	B	laborer
Cutler	Edward	22	Full Sgt.	1 HA	S	physician
Dakin	Abel Henry	29	Musician	39	I	cordwainer
Dakin	Arthur	22	Corp.	45	F	machinist
Daniels	Charles	22		20		harness maker
Darling	Gardner H.	30	Private	16	H	watchman
Davis	Solomon	36	Private	6	E	carpenter
Dean	George	18	Private	42	A	clerk
Dean	Otis	31	Private	29 HA		machinist
Dickey	George	35	Private	13	F	farmer
Dison	Charles	21	Private	56	K	laborer
Dooner	James	18	Private	26	E	farmer
Dooner	Michael	26	Private	26	E	farmer
Duley	Charles	18	Full Corp.	13	H	farmer
Dutton	Dana F	29	Sgt.	13	H	farmer
Dutton	Francis	26	Private	6	E	farmer
Eaton	John H.	24	Private	45	F	farmer
Eaton	Marshall	30	1st Sgt.	45	F	farmer
Fairbanks	Eugene	21	Private	13	H	farmer
Farnsworth	Edward	24	Private	Army		seaman
Faver	Thomas	35		20	R	barber
Fish	James F.	27	Private	13	A	shoe maker
Fiske	James W.	26	Private	26	E	boot maker

Fitzgerald	Michael	22	Full Corp.	60	B	boot maker
Fitzpatrick	Cornelius	23	Private	29 HA		laborer
Flood	George	18	Private	26	E	clerk
Forsyth	John	27	Full Sgt.	16	H	carpenter
Garfield	Francis	32	Private	35	D	farmer
Garfield	Josiah	21	Private	19	K	laborer
Garfield	Samuel H.	18	Private	13	F	farmer
Gay	Almer H.	27	Corp	13	F	shoe maker
Gleason	Josiah	38	Private	32	G	farmer
Graham	Richard	19	Private	2 Cav.	I	shoe maker
Greene	William	26	Private	13	B	shoe maker
Hall	George Harry	22	Private	35	D	machinist
Haynes	Charles E.	24	Private	13	F	farmer
Haynes	Elias	27	Full 2nd Lt.	26	E	carpenter
Haynes	John	18	Full Sgt.	26	E	farmer
Haynes	Leander A.	27	Private	13	H	farmer
Heaphey	Matthew	21	Private	29 HA		boot maker
Heffernan	James	19	Private	32	F	paper maker
Hemenway	Charles Bradley	26	Corp.	45	F	farmer
Henry	David	22		20		seaman
Hudson	Alfred S.	20	San. Comm.			
Hudson	John P.	23	Private	7 LA*		book keeper
Hunt	Edwin	23	San. Comm.			
Hunt	Frank H.	18	Musician	45	F	clerk
Hurlburt	Rufus H.	20	Sgt.	35	D	farmer
Johnson	Mortimer	19	Sgt.	13	F	farmer
Johnson	William	22		20		cigar maker
Jones	George A.	18	Private	38	I	farmer
Jones	George W.	22	Private	13	F	farmer
Jones	Theodoric A.	18	Private	45	F	shoe maker
Kelly	John			26		
Leavett	Jonathan G.	34	Private	4 HA	I	shoe maker
Lee	John	22	2nd Lt.	1 Cav.	L	blacksmith

Lee	Walter	38	Private	9		
Malone	Michael	22	Private	24	B	machinist
Maloney	James	22		20		cooper
McCluskey	John	27		20		boatman
McDonald	Patrick					
McDougal	Peter	38	Private	24	K	carpenter
Mison	Patrick			1		laborer
Moore	Albert H.	26	Private	35	D	farmer
Moore	Alfred M.	21	Private	59	I	farmer
Moore	George F.	20	Corp.	35	D	farmer
Moore	Henry F.	21	Private	13	H	carpenter
Moore	John Hayward	21	Private	13	F	farmer
Moore	John Herschell	21	Private	32	G	student
Morgan	John	23		20		seaman
Muller	Michael	29	Private	9	K	operative
Murphy	George	31	Private	22	A	laborer
Newton	Augustus	25	Private	6	E	fireman
O'Brien	John	18	Private	Navy		shoe maker
O'Donnel	John			26		laborer
Parmenter	Edwin S.	20	Private	18	H	farmer
Parmenter	Henry	21	Private	16	H	mechanic
Pingrey	Proctor	35	Full Private	13	H	butcher
Powell	Joseph	21		20		pressman
Price	Henry	39		20		seaman
Puffer	Alpheus	22	Private	45	F	carpenter
Puffer	John	33	Private	5	G	painter
Puffer	Marcus M.	21		26		laborer
Puffer	Rockwood	18	Private	6	E	laborer
Richardson	Albert B.	19	Musician	45	F	miller
Richardson	Osmond	19	Private	13	H	farmer
Richardson	Thomas C.	26	Band Master	13	band	musician
Robinson	Daniel	21	Private	5 Cav.	M	farmer
Robinson	William J.	21		20		steward

Rogers	Charles	26		20		laborer
Rogers	Homer	22	Sgt.	45	F	student
Roth	John	40		33	E	weaver
Rundell	James	19	Private	4 HA	I	clerk
Ryde	Benjamin	35	Full Corp.	59	D	fireman
Sanderson	Horace	21	Private	16	K	gilder
Sawyer	James M.	19	Private	39	A	farmer
Sawyer	John					laborer
Sawyer	William	19	Private	26	E	farmer
Scott	William	19	Private	45	F	farmer
Shea	Michael	21	Private	29 HA		shoe maker
Simpson	George H.	19	Private	13	B	machinist
Sinclair	Hartson D.	21	Private	2 Cav.	D	teacher
Smith	Curtis	21	Private	59	C	farmer
Smith	George T.	20	Private	13	F	farmer
Smith	Matthew	19	Private	59	C	farmer
Smith	Sidney	21	Private	4 HA	E	farmer
Smith	Spencer	21	Full Corp.	13	F	farmer
Smith	Thomas	28	Private	19	A	baker
Spaulding	Charles C.	24	Private	45	F	farmer
Stewart	Jeremiah	21	Full QM Sgt.	13	B	farmer
Stewart	John	22		20		carpenter
Stone	John E.	23	Full Corp.	13	H	carpenter
Taylor	Charles	22	Private	4 HA	L	carpenter
Taylor	Lyman	21	Private	5 Cav.	M	laborer
Walsh	James	29		20		seaman
Weeks	Albert	20	Full Sgt.	26	E	farmer
White	John	21		20		seaman
Wiley	John	22		20		stone cutter
Willis	Averill Frank	19	Private	1 Cav.	L	farmer
Willis	Eli H	21	Private	35	D	farmer
Willis	George L.	18	Full Corp.	13	F	farmer
Willis	Silas	22	Private	26	E	farmer
Willis	Stillman	44	Private	30	F	clerk

Wilson	Patrick	23		1		laborer
Witherel	Warren B.	22	Private	16	H	carpenter
Woodbury	George	18	Private	13	H	shoe maker

John Forsyth, Edwin Parmenter, and Horace Sanderson, were all killed in battle. Cyrus Barker, Thomas Corcoran, Abel Dakin, George Dickey, John Hudson, Hartson Sinclair, Curtis Smith, Thomas Smith, Silas Willis and Stillman Willis, all died in service due to disease or hardship.

* HA – Heavy Artillery, ** LA - Light Artillery

Appendix E

Timeline of the Thirty-fifth Regiment Massachusetts Volunteers with Maps

In the Thirty-fifth Regiment, during its service, ten officers and one hundred and thirty-eight enlisted men were killed or mortally wounded and one officer and one hundred enlisted men died by disease, for a total loss of 249 men.

1862
Call for volunteers published in the Boston Journal - July 4, 5, 1862

Arrival of volunteers in Lynnfield the end of July

Training August 1 to 22

Arms distributed to volunteers on August 20

Board trains for Boston and marched by Governor Andrews on August 22

Travel to Philadelphia

March into Maryland on September 6 to 12

Battles of South Mountain, Maryland on September 14

Battle of Antietam on September 16 to 17

Duty at Pleasant Valley from September 17 to October 27

Movement to Falmouth, Virginia, on October 27 to November 19

Warrenton, Sulphur Springs on November 15

Battle of Fredericksburg on December 12-15

1863

"Mud March" on January 20 to 24

At Falmouth until February 19

Moved to Newport News, Virginia, on February 19

Moved to Covington, Kentucky, on March 26 to 30

Moved to Paris on April 1

Moved to Mount Sterling on April 3

Moved to Lancaster on May 6 and 7

Moved to Crab Orchard on May 23

Moved to Stanford on May 25

Travel down Mississippi River to Vicksburg, Mississippi, from June 3 to 14

Siege of Vicksburg from June 14 to July 4

Advance on Jackson, Mississippi, from July 5-10

Siege of Jackson from July 10 to 17

At Milldale from July 17 to August 6

Moved to Cincinnati, Ohio, from August 6 to14

At Covington, Kentucky, from August 14 to 18

March to Nicholasville from August 18 to 25

March to Crab Orchard from September 9 to 11

March over Cumberland Mountains to Knoxville, Tennessee

Knoxville Campaign from November 4 to December 23

At Lenoir Station from October 30 to November 14

Campbell's Station on November 16

Siege of Knoxville from November 17 to December 4

Pursuit of Longstreet from December 5 to 19

1864

Operations in East Tennessee until March 20

Movement to Annapolis, Maryland, from March 20 to April 7

Rapidan Campaign from May to June

Battles of the Wilderness from May 5 to 7

Spottsylvania from May 8 to 12

Ny River on May 10

Spotsylvania C. H. from May 12 to 21

Assault on the Salient on May 12

North Anna River from May 23 to 26

On line of the Pamunkey on May 28 to 31

Totopotomoy and Cold Harbor, and

Before Petersburg, near Bethesda Church, from May 26 to June 12

Siege of Petersburg beginning June 16, 1864

Mine Explosion, Petersburg on July 30, 1864
Weldon Railroad from August 18 to 21
Poplar Springs Church from September 29 to October 2
Boydton Plank Road, Hatcher's Run on October 27-28
Fort Stedman from October 29 into 1864

1865

Fort Stedman from January 1 to March 25
Appomattox Campaign from March 28 to April 9
Assault on and fall of Petersburg on April 2
Occupation of Petersburg on April 3
March to Farmville from April 4 to 10
Moved to City Point and onto Alexandria from April 20 to 28
Grand Review on May 23
Mustered out on June 9
Discharged from service on June 27 1865

The timeline information is a compilation of information in the *History of the Thirty-fifth Massachusetts Volunteers, 1862 1865* listed in the bibliography and from the civil war website: www.mycivilwar.com/regiments/usa-ma/ma_inf_reg_35.htm (accessed on 12 Feb. 11).

Map of travels of George Moore during the Civil War, map by m. e. hoover

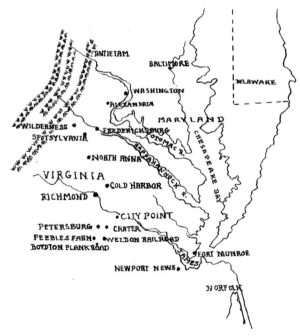

Virginia Battles. Map by m. e. hoover

Appendix F

Commissions during the Civil War

United States Christian Commission

The Young Men's Christian Association (YMCA) founded the United States Christian Commission in November, 1861, after the disastrous First Battle of Bull Run. The Commission was formed originally to act as a clearinghouse for all religious work in the armed forces. A secondary and later goal was to provide numerous social services and recreation along with spiritual support to soldiers of both armies, similar to our present USO. Commission delegates, who were often seminary students and ministers, also collaborated with the U. S. Sanitary Commission in providing medical services. During the war more than 5,000 volunteers delivered over 6 million worth of goods and supplies to men on the battlefields, in camps, hospitals, and prisons. Although relatively unknown, the benevolent work of the Christian Commission during the Civil War is a story of heroism and courage. (Meredith 120)

United States Sanitary Commission

The United States Sanitary Commission was a relief organization of volunteers formed by the Federal Government in June of 1861 in response to a delegation of civilians who lobbied the War Department to improve the medical facilities at the battlefields. It covered all types of aid including hospital medical inspection and ambulance service. It provided railroad hospital cars, and maintained and operated feeding stations. The executive secretary was Frederick Law Olmsted who coordinated the activities of thousands of volunteers, collected needed medical supplies, and recruited thousands of nurses. The Commission also furnished financial assistance to families of deceased or wounded soldiers. Dorothea Dix, who had observed

Florence Nightingale's hospitals, was active in the more than fifty hospitals which were opening in the Washington area. Wooden hospitals were built wherever space was available, and other hospitals were opened in schools and colleges including Georgetown University. Hospitals were also located on the present day site of the Smithsonian Air and Space Museum, and the south lawn of the White House. Although the Sanitary Commission was in large part financed by the Federal Government, its funds were inadequate to meet its needs, so private citizens made up the deficit by holding popular charity fundraisers and "Sanitary Fairs" around the country to raise money. (Keegan 315-316)(Meredith 120)

Appendix G

Governor Andrew and Generals
mentioned in the letters

John Albion Andrew (1818-1867)

A graduate of Bowdoin College, John Andrew took office as Governor of Massachusetts on January 2, 1861, and immediately placed the Commonwealth troops in a state of readiness to support the Union. Because of this, and under his leadership, Massachusetts troops were the first to arrive in Washington and the first troops to fight in the Civil War. In 1863, he sent a petition to President Lincoln to compel the army to accept the Massachusetts Fifty-fourth Regiment, formed entirely of black troops under the leadership of volunteer white officers. After the war Andrew advocated reconciliation and friendship with the South. (Commonwealth of Massachusetts Website)

Nathaniel Prentiss Banks (1816-1894)

Born in Waltham, Massachusetts, Nathaniel Banks received only a "common" education and served as a bobbin boy in a cotton factory in his early years. However, he was admitted to the bar at age twenty-three and served in the state legislature as a U. S. Congressman, and from 1858 to 1860 as Governor of Massachusetts. With no prior military service, Banks was in divisional and departmental command early in the war. In November 1862 he organized a force of 30,000 new recruits drawn from New York and New England and sailed from New York with this large force of raw recruits to New Orleans, Louisiana, as Commander of the Department of the Gulf. Although it was felt that he was not entitled, he was awarded the Thanks of Congress as one of its former members. After he was mustered out of the service, he returned to his political career and served in congress and the state senate until 1890. (Sifakis, 30-31)

Ambrose Everett Burnside (1824-1881)

An Indiana native, Burnside graduated from West Point in 1847 and served six years in the regular artillery. In 1853 he moved to Rhode Island, served as major general in the militia, and began manufacturing a breech-loading carbine. When this endeavor was unsuccessful, and with the outbreak of the Civil War, Burnside joined the Union Army serving as brigadier general. Throughout his career, he often refused promotions recognizing his own inexperience and inability to lead. He led troops at South Mountain and Antietam, in command of the IX Corps under General McClellan. In Antietam, his delay in attacking at Stone Bridge was in part due to McClellan's cumbersome placement of the two corps under his command. When General McClellan was removed from command at this time, Burnside reluctantly accepted assignment on November 7, 1862, as Commander of the army of the Potomac. The Union defeat at Fredericksburg and the disastrous "Mud March" resulted in Burnside's resignation. President Lincoln replaced him with Major General Joseph Hooker; however, because he was reluctant to lose General Burnside, Lincoln assigned him to the Department of the Ohio. For his courageous stand at Knoxville against Confederate General Longstreet, Burnside received the Thanks of Congress on January 28, 1864. Burnside's reluctance to commit his troops in various battles resulted in his being sent on leave from which he was never recalled. He resigned on April 15, 1865, and later served as Governor of Rhode Island for three years and as senator from Rhode Island until his death in 1881. (The term "sideburns" comes from the unusual pattern of whiskers that he wore).

Edward Ferrero (1831-1899)

Edward Ferrero was born in Spain, but was raised in New York and served in the New York Militia. He was a dance instructor at the United States Military Academy, and joined the army at the beginning of the war. He served as a division commander, primarily in the IX Corps. He led a brigade of the army of the Potomac under General Burnside in battles at Second Bull Run, Fredericksburg, South Mountain, and Antietam where his brigade was a part of the Union IX Corps that stormed Burnside's Bridge. For his personal bravery at Antietam he was promoted to brigadier general of volunteers on September 19, 1862. His career was marred by criticism of his leadership skills. On August 24, 1865, he mustered out and returned to his dancing instructor career. (Sifakis, 215-216)

Ulysses Simpson Grant (1822-1885)

Graduating from the United States Military Academy in 1843, Grant excelled only in horsemanship, and found the military life distasteful. He served in the Mexican War, frequently leading a company in combat. His returned to civilian life in 1854, however, was unsuccessful. His attempts at farming, selling real estate, and serving as a store clerk all failed. When the Civil War broke out, he restarted his military career. After varied successes and difficulties during the first several months of the war, President Lincoln promoted him to the rank of lieutenant general in the winter of 1863 and gave him command of all the Union armies. In December, 1863, Grant received the Thanks of Congress, one of only fifteen officers to receive that honor. In April, 1865, the Union Army captured Richmond, the Confederate capital, and General Grant pursued Lee to Appomattox, virtually ending the war. Elected President of the United States in 1868, he served two terms. He retired with the rank of general and wrote his autobiography, *Personal Memoirs of U.S. Grant*, which brought his family $450,000. General Grant died of cancer of the throat on July 23, 1885.

John Frederick Hartranft (1830-1889)

A volunteer from Pennsylvania, John Hartranft graduated from Union College in Schenectady, New York, with a degree in civil engineering. In July, 1862, he served as division commander in Burnside's IX Corps. He fought at Second Bull Run, South Mountain, Fredericksburg, and Antietam where he led the famous charge across Burnside's Bridge. He was promoted to brigadier general on May 12, 1864, after participating in the Wilderness Campaign and Spotsylvania. Mustered out on January 15, 1866, he was elected Governor of Pennsylvania in 1872. In 1876, he was a contender for the presidential nomination which eventually went to Rutherford B. Hayes of Ohio who had served with Hartranft during the Civil War in the same army corps. (Sifakis, 289)

Joseph Hooker (1814-1879)

A Massachusetts native, "Fighting Joe" Hooker, (a nickname he never liked) graduated from West Point in 1837, and after serving in the Mexican War, resigned his commission in 1839. At the beginning of the Civil War he was serving as Colonel of the Massachusetts State Militia, and offered his services to Washington. He served in various positions, among them as Commander Second Division III Corps Army of the Potomac. He went with McClellan's army to the Peninsula Campaign, earning the reputation of taking care of his men. He took part in battles at Second Bull Run, South Mountain, and Antietam. After the disastrous Mud March, General

Burnside was relieved of duty, and Hooker was given command. During General Hooker's time in the service, President Lincoln was concerned about Hooker's criticism of the officers and commanders, and his loose and negative talk about the management of the war. A heavy alcohol user, he was considered by many an immodest and immoral man. Throughout his service, General Hooker complained that others were given credit for his actions. Mustered out of the service in 1866, he spent the rest of his years in Michigan, Ohio, Indiana, and Illinois. On May 4, 1865, the coffin of President Abraham Lincoln was led in a slow march to Oak Ridge Cemetery by General Joseph Hooker. (Sifakis, 317-318)

John Williams Hudson (1836-1872)

A graduate of Harvard College in 1856, John taught school in Wayland Massachusetts for two years, studied law, and was admitted to the Suffolk Bar in 1858. He enlisted in August, 1862, with George and Albert Moore, and served in the Thirty-fifth Regiment Massachusetts Volunteer Infantry. Upon enlisting he received a commission as Second Lieutenant. Between his enlistment and November 1864, he was promoted to first lieutenant, captain, major and lieutenant-colonel. He served on the staffs of Generals Ferrero, Ledlie, and White, and fought in the battles at Antietam, Fredericksburg, Knoxville, North Anna River, Cold Harbor, and the various battles around Petersburg. After the war he married Sophia Whitney Mellen in March, 1865, and served as selectman in the town of Lexington, Massachusetts from 1866 to 1868. He died at the age of 36 on June 1, 1872. (Hudson, Charles)

Robert Edward Lee (1807-1870)

Graduating in 1829, second in his class at West Point, Lee did not receive a single demerit in his four years at the military academy and served as the cadet corps' adjutant. He served in the Mexican War and in various military positions as an exceptional officer for thirty-two years until 1861 when President Lincoln asked Lee to take command of the entire Union army. Although he did not support secession, Lee resigned his military commission as colonel in the U. S. Army to support the southern cause in his home state of Virginia. He served as senior military advisor to President Jefferson Davis, later becoming Commander of the Confederate Army of Northern Virginia. During his military service he was known as a superb military tactician. During the war he battled northern troops, winning victories over Burnside at Fredericksburg, defeating Hooker at Chancellorsville, and emerging victorious at Second Bull Run. His loss at Antietam, and the disastrous failure at Gettysburg resulted in almost certain eventual defeat for the South. In his final siege, Lee's forces held on to Richmond for ten months before he was forced to surrender at Appomattox. After the war Lee became president of Washington College (now Washington and Lee University) in Lexington, Virginia. He died of heart disease on October 12, 1870. Robert E. Lee remains the idol of the South and a popular figure in the North to this day.

Samuel Haven Leonard (1825-1902)

Born in Bolton, Massachusetts, on July 10, 1825, and listed as an "express man", Samuel Leonard was mustered into the Thirteenth Massachusetts Volunteer Infantry on July 16, 1861. He served as Colonel and Commander of the Thirteenth Regiment. Because of his high rank, he acted as Brigade Commander of the army of the Potomac, First Corps, Second Division, First Brigade at various times. During the winter of 1863-1864, Colonel Leonard was in command of the brigade picket for the advance guard of the army of the Potomac. He was known as a man of few words, but he had a clear booming voice and a reputation throughout Massachusetts as a drill master second to none. The four rifle companies of the Fourth Volunteers became the nucleus of the Thirteenth Regiment Massachusetts Volunteers in 1861. Because it cost a recruit $12.50 for the privilege of enlisting in the exclusive Fourth Battalion of Rifles in addition to approval by a vote from members of the Boston Militia group, most of these enlistees were Boston men from good circumstances whose employers promised to hold their positions until they returned from the war. Colonel Leonard led his regiment through three years of hard campaigns which gained for them an enviable service record. He was seriously wounded in Gettysburg on July 1, 1863, when his regiment suffered heavily on Seminary Ridge. After an hour of fighting the Thirteenth Regiment captured 130 Confederates, but as they fought their way back to their lines the Union defense line collapsed and they lost almost two-thirds of their men. They brought 284 men to the field but lost seven killed, seventy-seven wounded, and 101 missing. Colonel Leonard mustered out on August 1, 1864. He died on December 27, 1902, and was buried in Worcester Rural Cemetery. (Section 14, Lot 1)

James Longstreet (1821-1904)

James Longstreet, affectionately called "Old War Horse" by General Lee, was born January 8, 1821, in South Carolina, moving to Alabama as a young boy. He graduated from West Point in 1842. In June 1861, with a staff rank of major, he resigned his commission and joined the Confederacy. Longstreet made significant contributions to Confederate victories in Second Bull Run, Fredericksburg, and Chickamauga. He also fought in Antietam and the Battle of the Wilderness where he was severely injured. At Gettysburg, he supervised the disastrous infantry assault known as Pickett's Charge. A favorite of General Robert E. Lee, he remained with him throughout the war and was with him at the surrender at Appomattox. After the war Longstreet worked for the U.S. Government as a diplomat, civil servant, and administrator. He died in Gainesville, Georgia, on January 2, 1904, one of only a few generals to live into the Twentieth century. (Sifakis, 394-395)

George Brinton McClellan (1826-1885)
George McClellan first attended the University of Pennsylvania, transferring to West Point to graduate second in his class in 1846. He served in Mexico and later was sent overseas to study European armies. In 1857 he resigned his commission and had a successful career with the Illinois Central Railroad as chief engineer and vice-president. In 1861 he re-entered the military at the beginning of the Civil War. After the North's defeat at First Bull Run (Manassas) in July 1861, President Lincoln put McClellan in charge of the Union forces the following November. McClellan whipped 100,000 untrained volunteers into the powerful Army of the Potomac. The soldiers were enthusiastic about their new leader, and proud of themselves. It soon became apparent that General McClellan was a highly intelligent engineer and a good organizer, but he had difficulty commanding his army. His caution and delay in moving his troops caused President Lincoln to lose patience. In March, 1862, the President relieved McClellan of his post. Subsequently, at Antietam, although a Union corporal had found a copy of Lee's secret orders and passed them along, McClellan's customary caution caused him to delay for sixteen hours when an immediate attack on the enemy might have ended the war. General McClellan relinquished command in November, 1862, and returned home to New Jersey to await new orders which were never sent. He ran against Lincoln for President of the United States in 1864, but carried only three states, resigning his commission on Election Day. He served as Governor of New Jersey in the late 1870's and died in 1885. (Sifakis, 406-407)

Albert Augustus Pope (1843-1909)
Born in Boston, Massachusetts, Albert Pope was commissioned as second lieutenant in the Thirty-fifth Massachusetts Regiment in 1862. He served in this capacity until the close of the Civil War, and was mustered out as brevet lieutenant colonel. After the war, Pope became interested in bicycles and by 1890 controlled the central bicycle patents in the United States. At the height of the bicycle craze in the mid 1890's, Pope was manufacturing about a quarter million bicycles annually under his bicycle brand, *Columbia*. At this time he began to diversify into auto production renaming the *Motor*

Carriage Department as the *Columbia Automobile Company.* Albert Pope was married to Abbie Linder of Newton, Massachusetts. They had four sons and one daughter. Pope died on August 20, 1909.

William Starke Rosecrans (1819-1898)

Born in Ohio, Rosecrans graduated from West Point in 1842, ranking fifth in his class. After a series of peacetime promotions, he resigned in 1854, but returned to military service at the outbreak of the Civil War. He was assigned to the staff of George McClellan and fought in major battles, with varying success, commanding units in Virginia, Missouri, and Tennessee. He was one of fifteen Union officers who received the Thanks of Congress Award, as well as President Lincoln's "expression of gratification," for victory at Murfreesboro. Rosecrans was suddenly relieved of duty in December, 1864, and spent the rest of his career waiting orders which never came. He resigned in 1867 and settled in California where he was elected to Congress in 1881. In 1889 he was placed on the retired list as brigadier general. He died in California and is buried in Arlington National Cemetery. (Sifakis, 553-555)

William Tecumseh Sherman (1820-1891)

William Tecumseh Sherman's father died when the boy was nine years old. There were eleven children in the family, so a neighbor, Senator Thomas Ewing took him in. William Sherman was a lively red-headed boy with a middle name derived from his father's interest in Tecumseh, chief of the Shawnee Indians. When Sherman was sixteen years old, Thomas Ewing obtained an appointment to the military academy for him. Sherman did well academically but had difficulty with the rules and regulations. In his *Memoir,* Sherman writes: "My average demerits, *per annum,* were about one hundred and fifty which reduced my final class standing from four to six." He entered the army as a second lieutenant and was stationed in Florida, Georgia, and South Carolina. In the years before the Civil War, Sherman married the daughter of his benefactor, resigned his commission, and went into banking in San Francisco. Later he became president of a military academy which is now Louisiana State University. At a meeting in Washington, D.C. with President Lincoln, he expressed the thought that the North was woefully unprepared for war which he determined would be a lengthy affair. In May 1861 Sherman was commissioned Colonel of the Thirteenth Infantry Regiment. In the First Battle of Bull Run in July, 1861, he was grazed by bullets and began to have second thoughts about his participation in the war. Sherman's Atlanta Campaign in 1864, with the capture of the city, ensured Lincoln's presidential reelection and was a source of great elation in the North. Sherman's famous "March to the Sea" was a campaign in December, 1864, in which Sherman took 62,000 men to the port of Savannah, Georgia, causing enormous property damage as he marched across the state, capturing Savannah. Sherman retired from the army in 1884 and lived in New York City thereafter, giving speeches, painting, and quoting Shakespeare. (Wikipedia, *Memoirs of Gen Sherman)*

Edward Augustus Wild (1825-1891)

A native of Brookline, Massachusetts, and a graduate of Harvard College and Jefferson Medical College in Philadelphia, Dr. Edward Wild served as a surgeon in the Crimean War. He was one of the first to join the ranks of the army of the Potomac when Governor Andrew asked for recruits. Dr. Wild joined as a front-line officer, preferring to command troops rather than tend to their medical needs. On August 21, 1862, he was appointed Colonel of the Thirty-fifth Massachusetts Infantry and assigned to the army of the Potomac's IX Corps. He led his new recruits into combat during the Maryland Campaign. At South Mountain he was severely wounded in his left arm and directed surgeons to amputate. While recuperating, he was promoted to brigadier general and assigned to recruiting. He recruited black soldiers in Massachusetts and later led a brigade of black troops. During his army service he had various charges against him which may have stemmed from his belief that blacks were the equals of whites in all ways. After the war, he could no longer practice medicine due to his war injuries, and he engaged in silver mining in Nevada and traveled in South America. He died in Colombia and was buried in that country. (Sifakis, 7)

Biographical sketches on the following: Ambrose Burnside, Ulysses Grant, Robert E. Lee, Albert A. Pope, and Samuel H. Leonard are a compilation of information from a variety of sources including books by Roy Meredith, Stewart Sifakis, Geoffrey Ward, Ric Burns and Ken Burns as well as Wikipedia.com. All references can be found in the bibliography.

Appendix H

Money Subscribed by the Undersigned to be used for Buying Soldiers in Sudbury, Massachusetts*

From the Marion Hurlbut Eaton Collection

Appendix I

Payments to the Sudbury Soldiers of the Thirteenth Regiment

The following record of payment of the soldiers of the Thirteenth Regiment was located in a binder in the town hall vault. It is a handwritten page simply marked, Military 1865.1 Military Town Hall Records Sudbury. It reads as follows:

The Committee to investigate the subject of payment to Soldiers under vote of April 29, 1861.their former report having been recommitted with instructions to report the amount each soldier would be entitled to agreeably to said vote now report as follows:

According to the best information they have obtained they are entitled as follows:

John H. Moore	3 years	242.00
Leander Haynes	3 years	242.00
Jeremiah Stewart	3 years	242.00
Geo W. Jones	3 years	242.00
Spenser Smith	3 years	242.00
Geo L. Willis	3 years	242.00
George T. Smith	31 months	207.00
Mortimer Johnson	3 years	207.00
Francis H. Brown	18 months	116.00
James F. Fish	13 ½ months	84.50

Almer H. Gay	10 months	61.00
Citizens of Sudbury Total		**$2127.50**
Cyrus Barker	23 months	151.00
Lyman W. Brown	25 months	165.00
George W. Woodbury	19 months, 5 days	122.00
George H. Simpson	15 months, 10 days	97.50
Osmond Richardson	6 months, 20 days	36.00
Samuel H. Garfield	17 months, 6 days	110.00
George Dickey	7 4/5 months	43.00
Henry F. Moore	3 years	242.00
William Green	3 years	242.00
Belonging to other towns		**$1208.50**
Total Amount		**$3336.00**

Dana F Dutton, J.E. Stone, Henry Battles and Albert Conant, deserted, and no account in favor of them have been made up.

Respectfully submitted by the committee of
Abel Jones
Thomas Hurlbut
A. Balcom

According to records of the town, the amount of money expended on the Civil War not including any aid given by the state was $17,575. The state reimbursed the town $6,199.18 for money it raised to assist soldiers' families during the war.

Bibliography

Abbott, John S. *The History of the Civil War in America; Origin and Progress of the Rebellion of the Various Navel and Military Engagements, of the Heroic Deeds Performed by Armies and Individuals, and Touching Scenes in the Field, the Camp, the Hospital and the Cabin.* Vol. II. Springfield, Massachusetts: Gurdon Bill, 1866.

Bolton, Ethel Stanwood. *Moore Family,* Library of Congress, Collection Americana # 5860174. Boston: D. Clap & Sons, 1873.

Boston Daily Journal. October 13, 1864.

Boston Daily Journal. October 5, 1863.

Committee of the Regimental Association. *History of the Thirty-Fifth Regiment Massachusetts Volunteers, 1862-1865: With a Roster (1884).* Boston: Mills, Knight & Co., 1884.

Commonwealth of Massachusetts' official website, http://mass.gov/governorsofma.html

Compiled and Written by Members of the Federal Writers' Project of the Works Progress Administration in Massachusetts. *A Brief History of the Town of Sudbury in Massachusetts 1639-1939.*

Compiled by the Adjutant General, *Massachusetts Soldiers and Sailors and Marines in the Civil War.* Norwood, Massachusetts: Norwood Press, 1931.

Conklin, Edwin P., *Middlesex County and its People – A History.* Vol. II. New York: Lewis Historical Publishing Company, Inc., 1927.

Davis, Charles E. Jr. *Three Years in the army: The Story of the Thirteenth Massachusetts Volunteers from July 16, 1861 to August 1,1864.* Boston: Estes and Lauriat, 1894.

Garfield, Curtis F. *Sudbury, Massachusetts: 1890-1989, 100 Years in the Life of a Town.* Berryville, VA.: Berryville Graphics, 1999.

Genealogical Dictionary of First Settlers of New England. Goodnow Library, Sudbury, MA.

Hengen, Elizabeth Durfee. *Building the City of Homes and Industry, The Architectural and Historical Development of Everett, Massachusetts.* Everett, MA: Daniels Printing Company, 1994.

Hudson, Alfred Sereno. *The Annals of Sudbury, Wayland, and Maynard, Middlesex County, Massachusetts.* Self published, 1891.

Hudson, Charles. *History of the Town of Lexington, Middlesex County Massachusetts from its First Settlement to 1868.* Revised and Continued to 1912 by the Lexington Historical Society, Vol. II, Genealogies. Boston and New York: Houghton Mifflin Company, 1913.

Keegan, John. *The American Civil War, A Military History.* New York: Bonanza Books, 1988.

Kellogg, Robert H. *Life and Death in Rebel Prisons.* Hartford, Connecticut: Wiley, Waterman & Eaton, 1866.

Magnuson. Rosalind. *Trunks, Textiles & Transits, Manufacturing on the Mousam River.* The Brick Store Museum, Kennebunk and Portland, ME: Walch Publishing, 2005.

Mayhue, Justin T. *Letters of John W. Brendel.* Hagerstown, MD: Copyquick Printing and Graphics, 2006.

Meredith, Roy. *The World of Matthew Brady, Portraits of the Civil War Period.* New York: Bonanza Books, 1988.

Munden, Kenneth W., Henry Putney Beers. *The Union – A Guide to Federal Archives Relating to the Civil War.* Washington D. C.: National Archives and Records Administration, 1986.

Bradenton Herald. Sunday, July 11, 1948.

Concord Enterprise. January 30, 1929.

Maynard News. Friday, February 1, 1929.

Roddy, Edward G., *Mills, Mansions and Mergers: The Life of William M. Wood.* North Andover, MA: Merrimack Valley Textile Museum, 1982.

Rossiter, Johnson, John Tyler Morgan. *Campfire and Battlefield: An Illustrated History of the Campaigns and Conflicts of the Great Civil War.* New York: Byron, Taylor & Co., 1894.

Schouler, William. *A History of Massachusetts in the Civil War.* Boston: E. P. Dutton & Company, 1868.

_____. *The History of Massachusetts in the Civil War, Towns and Cities.* Vol. II. Boston: Published by the Author, 1971.

Scott, Laura. *Sudbury, a Pictorial History.* Norfolk, VA: The Donning Co. Publishers, 1989.

Selectman's Report. *Receipts and Expenditures of the Town of Sudbury from March 20, 1858, to March 10, 1859*

_____. *Receipts and Expenditures of the Town of Sudbury,* January 1865.

_____. *Receipts and Expenditures of the Town of Sudbury,* November 1864.

Seymour, Digby Gordon. *Divided Loyalties-Fort Sanders and the Civil War in East Tennessee.* Knoxville: University of Tennessee Press, 1963, revised, 1862 and 2001 by East Tennessee Historical Society.

Shaara, Jeff. *Civil War Battlefields,* New York: Ballantine Books, 2006.

Shaw, Linus H., Minister of the First Parish in Sudbury, *War and Its Cause,* Sermon Preached at Sudbury, Massachusetts on Nov 21, 1861.

Sifakis, Stewart. *Who Was in the Civil War,* New York: Facts on File Publications, 1988.

Smith, Timothy L. *Togus Down in Maine, The First National Home.* Charlston SC: Arcadia: 1998.

Sudbury, Massachusetts. *On Thanksgiving Day, Nov. 21, 1861, at a Union Meeting of the Religious Societies of the Town.* Waltham: Press of Josiah Hastings, 1861.

Sudbury Chamber of Commerce. Sudbury, MA 01776, http://www.sudbury. org/townof.html.

Sudbury Town Report. Town Hall, Sudbury, Massachusetts, November 1864, to January 1865.

Sudbury Vital Records. Vital Records of Sudbury Mass to 1850. Boston: N. E. Historic Genealogical Society, 1903.

The Town of Wayland in the Civil War of 1861-1865 as Represented in the army and Navy of the American Union. Wayland, Prepared and published by order of the Town of Wayland, Boston: Rand, Avery & Frye, 1871.

Town of Sudbury. Report of Committee Investigating Payments to Soldiers per vote of April, 29, 1861. Town Clerks Office, Town Hall, Sudbury, MA.

Ward, Geoffery C., Ric Burns and Ken Burns. *The Civil War – An Illustrated History*, New York: Alfred Knopf, 1991.

Wikipedia. From *Memoirs of General William T. Sherman*, Written by Himself (1875) 2nd ed. The Free Encyclopedia, http://en.wikipedia.org/wiki/William_Tecumseh_Sherman.

Wilson, John Laird, *Pictorial History of the Great Civil War: Its Causes, Origins, Conduct and Results,* Philadelphia, Pa., Chicago, Ill., St. Louis, Mo., Atlanta, Georgia: The National Publishing Company, 1878.

Mary Ellen Hoover, a member of the Sudbury Historical Society, participated in the transcription of the Moore collection, and has researched the roll of the Thirty-fifth Regiment in the Civil War. Mary Ellen is a graduate of Russell Sage College and resides with her husband in Sudbury, Massachusetts.

Elin Williams Neiterman holds a Masters Degree as a Nurse Practioner and is an active member of the Sudbury Historical Society. Her research followed George Moore's family from the 1600's to the present day. Elin resides in Sudbury, Massachusetts with her husband and two sons.

E. Dianne James is a former high school English teacher who has studied Civil War history and traveled to battlefields throughout the country. A graduate of Wellesley College with a Masters degree from Lesley University she has taught writing to high school students and adults. Dianne lives with her husband in Hyannis Port, Massachusetts.